# The Anatomy of an Entrepreneur

A publication of
the Center for Self-Governance

# The Anatomy of an Entrepreneur

*Family, Culture, and Ethics*

Joseph J. Jacobs

ICS Press
ICS
San Francisco, California

Macdonald

A MACDONALD BOOK



First published in 1991 in the United States of America by the Institute for Contemporary Studies

*The Institute for Contemporary Studies is dedicated to promoting the self-governing and entrepreneurial way of life through its Center for Self-Governance which conducts an ongoing program of research, publishing, and training.*

*Please contact the Center for Self-Governance for more information, 243 Kearny Street, San Francisco, California, 94108, U.S.A. (415) 981-5353, Fax (415) 986-4878.*

This edition published in the United Kingdom in 1991 by
Macdonald and Co (Publishers) Ltd
165 Great Dover Street
London
SE1 4YA
A member of Maxwell Macmillan Publishing Corporation



*British Library Standard Data*

A CIP catalogue record for this book is available from the British Library.

ISBN 0-356-20775-7

Printed and bound in Great Britain by
BPCC Hazell Books Ltd, Aylesbury and Paulton.

*Fifty years ago she edited and typed a thesis for me. For the many times since that I failed to acknowledge my debt to her, this book and my life are dedicated. With a modesty that belies the great woman she is and loyalty that I cannot live without, Vi is the heart in the anatomy of this entrepreneur.*
*Because of her, I breathe.*

# *Contents*

# *A Note from the Publisher*

With the publication of this book, the Institute for Contemporary Studies, through its Center for Self-Governance, launches a new series of books on entrepreneurship. Let me tell you why this book and the subject of entrepreneurship are important.

In many ways, Joe Jacobs's story is similar to those of other successful entrepreneurs whose autobiographies line bookstore shelves. What is different about this book is that Joe has told us the *whole* story, letting us into his mind and his heart as well as his business. He reveals the human side of a productive community.

Joe tells a compelling personal tale of success and failure, of difficult business choices, of the value of family. He reminds us that in business the "process" is frequently more satisfying than the results and that community, culture, and ethics are at the core of every successful entrepreneur.

Successful entrepreneurs as well as those just starting a business career will want to read Joe's tale because it goes beyond spread sheets and strategy to community and values. We believe its message is one that business and government leaders would do well to take to heart.

Self-governance and the entrepreneurial spirit—as exemplified in *The Anatomy of an Entrepreneur*—have animated much of what is good in America today. We are proud to publish this book about a man who has lived a self-governing life by working within his family, business, and culture to make a better world for himself and for his communities.

Robert B. Hawkins, Jr., President
Institute for Contemporary Studies

# *Foreword*

*The Anatomy of an Entrepreneur* is inspiring and informative on several levels. At its most direct, it is the story of a first-generation American of Lebanese ancestry who grasped the opportunities available in the United States and enjoyed substantial material success as a result of his own hard work and personal drive.

Those interested in subjects as diverse as capitalization of a private firm, business opportunities in the Middle East, and management theory in a mature organization will find plenty of personal reminiscences in these pages. The book tells us not only how Joe Jacobs made his money but also how he spends it—a topic which, as he accurately observes, receives far less attention than it should.

But it is as a story of America that this book is most compelling. Americans are as diverse a national group as any on earth. Our ancestors came from every world region, speaking virtually every known language, with faiths and traditions varied beyond imagination. Some came hundreds of years ago; the ancestors of future generations continue to arrive today.

Yet the common thread that makes every American an American, not a Lebanese or a German or a Mexican, is our shared experience of a national ethic that is reflected in our founding principles as well as in the lives of our people.

Joe Jacobs gives enormous credit to the traditions and values of his parents. The early chapters of this book reflect a sense of pride and love for his family that is one of the truly universal human characteristics. That sense of tradition runs like a thread throughout the narrative, following Joe in his travels from Brooklyn to the West Coast to the tragedy that is today's Beirut.

The lively Lebanese communities, a family life combining unquestioned parental authority and enormous parental love and sacrifice, the constant family demand that the children better themselves, the memories of familiar music and the instantly recognizable aroma of the food are all things that every person of Lebanese heritage carries throughout life. These are the familiar ingredients of our lives.

Yet, great as the influence of family and tradition and community is in every life, Joe Jacobs's story is an American story that could only have happened in America.

It is the unique American contribution to human history to have created a haven where both tradition and individuality are respected and play a role. It is only in America that a Joe Jacobs could, in fact, achieve the enormous material and personal success he has achieved without being forced to deny or abandon his background.

It is that unique blending of two very different sources of energy and vitality that is the American experience. The power of individual action, the ability to make decisions and correct them when they're wrong, the space in which to test different assumptions and try out alternative approaches—all are factors in the American system.

In the last century, the frontier was the arena in which the American experience was most often played out. In this century, it is the arena of human ingenuity and will. No other national tradition favors human action in quite the same way.

So although, like Joe Jacobs, I give great credit to my own family and upbringing for many of the values and habits I have found must useful in adult life, I believe that the entity to which the greatest share of credit must go is this nation.

In that respect, Joe Jacobs and I have reached different political conclusions from the same premises. I believe most strongly that it is through our governing structures and principles that Americans have remained free and have achieved the level of prosperity, justice, and personal freedom we enjoy.

Although it's tempting to suggest that something in the air gives Americans, as a group, the political genius to resist dictatorship and to preserve an open economic system, I think it's more accurate to give credit for those results to our founding principles and to the people who have for two centuries worked to maintain those principles.

That we have been true to those founding principles for 200 years has given us, I believe, the unprecedented ability to become both a wealthy and militarily powerful nation and the world's preeminent exporter of culture and ideals. Other nations reward personal drive and energy. Other systems allow room for individual achievement. Many nations nurture and preserve traditional lifestyles and communities.

But only America does *all* these things and, at the same time, finds its borders thronged by those who want to enter and live their lives as Americans. That is because our nation provides not only economic opportunity, but the greatest opportunity of all: the opportunity to live a free and fully realized human life. Those who, like Joe Jacobs, have succeeded in America because of the opportunities and their own hard work are an integral part of the American story. Their success is an inspiration to others. Their paths to the top are a guide to others following in their footsteps. Their efforts have bettered the lives of their communities as well as their employees and stockholders. They deserve the respect with which the American community treats them. I hope the readers of Joe's book will take away with them the sense, not only of a life lived with vigor and enormous personal energy, but of a national environment in which such a life could be successfully lived. This book is, ultimately, Joe Jacobs's ode to America, a good man's tribute to a good nation.

George Mitchell
Majority Leader, U.S. Senate

# *Acknowledgments*

The path of an entrepreneur may be laid out by him, but it is constructed and maintained by others. I acknowledge the early efforts of a small band of fewer than 30 new employees who worked together in the early fifties to make a success of our first sizable project. To Tony Ferraro, Bob Shapiro, Ted Goobic, Bill Day, Jack Carter, Earl Thompson, John Buehler, and others—you were there at the start. Stan Krugman, my first and long-time associate, left an indelible imprint on our company. His high standards of performance are still part of our persona. His contributions to our company's growth in its first 25 years cannot be overestimated. But most of all, there are the thousands of people who were and are part of our company; they have enhanced its reputation and thus do honor to my name.

My heartfelt gratitude to my close friends, Noel Watson and his team of senior executives, who were portrayed in our recent annual report and who engineered the resurgence of our company in 1984 and set it on its path of spectacular growth, which continues unabated today. My entrepreneurship is but a reflection of their hard work and dedication.

All the members of our board of directors, past and present, are my friends and, as such, have worked hard to prevent me from making more of a fool of myself than I otherwise might have.

Alta Wall, Betty Jones, and Janice Pate have made order out of my business life. The bulk of this book was transcribed by Betty Jones from my mostly illegible scribbles, written at odd moments on airplanes and other places. To all three fell the task of correcting my many misspellings and editing out the repetition of words I had momentarily fallen in love with.

An acknowledgment is due the Institute for Contemporary Studies, the think tank and publisher that liked my memoirs enough to publish them and to use this book to start a series on entrepreneurship.

To Frances Bowles, the editor with whom I argued constantly and who turned out to be right most of the time, a special thanks for tolerating my opinionation; and thanks as well to Janet Mowery of ICS Press for her many constructive suggestions.

One cannot live 75 years without acquiring an enormous debt to thousands of people. To all those unmentioned, heartfelt thanks and gratitude.

# *Prologue*

When I was growing up in the Lebanese-American community of Brooklyn, New York, the metaphor of the "melting pot" was in common use as we struggled to assimilate. But, looking back, I see that we did not melt, much less dissolve. At most we were amalgamated, and that is different. Our cultural background is clearly apparent as a discrete, inherent strand in the fiber of our makeup. Ethnic memory and ethnic values were woven into the very fabric of all of us of the first and even the second generation, who, on the surface, became indistinguishable from other Americans. We carry with us into our business and social lives a core of values that reflects the immigrant experience. This is true of most other ethnic groups as well. Among just my own "cousins," I have been amazed to see how many of the estimated two and a half million of us all over this country are entrepreneurs in the classic sense. The similarity of our stories can only reflect a common ethnic inheritance. More recently, at meetings of the American Task Force for Lebanon, a group whose role is to interact with the U.S. government in support of the sovereignty and independence of Lebanon, I have met many others who have reinforced these observations. Even among those who have chosen to enter the professions, the number who carry on entrepreneurial activities in their spare time is surprisingly high.

In multiracial America, many people will identify with the ethnic values that propel and guide the adventurous entrepreneur. We are what Michael Novak calls "the unmeltable ethnics" and are close enough to our immigrant forebears to have been influenced deeply by their ethnic mores.

As I considered those values, ethical standards, moral fiber, courage, and the need to reach for seemingly unattainable goals in an attempt to define my inner drive, I kept coming back to family and community. They are what shaped me and, therefore, shaped the way I conducted business. To the extent that those influences were ethnic and derived from my immigrant parents and friends, I suspect that they are shared by a large number of the entrepreneurs in this wonderful country of ours. Business as an expression of culture and morality *is* intrinsically socially responsible. The invisible wedge that has been driven between business and culture must be eliminated.

The strong emphasis upon character, morality, and the sanctity of one's "reputation" that I learned from my parents and the Lebanese ethnic enclave in which I grew up was a source of strength that nurtured the entrepreneurial accomplishment. We of the first generation are fortunate and have a star over our heads. Consider for a moment our role models: fathers and mothers who took enormous risks to come to this country and who prospered despite the disadvantages of a language barrier, a lack of education, and the need to adapt to a strange culture. We have all the advantages our parents lacked. We are educated, we speak the language, we move easily in the American mainstream. But we know we are different. We remembered as children being ashamed of our parents' accents. Later we learned to be proud of our heritage. We were raised with rigid codes of behavior; our parents' do's and don'ts of morality were not questioned. We learned by osmosis many things—to venture, to take risks—that became an unconscious but vital part of our ability to succeed and contribute substantially to what America is today—an America of which I am very proud. I am an unabashed patriot.

My family has business in its blood. In the Lebanese-American community of my youth, the first question two newly acquainted Lebanese immigrants asked each other was, "What business are you in?" Being in business *for yourself* and not working for others was assumed to be the natural condition. Business was the path to financial improvement, but more important than that, it was the entry point into American society. It was the means by which my family and many others came to feel that we are full partners in the American experience.

I am an entrepreneur by any definition, but not in any heroic sense. I had no brilliant flashes of inspiration, no spectacular recognition of market need, no marvelous coincidence of being in the right place at the right time. I slugged it out in my chosen profession, making lots of errors and, fortunately, lots of good decisions. But my story is more representative of the entrepreneurial process than that of the more celebrated examples one reads about—and there isn't a system more amenable to the relentless energy of the entrepreneur than ours.

Not surprisingly, I am a passionate advocate of the free-enterprise system. As an entrepreneur, I have seen its inner workings and have benefited from it substantially. In parallel with my business life, I have been an activist in promoting the understanding and appreciation of capitalism and the free-market system as a dynamic wellspring of energy for human good. Over the years, as board chairman of the Institute for Contemporary Studies and in other groups, I have supported reflective and scholarly studies of this vital social force.

How could it be otherwise? It started with my father, who came to this country in 1886 at the age of 16, uneducated and penniless, from what was then Syria and is now Lebanon. The great wave of immigration in which my father was but a droplet nourished this country's growth and made it the model for the world. No system other than ours could have accommodated these people with hunger and fire in their bellies—and my own story is but an extrapolation of theirs.

How do you define an entrepreneur? Certainly not by accomplishments alone, nor by a summary of business defeats and successes, but rather by the ways in which he handles success and failure. The narrow focus and the drive to succeed are necessary parts of his persona. But, though the entrepreneur's motives are entirely self-centered, the social good that is a by-product is still enormous, a point often sadly missed by the many critics of businessmen.

The relationship between my personal development as an entrepreneur and my belief in the free-market economy evolved as I explored what made me what I've grown to be. There is an unrecognized feature that may be the greatest strength of the free-market system, and that is its ability to draw upon culture and community. Socialism, on the one hand, tends to try to shape culture—to mold community values to some elitist blueprint. Our system, on the other hand, draws upon more traditional cultural values while allowing them to mature independently within the social system. Capitalism grows from the bottom; socialism is imposed from the top. Capitalism, in my view, is the economic system that most accurately reflects democracy—and there is no longer any doubt that economies managed from the top fail to meet either the material or the psychological needs of the people. The political system called "democratic socialism" may be internally contradictory—in common parlance, an oxymoron.

American capitalism has a special quality, an energy that is duplicated nowhere else in the world. I am convinced that this derives from the successive waves of immigrants whose striving has reenergized the process and prevented it from ossifying. I am also thankful that that dynamic input is continuing.

It is in the lack of recognition of the connection between cultural (and ethnic) mores and the free-market system that the troublesome aspects of business appear. The emphasis has too often been on results. Not enough stress has been placed upon the values inherent in the way in which one gets those results. This is the narrow focus on "the bottom line" that is so common. It is indeed a whole methodology taught in business schools and called "management by objectives" (MBO for short).

This may seem a strange criticism for one trained as an engineer to make. Few professionals are more attuned to the need for coming up with hard, bottom-line answers. Yet an existential view of the *process* by which one reaches the bottom line will reveal the humanity, the emotional content, and the moral fiber that are so necessary to achieve results and that can only be derived from one's roots. I use the term *anatomy* to try to define those characteristics that determine how the game will be played, not necessarily what the end result or bottom line will be. Just as in athletics, where hand and eye coordination affect the number of hits a baseball player gets or how far a golfer drives a golf ball, so these inner characteristics are more important than a recitation of wealth acquired or any other quantitative measure of accomplishment.

I did not intend this book to be a polemical treatise. My motives were simpler. I wanted to explore the sources of the entrepreneurial drive that shaped my life. But, as I kept discovering the influences of my ethnic roots and the values derived from my immigrant parents and their friends, a relationship to some of the troubling aspects of business and capitalism began to be revealed.

When describing my political and social views, I have always been troubled by the term *conservative,* for the images of insensitivity and rigidity that the word invariably evokes do not apply to me. I'd rather describe my views, and the views of most of my business friends, with the compound term *compassionate conservative,* thus challenging the liberal viewpoint that the moral high ground of compassion is exclusively theirs—for that very noble feeling of compassion is, in fact, clearly compatible with capitalism. Whence came the compassion that is an intrinsic part of me? I am convinced that its source is the tribal memories of our immigrant forebears, of oppression by cruel masters—in my father's case the fiercely ruthless Ottomans who ruled Lebanon for 400 years—and of countless other deprivations they struggled to overcome when they emigrated.

That ethnic and immigrant strand has given American capitalism its special cast. The ambivalent tension all immigrants feel between individualism and community—between wanting to belong and wanting to remain separate, between achievement realized in financial success and the other social values that ultimately animate their traditional values—was at the heart of my entrepreneurial experience.

At a time when the American business system is being questioned on many fronts and is meeting growing opposition at home, it faces a severe challenge to rediscover its soul. I hope this story of one man's experiences as an entrepreneur reexamining his cultural roots can help the process.

# I
# The Formative Years

ONE

# Origins

Qatar is a country not very well known. Few people can spell it and still fewer know where it is. I do. It is etched in my memory because, in a stranger's living room in Doha, the capital of Qatar, I was able to trace the origin of my father's family back to the thirteenth century. I'm sure my father had no inkling of his roots, because when I was a child, my father's and mother's origins in Lebanon were only occasionally alluded to in isolated stories. The Lebanon I knew came from the cultural mores, the taboos, and the behavioral codes I had to live with.

For most immigrants, family history seems to begin with that first step onto alien soil. The significance of a new life is so overwhelming that whatever happened previously tends to pale. I knew little of my father's past other than a collection of disconnected stories I had heard since childhood. I heard vague stories of his having killed or maimed a Turkish soldier, stories that I have trouble reconciling with the gentle, reserved man I remember. The Turks had been harsh rulers of much of the Arab world for almost 400 years. Whether he really was a fugitive or he simply wanted to avoid going into the Turkish army, he never said. I do know that he was born in Beirut and had no more than a third-grade education, if that. But he was not lacking in courage—a trait I admire and marvel at to this day. In 1886, at the age of 16, part of the earliest wave of Christian Lebanese to emigrate to this country, he set sail alone for the United States. Like so many others, he came penniless and speaking no English. He did not, I am sure, believe that the streets were paved with gold, but the land of freedom and opportunity beckoned to him as it did to millions of immigrants at the time. I am sure that I would not have had the guts at that age to embark on such a venture to a strange country half way round the world.

When he arrived at Ellis Island, my father was asked his name. He replied, in Arabic, "*Yussef Ibn Yakoob*" (Joseph, son of Jacob). Throughout the Arab world and among the villages of Lebanon, family lines are often blurred. In some villages there may be only three or four family units and a long history of intermarriage among those families. Within the family units, children are usually identified, for convenience, by the first name of their fathers. Thus, in a family of four or five brothers, each of the sons is often identified by the first name of his father, to distinguish him from cousins with the same family name and lineage. Often the main family designation is simply dropped. At Ellis Island the translator condensed my father's Arabic name and came up with Joseph Jacobs in English.

A friend of the family, George Malhame, who had come from Lebanon earlier, took my father in hand and gave him a suitcase full of notions (needles, thread, scissors, and so on) on credit. He showed him how to go from door to door and peddle his wares. Most immigrant Lebanese from those days became peddlers. This giving of a helping hand to newly arrived immigrants was a tradition in the Lebanese community that continues to this day. My father quickly learned enough English to get by and, of course, learned the monetary system. Years later he used to describe his pricing formula: "I simply made 1 percent on every sale. If I bought it for a dollar, I sold it for two. That's 1 percent profit, isn't it?" he would ask, his eyes twinkling.

The Lebanese peddler is a standard character in any description of early twentieth-century American rural life. Living frugally, he traveled this whole country, walking or riding on horseback, wagons, trains, whatever was available. I have a copy of my father's citizenship papers, issued in Denver, Colorado, in 1890. I remember being told of his traveling through the old West on horseback or horse-drawn wagon, but I still find it difficult to imagine the kinds of trials he went through in those days.

A cultural network throughout the country welcomed the Lebanese peddlers with typical, traditional Lebanese hospitality and, when he was on the road, my father would often board with other Lebanese families, among them the Forzley family in Putnam, Connecticut. Their younger daughter, Affifie, fair-skinned, with beautiful curly hair and fine features, was a serious child who by all accounts acted much older than her age. She kept house for her parents, an older sister, and two brothers who worked in the knitting mills. The family had come from the Bekaa Valley of Lebanon (the site of the famous Roman ruins of Baalbeck) to this country when Affifie was nine years old. In her case, the family name was derived from the name of the place of the family's origin, a small town called Forzel, near Zahleh, which is northeast of Beirut. As was not uncommon in that culture, Affifie never went to school and was illiterate. My father was 15 years older than she when they married (she was 14) and they had seven children, of whom I am the youngest.

Because my father had no relatives in this country, my mother's relatives provided us with the extended family that is so important to the Lebanese. I knew my maternal grandfather, a tall, handsome man with a handlebar mustache, only slightly; he died when I was very young. My grandmother I knew better, but most clearly I recall watching her hobble around on crutches after her leg was amputated when diabetic gangrene set in.

Affifie had done the accepted thing by marrying a Lebanese who was in business for himself. The rest of her family strayed from the path and managed to incur the community's censure in one way or another. Rose, my mother's sister, was the fun-loving one. My mother disapproved of Rose's frivolity and was especially critical when she married a younger man after her first husband died. Proper Lebanese widows wore black for the rest of their lives and rarely remarried, let alone to younger men. Both her brothers, unfortunately it was felt, married "Americans."

Uncle Al married a young Irish girl, Loretta Clancy, who was a lingerie buyer for R. H. Macy's department store in New York. She later provoked an incident that made a deep impression on me at the time and has influenced me since. One of Macy's suppliers was Helene Lingerie, a company formed in his later years by my father. The company's designer was my sister, Helen (hence the name). In the 1920s she designed an undergarment that was copyrighted under the name of "Tomboy." At the time Aunt Rose ran a contracting operation, supplying sewing services to garment manufacturers. Loretta induced Rose to copy the Tomboy design so that Macy's could sell the garment without dealing with Helene Lingerie. Of course she was found out, and I remember Loretta coming up the stairs of our house with tears streaming down her face to beg my parents not to report her to her boss. After the outrage and anger had subsided, they decided to do nothing about the incident although it violated all of their standards of integrity. Their overriding motive was to protect the family name. This reaction made a considerable impression upon me. Morality, I learned, was not always a matter of distinguishing between right and wrong and then acting uncompromisingly. Other considerations were important, and even when the distinction seemed obvious, one's choice of action was not always clear. Often I have been hotly angry about some injustice, but most of the time (not always, though), I have held back for fear of demeaning my name. This ambiguity is tolerable within a family, but it can cause trouble in other circumstances.

My mother's brother, Elias, was the epitome of a professional traveling salesman—tall, handsome, and charming. He always earned good money, but spent it all. In the eyes of the family, his success was somewhat diminished because he was not in business for himself. And he too married an "American," thereby losing even more status within the Lebanese community. The fact that his wife came from a Main Line, Philadelphia, family made no difference at all. He is reputed to have had the first electric refrigerator in Philadelphia; it was said, by our family at least, that he had the first automobile, electric iron, or whatever other appliance was under discussion. In 1926, as a 10-year-old, I remember being taken to the Sesquicentennial Fair in Philadelphia (the 150th anniversary of the signing of the Declaration of Independence) and seeing Uncle Elias buying every new gadget in sight—a potato peeler, an electric ice-cream maker, a toaster, and more.

Uncle Elias has left his imprint on me, not only because of his personality and presence as a salesman, but also because he was a pioneer and an experimenter. By observation, by anecdote, or by some mysterious gene transfer, I seem to have acquired his yearning to try new things, new ideas. I welcome innovation and will go to some lengths not to do something the conventional way. This quality is in some cases of doubtful virtue, but has contributed substantially to my business career.

I have learned from experience that, unfortunately, every novel idea is not a panacea. But the urge to innovate, to be first, to disregard the tried and true is an important part of my makeup. Uncle Elias did much to foster it.

My father's family is more shadowy. I have met only one member—a cousin, Salim Mokarzal, the son of my father's older sister, whom I saw briefly in Beirut in 1962 when he was about 60. At the time he was running a resort hotel in Sofar, a town in the mountains of Lebanon. His English and my Arabic were both halting, but his French was fluent and my sister-in-law, being fluent in all three languages, translated for me. Salim revealed that our original family name was Nacouzi and that the family had originated in a small village, called Sah'el Alma, in the mountains above the Bay of Junieh, about 20 miles north of Beirut. Apparently my father's branch of the family were the descendants of Jacob Nacouzi. My cousin said that this information came from a handwritten diary that he had seen when he was a youngster. The diary was written in the early 1800s by our great-great-grandfather who had moved from the mountain village to Beirut. Salim did not know what had happened to the diary, but did remember several entries. My paternal forebears were Maronite Christians, a distinct sect of the Roman Catholic Church that differs in that Mass is not said in Latin but in Aramaic, the language Christ spoke but that is now dead except in the Maronite ritual. The Maronites like to claim that they descend from the original Christian disciples. The diary related how the Christians in Lebanon were treated as inferiors by the Ottomans. For instance, when a Christian died he was reported to have "suffocated"—Christians were not, it seems, worthy of peaceful deaths. When a Christian bought a new *abah*, the traditional robe or outer garment that is still worn in many desert communities, he was forced to put a right-angled tear in the left sleeve, not only to identify him as an inferior Christian, but also to symbolize his unworthiness to wear anything new. "'Twas ever thus."

This is as much as Salim could tell me, but it was enough to enable me to pick up the threads of the story again in Qatar in 1969. I was on a business trip to the Middle East and had spent about two weeks pounding the pavements, what few there were, in Kuwait, Bahrain, and Saudi Arabia looking for work for my company. I had thought, rather foolishly I found out later, that my Arabic-speaking background and heritage might give us a competitive advantage over those much larger companies, such as Fluor and Bechtel, who were doing very well selling engineering and construction services to the Arab countries. In Qatar I had met the minister of industry who was also a not-so-silent partner of the agent who wanted to represent us. (Such an arrangement is not uncommon in Arab countries.) One day the minister, a short, swarthy, desert Arab in Bedouin dress and with a diamond-studded gold watch on his wrist, asked mischievously if I missed having a drink. I allowed that, after two weeks in strictly Moslem countries, a scotch whiskey might not be unwelcome. He said, "Be my guest tonight at the Shell Club. I am a member." Shell Oil was the principal foreign oil company in Qatar and had about 10,000 employees and their dependents living within a fenced compound there. They had a dining room and a bar where alcoholic beverages were served. Islamic law forbids the use of alcohol, but the authorities apparently averted their eyes from transgressions inside the Shell compound.

At the bar, when I was introduced to Shell's personnel manager, a Lebanese, I said in Arabic, "How is your health?" He looked startled and then, in English, he asked, "You're Lebanese, aren't you?" I said, "I am an American, but my father and mother were both born in Lebanon. How could you tell?"

"You speak with a Lebanese accent." As halting as my Arabic is, it revealed my heritage! His next question was as startling and perceptive. "It's obvious that your Lebanese family name could not be Jacobs. What is the real family name?" I told him the story as well as I knew it, finishing up with the observation that the family name was probably Nacouzi. "Ah," said my new Lebanese friend, "I believe you have a relative here in town." He told me that Jamil Nacouzi was the manager of Spinneys Grocery Co., a prominent British purveyor of food that has branches throughout the Middle East. He gave me Mr. Nacouzi's telephone number and urged me to call him.

When we met in the lobby of my hotel, Jamil took one look at me and exclaimed, "You are a Nacouzi!" "You have our nose," he said, "and the shape of your eyebrows is characteristic of our family." In him I could see a remarkable resemblance to my brother Albert in spite of the difference in coloring. Jamil is dark; my brother blond, like the rest of my family, and blue-eyed. We were not at all like the stereotypical dark-skinned Lebanese or Syrian. In fact, there has been a running joke in our family for as long as I can remember that the Crusaders who were away from home so long dallied a bit in the mountains of Lebanon. Stories of the Crusaders' exploits usually involved two of them and, of course, they were always knights, though in truth they could just as well have been cooks or horse handlers. I told Jamil what I had learned from Salim and we compared other notes. "There is no doubt," he said, "that we are from the same family. Would you like to know about the origins of your father's family?" Would I indeed!

Thus it was that I found myself in the comfortable living room of a house in the remote, little-known country of Qatar, listening to a man who was both a stranger and a relative trace the history of my father's family back to the thirteenth century. I sat stunned and open-mouthed as the tableau unfolded. Of this lineage I am intensely proud, even though I am the first to acknowledge that it has nothing to do with any achievement I can claim. The search for roots is universal. This augments the pride of the immigrant, the man who came to these shores penniless and alone, the man (and his family, in due course) whose achievements had to be not only material, but also social. Having no one to speak for us, no family, no references, we worked doubly hard to become accepted, to demonstrate our worth to the establishment, those scions of the *Mayflower*, those third-generation WASPs who looked down on the "Syrian" immigrants and, by their very presence, seemed to taunt us with our lack of status. The immigrant had no family history to give him security—his life only started when he landed at Ellis Island. The rejection we felt was exaggerated but was part of our motivation. I remember that I used to ask my mother and father not to speak Arabic in front of my American friends, and when my parents spoke to me in Arabic, I would answer in English. How desperately we wanted to belong. Subsequently, I have rarely found that those whose origins are securely established are therefore to be admired or envied; they too, "put on their trousers one leg at a time," as the saying goes. The cloak of privilege often conceals the same imperfections that we all have. But to be accepted into a social group one was not born to is a deep yearning. The fact that, once one has been accepted, the position may be much less satisfying than expected does not diminish the yearning a bit.

Jamil told me that his uncle was a Maronite priest who had spent his life tracing the lineage of our family. He started at the beginning. It seems that, during the thirteenth century, two brothers from the island of Cyprus committed some serious crime and had to flee. As fishermen, they knew of a land not far to the east where rugged mountains rose practically out of the sea. In their commerce with the Moslem people who lived on the narrow coastal plain, they had heard that (Christian) refugees living up in the mountains were able to resist the authority of the Arab rulers below. Our Cypriot forebears fled their island, landed somewhere in the Bay of Junieh, and immediately went into the mountains of Lebanon where they would be safe. There they settled down, married, became Maronites as were the rest of the villagers, and started the family line. The Arabs knew they were up there, and when these descendants made their occasional defense of their homes or their frequent raids on the Arab authorities, the Arabs referred to them, in Arabic, as *el Nacouzi*, "the people from Nicosia" (the principal city of Cyprus).

To this day I get goose bumps as I recreate my feelings while sitting there in Qatar, 12,000 miles from home, discovering I had roots as deep as those of any of the privileged members of the society I strove to be accepted by.

Though the discovery of family genealogy was a one-in-a-million chance happening, my father's story—the one I grew up with—was anything but unusual. In fact, I have discovered that the principal elements are common to most immigrants. Our forebears usually lived obscure lives in other parts of the world; one member ventured or fled to this country, and from inauspicious beginnings made a new life for himself and his descendants. This readiness to take risks and to make good has long been characteristic of the immigrant and is the benchmark of the entrepreneur. Despite the intense conservatism of the Lebanese family, in which traditional customs are revered, the new life into which the immigrants were thrust seems to have spurred the drive of entrepreneurship.

For the original immigrants, it was a challenge merely to establish an economic foothold in the country; they had little time or energy left over to take part in the American way of life, to become, even if only intermittently, assimilated. For the most part, traditional custom and expectations still held. For us of the next generation, it was so much easier to join the mainstream of American society. But we bore another burden. Because we had to reject some of the ethnic taboos our parents clung to for comfort in a strange land, we also incurred their disapproval. In such an atmosphere, we were doubly driven to succeed: to show our parents and to show our peers. Not being able to appreciate the physical and cultural distances our parents had covered, and envious of the easy familiarity of our American peers, we were spurred on by dissatisfaction and the need "to show them."

It seems to me that this force in our American culture has not been appreciated widely. It lies at the base of much entrepreneurship and was largely responsible for the energy that has fueled the remarkable history of this country, especially during the past 100 years. If one couples this desire to succeed and to be accepted with the overlay of the familial cultural values that gave us moral guidance, it's no wonder that we first-generation children of immigrants have become such a potent force in American business and American culture.

TWO

# *What Business Are You In?*

My father was born in Beirut; I was born in Brooklyn, New York, the youngest of seven children. My brothers and sisters were born in various New England mill towns. My father was on the road, peddling, most of that time. When he opened his first permanent office, the family settled in Brooklyn for good. Parents and children spoke different languages, but the bonds of family are the strongest I shall ever know.

Growing up in a divided culture, we were introduced to tensions shared by all the ethnic enclaves scattered through New York City, the immigrants' haven in the early twentieth century. As immigrants and outsiders we Lebanese clung as best we could to what we knew—our immediate families, relatives, and anybody else who was Lebanese. For us the concept of family was so extensive as to become synonymous with an entire people. If you were Lebanese, you were one of us. We were "cousins." It is clear that the influences that determined my values and helped me become an entrepreneur came, not only out of my immediate family, but also out of the entire ethnic community in which I was raised.

The consciousness of community gave tremendous weight to the mores of that community; the sanctions were real and binding. Anonymity was not possible—too many people knew you and too many people cared to allow anyone of Lebanese descent to walk through life alone in those days, even by choice. We saw the rugged individualism of the "American" way as a constant challenge, an enticement for us, who felt circumscribed by our heritage. Our parents, I think, regarded it with some dismay—and yet with fervent admiration.

Their relationship to "Americans" was marked by ambivalence. (Even the word seemed to be bracketed with quotation marks as it was spoken, perhaps to accentuate the difference between "them" and "us.") Admiration, envy, and a desire to become American were underlying emotions, but rejection was another. America as a country was venerated and the freedom from tyranny and injustice was appreciated, discussed, and gratefully acknowledged by those who had fled oppression. Our parents wanted us to be Americans, but not at the expense of our own heritage. They distinguished so sharply between the two cultures that they developed an almost dualistic outlook.

Americans were different, they were outside the tribe. Most of the ethnic immigrants, the Italians, Poles, Germans, Scandinavians, and others, tended to live in enclaves where the mother tongue was the everyday language and English was kept primarily for commerce with Americans. So did the Lebanese.

As all families do, we squabbled. Even in Brooklyn we had time for tribal and religious differences. Most of the Lebanese we knew were Christians, either Maronite or Eastern Orthodox. Between these two only slightly differing churches there was a pronounced rivalry that was a pale reflection of the ancient tribal feuds that have virtually destroyed Lebanon today.

Philip Habib, the well-known and celebrated diplomat who was also born in Brooklyn, tells an amusing story. As a special ambassador sent to solve the Middle East crisis in 1983, he crossed swords a number of times with Hafez Assad, the president of Syria. During one heated exchange, Assad said: "Mr. Ambassador, you keep talking about Lebanon as a country. It is really part of Syria. If you don't think so, go look at your father's passport when he emigrated to the United States." Of course, it gave the port of embarkation as Beirut, Syria. "But," Habib said, in his typical brusque and direct manner, "if you want to go back that far, then the origin was really Beirut, a city in the Ottoman

Empire!"—implying that, by Assad's reasoning, he could be called a Turk as easily as he could be called a Syrian.

Being so grateful for my heritage, I am an interested observer and, at the same time, a saddened critic of the country of my forebears. I see an exponential escalation of the tribal and religious rivalries I saw in Brooklyn as a child. We had, however, that powerful unifying force of being Americans as well, a force that prevented the early immigrants from perpetuating the tribal and religious rivalries that they inherited. Thus the rivalries were reduced to petty annoyances that were buried beneath the overwhelming sense of being American. In Lebanon itself, nationalism, the identification with country as the primary loyalty, is new and I fear superficial. Certainly it is not strong enough to overcome tribal and religious rivalries that have existed for thousands of years. People in Lebanon today have great trouble thinking of themselves as Lebanese first and Maronite, Sunni, Shi'ah, Druze, and so on, second. Until they do, Lebanon will not easily become an independent country.

Descendants of the ancient Phoenicians, the Lebanese perpetuated the tradition of trading for which the Phoenicians were celebrated. The behavioral standards of the trader, as transmitted to us, placed great importance on pride, reputation, and integrity. The Phoenicians, I was taught, could not have existed as a trading society for as long as they did without upholding the sanctity of a man's word. The Phoenicians invented the alphabet, no doubt to record details of the trades they made.

Pride, and reputation, and integrity—those qualities were as ingrained in my father as they are in me. I often wonder where the myth arose that a necessary ingredient for successful trading is dishonesty or deviousness. Nothing could be further from the truth. The trader gets good value because he is able to offer good value. In a good trade, both buyer and seller are engaged in what is now called a "win-win" situation.

In the great American supermarket of opportunity, each ethnic group tended to gravitate toward particular segments of the American economy: the Irish to bricklaying as a trade, to contracting as a business, or to civic work—police, politics, and so on;

the Polish to steel mills and manufacturing as a trade and to machine shops and parts fabrication as a business; the Lebanese to trading—buying and selling—mostly in soft goods or "dry" goods, such as linens, lingerie, dresses, clothing, oriental rugs.

Vivid in my memory is the question asked by one Lebanese of another on meeting for the first time: "What business are you in?" Never, "Who do you work for?" or, "What is your trade?" Oh, there were people who worked for others—usually their Lebanese relatives—but it was understood that they were only getting together a grubstake in order to start their "own business." So the cultural thrust made "being in business for yourself" the basis of immense drive among our people and in me. It seems that my whole life was geared, and warped, and shaped so that I might produce a satisfactory answer to the perennial question, "What business are you in?"

I have heard the story repeated thousands of times by Lebanese all over the country—in Wichita, Kansas; Vicksburg, Mississippi; Austin, Texas; Seattle, Washington; and in the most unexpected, out-of-the-way places. Time after time, I've asked the question, "How did your father [or grandfather] come from Lebanon and wind up in Littleton, New Hampshire [or Natchez, Mississippi, or any one of hundreds of other towns] to own the most prosperous clothing store [or automobile agency, or feed mill] in town?" The answers would fill volumes, but all had the underlying cultural thrust of adventure, daring, and "being in your own business." In all those scattered places, the historical and cultural backgrounds of Lebanese immigrants were the same as those I grew up with in Brooklyn. The pattern was repeated over and over again. Come to the United States penniless, go "on the road" to peddle, settle down in some hospitable place or where others of the family lived, and open a store or shop and prosper.

Let me describe my father. He was a gentle man, universally liked by all who met him. According to my older brothers and sisters, he was away from home a lot in the years before World War I, carrying his suitcase (*shenta* in Arabic) selling his wares, and making his "1 percent" profit. I remember little of his traveling because, by the time I was old enough to be aware of his work, he had an office in lower Manhattan and sold to other peddlers. Often on Saturdays, when I was about six or seven, he would take me by streetcar to the office for half a day's work, to look at the mail, and then we would go on to the Washington Market in lower Manhattan. The farmers brought their produce to a large warehouse building and the brokers or wholesalers and the grocery store owners of the city would come in at 4 or 5 A.M. to pick over the offerings and buy their fresh produce for the day.

The market was an exotic place where one could buy all sorts of unusual delicacies, such as squid and sea urchins, those spiny, hard-shelled mollusks whose orange flesh my father enjoyed, and rare fruit, such as prickly pears, the fruit of a cactus, that had to be washed and scrubbed while one wore thick gloves to avoid the spines. Then we would cut the skin and savor the sweet, cold flesh. Stalls in the building catered to retail customers who bought fruit and vegetables by the case and, with each box of figs or apricots he bought, my father would regale me with his exaggerated memories of the superior fruit in Lebanon. These were great outings for me, for I had Pop to myself for a whole morning. In a family of seven children, those were times to be cherished. I played with the typewriter in his office, scribbled on his note pads, and went home happy in the open-air streetcar, weighed down with cases of fruit, unusual meats, and all the Middle Eastern ingredients Mom needed to cook her marvelous meals.

Better still were the occasions when just the two of us would go by streetcar to Sheepshead Bay near Coney Island and board a "day" boat for a day of deep-sea fishing. My memories of him are clouded with nostalgia.

A series of heart attacks left him an invalid for the last years of his life. When he died, in 1933, I was just past 16. The psychological "transference" that every boy needs to make was incomplete and his death scarred me noticeably, but I remember him as a gentle, caring man who loved his children and revered his family. His image as a successful businessman was constantly reinforced in stories told by my mother and siblings. It is curious that these images should survive so strongly because, beyond those childhood excursions, most of my conscious memories are

*Jacobs family portrait, 1913. Front, left to right: Evelyn, Ed, Ted, Mom, Pop, Albert; back: Margaret, Helen. Mom designed and sewed all the family's clothing except the men's suits.*

from the period when his financial fortunes had been eroded severely and he was, in the last five years of his life, a cardiac invalid. The failure of his final business, Helene Lingerie, the Depression, and the years of his invalidism were traumatic, painful, and suffocating for me. But I never lost the image of my father as a successful businessman who had an office and provided very well for his family.

His original business developed from one of the products he carried on his sales trips: straight razors made by the Geneva Cutlery Co. in Geneva, New York. Eventually he had a minority interest in the company, became their exclusive sales agent, and opened the office in Manhattan. He continued the tradition of helping newly arrived Lebanese by giving them a stock of razors on credit and sending them on their way to peddle.

Before World War I, almost all straight razors, except for those made by the Geneva Cutlery Co., were made in Solingen, Ger-

*Pop at his office on Canal Street in New York City about 1918.*

many, and were known as "Solingen razors." Even the output at Geneva Cutlery was the work of craftsmen brought over from Solingen. Along came World War I and imports of razors from Germany were abruptly cut off. Suddenly my father had a virtual monopoly. I remember hearing stories of people coming to his offices to help open cases of razors for the privilege of buying a dozen that they then resold at exorbitant profit. In contrast, because wholesale prices provided an adequate profit, my father never charged his customers an extra cent, though his razors were in such demand that they were rationed to his regular customers. He boasted with pride of that many times. He was determined not to be a profiteer. Even so, he became quite wealthy by the standards of those days.

To me, the lesson in integrity was clear. A business should be run at a profit (whether the much-repeated "1 percent" was the standard or not, I don't know) and customers treated fairly. To take inordinate advantage of a temporary situation was as reprehensible as not making a profit. My father was universally praised as a man of integrity and his example is imprinted in my psyche.

We lived in a large, four-story brownstone in the Park Slope section of Brooklyn. We had moved away from the Lebanese ghetto of Atlantic Avenue in Brooklyn Heights to the more affluent neighborhood near Prospect Park, as had a number of other newly successful Lebanese. I vaguely remember many fancy parties and balls at which my mother would preside as the *grande dame* with a dignity and flair, acquired from I know not where, that would have been admired in any society group. Only the Arabic, the accented English, and the exotic Middle Eastern food would have differentiated the occasions.

Right after World War I, King Gillette (one of those storied entrepreneurs) invented the safety razor, and my father's business was wiped out almost overnight. He retained enough money, however, to start a new business, Helene Lingerie, that became reasonably successful until the Depression, when it finally had to be liquidated. This business was based on my sister Helen's emerging talent as a designer of clothes and lingerie. She, along with my other sisters, had inherited my mother's taste and natural sense of style.

In the years of my adolescence, however, my role model was not so much a father as a legend, a man remembered for his past accomplishments and in my mother's description of his masculinity and courage.

And how should I describe my mother? She was a remarkable woman. She never did learn to read or write; but despite that, she was a *classy* lady. She had impeccable taste and invariably comported herself with a natural and palpable dignity. In addition, she had a driving ambition for her children—all of whom made a significant mark in life. When I describe my mother as classy, I mean that she had an innate sense of taste and even elegance about her. It was reflected in her clothes, in the furnishings in our home, in the way she entertained guests, and in her almost regal carriage. All the girls' and children's dresses in the family picture made before I was born were hand sewn by her.

Pride, reputation, and integrity were constantly recurring themes with her, too. One simply did not *do* certain things. What would people say? No matter what sacrifices were needed, one's reputation for honesty and loyalty was paramount. One must not bring shame upon the family. The Arabic word for shame, *eyb*, has the extreme force of a tribal taboo. It carries with it all sorts of nuances of punishment and ostracism comparable with the "A" for adulteress that was forced on Hester Prynne.

For instance, when Helene Lingerie went bankrupt, the company owed the Chase Bank a small amount of money. I understood that there was absolutely no legal liability for that loan, but my father from his sick bed and my mother even more vehemently insisted that this loan be repaid. Their pride and the reputation of the family were at stake. My sisters were earning barely enough for us to get by, but each week they would send a small installment to the bank. Finally the loan was paid off and Helen, as the older sister, received a letter of acknowledgment and admiration from the bank. For years my mother, beaming with pride, would show this letter to the family. Today I have it framed and hanging in my den. The words are engraved in my mind: " . . . filial devotion of this kind is so rare. . . . "

How many times in my business career have I accepted moral responsibility when there was no legal one? How many times have I fought expensive legal battles because we were morally right, if legally weak? How many times have I gone to extraordinary efforts to save our honor? Such actions have been the result of moral, rather than economic or expedient, decisions; they have arisen, not from some deeply reasoned analysis, but rather from my instincts and early training. Yet the stance has paid off. I am certain that our company would not have prospered as it did if, as a youngster, I had learned more cynical standards of behavior. I can cite numerous times during my business career when we have gone to extraordinary lengths to make a project right or to correct deficiencies for which we had no legal obligation. Honor and principle are not as incompatible with success in business as many people think.

Each company develops a personality of its own. Jacobs Engineering is no exception. My imprint on the company is clear. That imprint is, just as clearly, a reflection of my heritage and my family's cultural standards. The Chase Bank story and my father's refusal to become a profiteer illustrate the importance that we accord responsibility to one's business associates, whether customers or suppliers. Such attitudes influence our business style and, I believe, contribute to our success.

The success of our fellow countrymen in the United States was a common topic of conversation at Lebanese gatherings. Success was usually defined in terms of business and financial accomplishments and measured by estimates of wealth; in the new capitalist world of America that was the way we kept score. Oh, we also talked about Lebanese intellectuals: Professor Phillip Hitti of Princeton and, of course, the revered Kahlil Gibran, a poet, philosopher, and artist who became a cult figure to many intellectual Americans. More recently, we talk about Dr. George Debakey; Senator James Abourezk; Governor Victor Atiyeh; Governor John Sununu, now the White House chief of staff; Senator George Mitchell; former ambassador Philip Habib; and many others. But most of the stories told then were about Lebanese like my father who came to America and became outstanding businessmen. It was unproved, but widely accepted, that a higher percentage of successful businessmen was to be found among the Lebanese than among any other ethnic immigrant group. Such stories and folk tales heard by my youthful ears were indelibly imprinted upon my impressionable mind. It is no wonder that going into business for yourself, establishing a business and making a success of it, was for me a given. I never doubted that, in the future, I must be able to answer the recurring question, "What business are you in?"—and to answer it with pride!

To illustrate that this thrust was a cultural one and not necessarily confined to my own family's ethos, I'll repeat a story I've told many times. I have a Lebanese-American friend, Alex Massad, whose parents immigrated to Oklahoma City. His father was not a businessman but a member of the clergy, a priest in the Orthodox church and, although a gentle, kind, and revered man, he was certainly not a role model for the potential entrepreneur. Yet the expectations of Lebanese culture, even in that small but closely knit ethnic community in Oklahoma City, influenced his mother. Alex himself has told this story many times and always with relish, humor, and an obviously deep love for his mother (characteristics that, by the way, are the antithesis of those *Fortune* magazine used to describe him as one of America's toughest executives).

When he graduated as a petroleum engineer after World War II, Alex accepted a job with Mobil Oil Co. His mother was disappointed. She would ask him plaintively, "Alex, my son, why don't you go into business for yourself? Why don't you open a store?"

"But Mama," he would say, "I've been trained as a petroleum engineer and I want to practice my profession." She would brush that response aside and insist that he open a store, perhaps a grocery store, or an oriental rug store. To her, that would mean that he would be "in business for himself," and then she could be proud of her son, and her stature in the community would thereby be enhanced considerably. Every time he went home during the years when he was a rapidly rising star at Mobil, Mama would ask him when he was going to quit working for that big company, open a store, and go into business for himself. Finally, on one visit home, Alex (then executive vice-president of Mobil Oil and probably number three or four in the hierarchy of that giant enterprise) announced triumphantly, "Mama, I *have* bought a store." Her elderly face brightened at the news. At last! Alex had taken her advice; her son would finally be judged a success in her community. "Yes, Mama, I have finally listened to you. I bought a store! I bought Montgomery Ward!"

Her smile changed to a disappointed frown. She was unimpressed and said, with despair, "It's not the same thing. I meant your *own* store!" Such is the depth of our cultural heritage. Alex and I laugh about this every time we see each other, but a respect and love for his mother and for our common heritage underlie every retelling.

When I was growing up, there was no escaping my mother's driving ambition for all of us. This demand for success and the admiration of the community falls heavily on the oldest son and is reflected in the Lebanese custom of identifying older women and widows as "the mother of" (*Im* in Arabic), the name of the oldest son. My mother, by this tradition, would have been *Im* Edward, *Im* being pronounced with a short *i* as is *Ibn*. In this

*JJJ about 1918.*

context, the son's name would be shorthand for all of his achievements, and the salutation a recognition of the honor he had brought upon the family. She would shine in the reflected glory.

These aspirations were born out of my mother's illiteracy and her drive to rise above the hard life of an immigrant family, which she obviously projected upon her children. With every one of us she never quit. We could always do better! We must risk and taunt failure for we were her children and we should and could be better than anyone else, better even than we ourselves may have wanted to be. We reacted in different ways.

The main focus of her ambition for the family was directed at my oldest brother, Ed. According to her inflexible tradition, he was destined to carry on the family business and the family name. My mother tried to invest in him all her determination to restore the fortune and social stature that we had lost after my father's business declined. Custom required that the oldest son

*JJJ with sister Helen at Jones Beach about 1930.*

enter the family business and that he take over the leadership of the family upon the father's death.

Ed inherited my father's gentleness as well as his remarkably fertile and imaginative mind and grew in his later years to be much like my father. For me, he must often have substituted for the father I missed so much in the years of my young manhood. I suspect that he had a lot of my mother's drive and determination, but used most of it up in rebelling against the crushing burden of being the oldest son. I'll never forget my mother's almost hysterical reaction when Ed said that he intended to marry an American—a choice that symbolized his rebellion against his mother and the demands of his heritage. In a perverse way, even this rebellion against my mother's rigid standards of what was proper and correct served as an example to me, of courage, determination, and a willingness to defy conformity. I have been a long time in recognizing how much courage Ed showed in contravening the rigid customs of a close family and a tight-knit community, but subconsciously I must have learned from it. If my mother's iron will could be defied, could other challenges be so very daunting?

By her own standards, my mother had better luck with my brother Ted, who is four years older than I am and was an outstanding athlete at school. He had been offered a football scholarship at the University of Alabama. My mother persuaded (maybe bullied) him to forgo that, attend the University of Buffalo, and to save boarding costs, live with my oldest sister, Margaret, who lived there with her husband and family. He became a physician and a well-known and accomplished surgeon.

Two of my sisters, Helen and Evelyn, also had their lives influenced and proscribed by my mother's expectations, but the decline in the family fortune gave them less scope anyway. Self-confident and talented, Helen had become a lingerie designer and made her mark while designing for Helene Lingerie. By the time Evelyn left school, the family was in dire financial straits and it was assumed that Evelyn, who had always lived in Helen's shadow, would get a job. After all, the boys—my brother Ted and I—were still to be educated, so the girls would go to work. I don't think it occurred to anyone to consider further education for the girls. I recall many instances in which, when a woman bore a daughter, the neighbors would say, "Too bad. Maybe the next one will be a son." Yet ours was, in many ways, a matriarchal society that bestowed immense powers upon the mother. She molded the character of the family, she set the standards, she exerted the discipline, and her approval of the marriages of her children was absolute, final, and overriding.

I do not know whether it ever occurred to Helen or Evelyn that they might have gone to college. My mother would have found the idea preposterous. Even so, she insisted that Evelyn was not to take a job as a shop girl or anything else so menial. She must become a designer as Helen was. Evelyn pleaded that she knew she had no talent; she could not become a designer. I remember many tearful arguments between the two, with my obdurate mother insisting that Evelyn could indeed be a designer and that she must try. Of course, Evelyn succumbed to the pressure, did try, and did become a designer—an outstandingly successful one. Indeed, she became one of the most famous designers of lingerie in the garment industry. The "I told you so" from my mother was unspoken, but always there as she proudly talked of Evelyn's success.

Several years later, after Helen married and moved to China, Evelyn became almost the sole support of the family. Long before "women's lib," she was looked upon with awe by our whole community. Influential and highly paid, she was the quintessential career woman a generation ahead of her time. I am sure that she was envied by many women who had dutifully followed their preordained destiny of marriage and children, and she was certainly admired by the whole community and became a great source of pride to my mother in the many years of her widowhood.

Shortly before Helene Lingerie went bankrupt, my father fell down the steps to the basement at home and broke his leg. After sitting in a wheelchair for six or eight weeks, he was about to get up when he had a massive heart attack. I remember running all over the neighborhood looking for a doctor while we were waiting for "Doc" Scanlon, our family doctor, to arrive.

Doc Scanlon was my idol. He was calm, reassuring, and besides, he had been a well-known pitcher for the Brooklyn Dodgers and could I be anything other than a rabid Dodgers fan? He was nicknamed "Doc" even when he was an active ball player because he was attending medical school at the time. To an adolescent boy in Brooklyn, the Dodgers, among them Dazzy Vance, Zack Wheat, Robby Robinson, and the legendary Doc Scanlon, were a collection of Bunyanesque superathletes.

When Doc arrived, he injected a massive dose of morphine into my father and the situation was incredibly tense for ten days or so. Twice I was summoned in the middle of the night to say goodbye. Though he recovered from that heart attack, Pop was an invalid for the next four or five years until his heart deteriorated completely. During his invalidism, he aged perceptibly and needed repeated doses of nitroglycerine to relieve angina pectoris. (I had occasion later to become quite familiar with that product.)

In an effort to help our failing family business, my mother pitched in frenetically. She took the streetcar every day to our factory to collect cut but unsewn garments, which she would then take to the Puerto Rican section of Brooklyn to "home workers" who would sew them together. She went back, picked up the finished garments, paid the workers in cash, and left more work. Everyone marveled at her courage. They simply didn't know Mom—she'd have withered any hoodlum with a stern look. Simultaneously, she ran our house smartly and cooked the wonderfully tasty and fragrant Middle Eastern food for which she was celebrated throughout the Lebanese community. Even in the pit of the Depression she set a sumptuous and fancy table.

By this time, Ed had married and left home. After the business closed, Helen and Evelyn had both found work as designers for other firms and, along with my brother Albert, who was to be married shortly, were supporting the family. For Evelyn, submission to the expectations of her mother in particular and the community in general did eventually give her a life of her own. For many Lebanese women of our generation, the freedom of America was somewhat illusory.

For instance, when Albert married a Lebanese girl, they did what an American girl would have balked at: moved into our house. Because she came from the same Lebanese culture and could understand the maternal and family pressures, Emily Tweel, Albert's young bride, did the dutiful thing. I imagine she resented it, but she smilingly accepted what must have been a disappointing and probably humiliating situation.

Perhaps because I was the youngest and had a chance to observe Evelyn, Ed, and others in the family, I was better able to cope with the pressure to achieve and to meet my mother's high standards. When she was applying the pressure, however, it was confusing and traumatic. It shook my youthful illusions and caused much unhappiness when my siblings defied, railed at, resented, resisted, or capitulated to Mom, while seeking Pop's affection and support. Only after years of introspection and in hindsight can I see how these emotional dramas sifted through a young mind and became synthesized into a behavioral pattern that was the foundation for my decision to go into business for myself. My siblings have taken a great deal of pride in what I have accomplished. They little realize that they can take credit for contributing, in many subtle and probably unconscious ways, significantly to those accomplishments.

If my attitude toward my mother sounds ambivalent, it reflects my adolescent feelings accurately. Much of my early uncertainty and subsequent aggressive drive were undoubtedly spurred by a need to please my mother and to meet her high standards. It took some time before I adopted her standards on their own merits and not because she espoused them. My eventual ability to integrate them into my own personality and to separate that admiration from her parental authority was important to my career as an entrepreneur.

THREE

# *Youth and Adolescence*

Our home in the center of populous, teeming Brooklyn was near Prospect Park, an oasis of green grass and woods. We had our Robin Hood fantasies there (we called our secret hiding places in the woods of Prospect Park "Sherwood Forest") and our rough-and-tumble fights on the fields.

There was a merry-go-round in Prospect Park, a boathouse on a lake, and a number of restaurants and concession stands run by the Robinson brothers, who were rumored to be "wired in" with Tammany Hall, with all that implied. It was there that I started working at the age of 12—and I have been working ever since. My first job was behind the counter of the soda pop and snack stand near the grass tennis courts. On summer weekends we'd sell hundreds of cases of cold soda, peanuts, Cracker Jack, and so on. On off days, when it rained, we filled the peanut bags from 100-pound sacks of peanuts in the shell. This was my first lesson on form versus substance. If you took, say, a cup of peanuts and simply stuffed them into a thick paper bag with the word "peanuts" printed on it, it was a pretty small package. Ah, but if you took the bottom corners of the bag, one in each hand, and then pressed upward with your thumbs in between the corners, you formed a U at the bottom. Then the same quantity of peanuts filled the bag to the top! There is a fine line here between deception and proper presentation. How you package something is important. If the peanuts were a good value for the price, the presentation only enhanced it. A good quality product ought to be packaged attractively.

I learned a different lesson when I graduated to working behind the soda fountain. I was making an ice-cream cone once and Mr. Robinson said impatiently, "Let me show you how to make a cone." I had been forcing the scoop into the ice cream to fill it thoroughly before putting it on the cone. He showed me how to use the edge of the scoop to cut only a thin layer of ice cream into the scoop. With practice, one could turn out a perfectly formed ball of ice cream that was hollow in the center! That was deception. Though I learned to do this, I was embarrassed enough to take a much thicker slice when he wasn't looking and therefore to leave practically no air in it. That such duplicity exists cannot be denied, as this and other examples show; but it is not representative of the overwhelming majority of business people I have met in the past 50 years.

Oh, at that age I was no moralist. I was still learning values. My pay started out at two dollars a day and over several years grew to three dollars a day for a good 12-hour day (from eight in the morning to sundown in summer). Mr. Robinson paid me in quarters taken out of the cash receipts, which I promptly gave to Mom, as part of the communal pot. Understandably, I resented this arbitrary expropriation of the money I earned; but with my mother's standards of what was proper and what was improper, such decisions were automatic and inviolable and my protestations were in vain. So I was not above stealing the odd quarter from Mom's cash box to spend on myself. To this day I remember the constant fear that I would be caught.

For me, dishonesty undiscovered was not a victory, as it is for some, but a painful burden. What undoubtedly started out as fear of punishment, changed over the years to fear of loss of self-esteem. What "other people" think of you is an important motivator. This was a logical extension of my mother's emphasis upon pride and reputation in the community—the need to "pay back the bank," to avoid the "shame." Whether motivated by fear of being caught, or of shame, or of lowered self-esteem, honesty

*The Public Speaking Society at Brooklyn Technical High School, 1932.*

characterizes most businessmen—the stereotype not withstanding. No apology is needed for seeking other people's admiration for probity. The results are what count. One must, however, strike a balance between smug self-satisfaction and the avaricious seeking of public approval.

I attended several public grade schools in Brooklyn and still have my "autograph" book from my eighth grade graduation, in which classmates wrote fond farewells to one another with silly doggerel. In the front of mine was a printed page where one listed "favorite songs," "favorite books," etc. Under the heading of "I want to be," I wrote, "an engineer." At the age of 13 did I really know that I wanted to be an engineer? I don't think I really knew what an engineer did, but I do know the origin of that expressed desire.

When I was quite a bit younger, we had a visitor to the house who was introduced as an engineer—a civil engineer, I believe—who had just come back from four years in Brazil. He had pictures of himself in puttees, high-laced boots, and a sombrero. What romance! That was what I wanted to be! Also, because I was good at arithmetic, engineering seemed to fit. So I enrolled at Brooklyn Technical High School—the first high school designed specifically to prepare its students for engineering college.

Why did I ultimately choose to study chemical engineering? Mr. Seroto, my first chemistry teacher in high school, took an interest in me and allowed me to do extra experiments in the lab when my curiosity was piqued. Therefore, when I went on to college at the Brooklyn Polytechnic Institute, I enrolled as a chemical engineer.

Times were tough. Near the school we had a "day old" store where the excess baked goods from Dugan's, a door delivery bakery, were sold at distress prices. Half a dozen slightly stale doughnuts and a bottle of milk made a cheap, filling lunch. How about a french fried potato sandwich? We high school kids, short of money, often had one for lunch. As a budding engineer, I was fascinated to see how the skins were scraped from the potatoes when they were rotated against a hardened abrasive wheel in the potato peeler. Crosscut, fried, and piled on a long piece of French or Italian bread, doused liberally with ketchup, and downed with a root beer, potatoes made a good lunch for 15 cents. But the best bargain was at another small stand. That guy served four skinny boiled hot dogs on the same kind of bread, piled them with sauerkraut, and offered all the root beer you could drink for 20 cents.

High school and adolescence were rough on me. Skinny, gawky, and incredibly shy, I found the passage through puberty to adolescence difficult and often traumatic. Because Brooklyn Tech was a boys' school and I worked most of the rest of the time, I had no opportunity to learn how to interact with girls. At home my role models were my serious and sometimes forbidding mother and two extremely competent and hard-working sisters. What with my "bookishness," a self-image of being "not good looking," and my shyness, my emotional life was a stormy turmoil during the high school years. Later, I was to find out that these were the kinds of powerful forces that always seem to underlie driving ambition. The causes of rejection may vary, but I am certain that within every entrepreneur, some rebuff provided the drive—the ambition, if you will—to succeed and to demonstrate that the rejections were unwarranted. The celebrated "fire in the belly" that characterizes successful businessmen may well have been ignited to burn away the bitterness and agony of youthful pain.

That timidity and lack of self-confidence made me miserable, but I was not entirely paralyzed. I was tough enough to cope with long hours of work and tough enough to stick to my principles when it really mattered. I was invited to join a high school fraternity; the pledge period included hazing, adolescent cruelty, and humiliation, and I rebelled. Although I wanted to "belong," I found the humiliation unacceptable, so I abruptly withdrew. Of course I was called a poor sport. I wanted to be "one of the guys," but not at any price. I don't think it's farfetched to say that I was showing the glimmering of a character trait an entrepreneur should have—to be willing to be different, not to follow the herd, to be unconventional, not to allow the all-too-human need for approval to overcome pride or principle. Perhaps I am glamorizing this simple act of rejection—I never did join a fraternity, even in college—but I think I am not exaggerating the connection between that instinctive experience and my makeup as a businessman.

I had another social problem in high school, caused by my Jewish-sounding name and the prominent Jacobs nose. I suffered some anti-Semitic slights and for a time considered changing my name. However, the sense of family, of pride, of not running away from a challenge prevailed. Of course, I ultimately recognized the triviality of the whole issue, but I've always had much sympathy for Jewish Americans as a result of these experiences. We can be thankful that overt anti-Semitism is gradually fading from our society.

Our neighborhood was essentially an ethnic enclave made up of a substantial number of Lebanese, Irish, and Italian immigrants—almost all first-generation—and only a smattering of "old Brooklyn" families. Those of us from Lebanese backgrounds were generally from a more affluent segment of our ethnic community—though during the Depression that was only a relative term. We had gone "uptown," unlike some of our relatives who stayed "downtown" around Atlantic Avenue.

My two closest pals from grade school through high school years were Michel and George. Michel's family was the more intellectual (his father, who had died early on, had been a merchant) and they had become almost as Americanized as my family. In contrast, George's family was more earthy and retained more of the "old country" characteristics. His father was alive but sedentary and unemployed, ostensibly retired. His mother worked at odd jobs to support the family. They were more like the families who had stayed downtown.

Many of our values arose from interchanges of our very different personalities. Because we were so close from childhood through adolescence into early adulthood, I had two role models that I could observe with no overlay of family authority. With them I was able to be more critical of what I saw, to admire, but also to reject. I did admire many things about both of them, but my hazy memory now is mostly of what I learned not to be—what I decided not to adopt as part of my developing person.

Olive-skinned, tall, and with a charming, even dazzling smile, Michel was multitalented. He could write beautifully, he was an artist—he could dash off sketches of people or scenes with a broken pencil—and a gifted conversationalist. With another friend, he even wrote an original play, *Ya Dilly*—Arabic for "My Goodness"—that our Lebanese community produced, acted in, and staged at the Brooklyn Academy of Music for a charity event. Bohemian in his outlook, he was as unconventional as I was straitlaced. Above all, Michel was handsome in a sultry way and women were enormously attracted to him.

How George and I envied him as we stumbled our way around learning about women! A man of the world, Michael made conquests that we could only dream about, particularly among older women, who were mesmerized by him. Girls of our own age seemed not to be impressed at all. But Michel was a dilettante, and that is the point of his character that influenced me most. My wide-ranging intelligence and even wider span of interests make me a quick study, but I can be quite superficial if I don't discipline myself. Not having Michel's natural talents, nor the opportunity to use them to mesmerize women, I concentrated on expanding my knowledge. I stressed intellectuality and gradually battled my way out of shyness—and it was a battle—by using language, words, and imagery. I learned to be interested in people, in their needs and their desire to be admired, and to be interesting to them. Unlike Michel, I spread this interest broadly and did not (perhaps could not) concentrate it on women.

I was motivated by a need to know, perhaps a need to know myself as I got to know other people. But the image of Michel as a dilettante is the most lasting impression I have of my friend. I am far from single-minded and have allowed myself to indulge those broad-ranging interests to some extent, but have almost always been able to keep them in perspective. When I write on Middle East politics, I have no illusion that I'm a foreign policy expert. In correspondence with Sidney Hook, the celebrated American philosopher, though I may stumble through philosophic thoughts, I have no illusions that I am a philosopher—even when Sidney applauds something I've said. When I write or speak on social theory, economic themes, or education, I do not delude myself that I am an expert.

In business, however, I'm willing to be measured; that is the area in which I am *not* a dilettante; that is the area in which I put it all on the line. One can be interested in many things, but the refusal to commit oneself to a primary enterprise is immature, a little cowardly, and an avoidance of responsibility—that is the curse of the dilettante.

I have no doubt that my wide-ranging interests, my imagination, my superficial acquaintance with philosophy, economics, education, politics, and psychology have contributed to the success of our business. The difference between a dilettante and others with equally scattered talents is simply focus.

George was short, muscular, athletic, and intensely ambitious for material things. He had enormous energy and drive and was single-minded: He was determined to be "somebody," to be admired for his accomplishments, athletic or otherwise. This sort of drive I recognized; determination was one of the hallmarks of my mother's character. What George showed me was that this sort of ambition can also corrupt.

In high school he decided to run for a school office and enlisted me as his aide. Somehow he was able to get at the ballots and proceeded to stuff the ballot box while I stood by and watched. He was elected and seemed not to be bothered at all that

POLYTECHNIC REPORTER, MARCH 3, 1937

**Full Program Of Inspection Trips Planned**

**Louis Everett '37 To Read Paper On Electrolytic Production of Chlorine**

(Continued from Page 1)

speak on "Some Modern Aspects of the Petroleum Industry," and Mr. Marshall will address the gathering on "Professional Development After Graduation."

**Everett '37, To Speak**

Saturday morning features more inspection trips, and in the afternoon the student prize contest will take place in the chapel.

Lewis B. Everett '37, was chosen as local entrant in the contest. He will deliver a paper on "The Electrolytic Production of Chlorine."

The two prizes of fifteen and ten dollars, respectively, will be awarded at the closing banquet, to be held

**AIChE Convention Chairman at Work**

Joseph J. Jacobs, Jr., chairman of the AIChE convention committee, makes a few last minute checks on the plans to accomodate 250

**IRC Members Neutrality F**

**Students To Hol Legislation Di**

The first meeting of t tional Relations Club of term will be held in the A group discussion on ne islation will be led by D orga '39.

The present neutrality Congress will be discuss forum. The principal bill mandatory neutrality wh place an embargo on all go to warring countries. (2) bargo which would limit s peacetime level and would shipment of implements o (3) discretionary neutral would permit the Presider cise full power in determ could be shipped to warri

Enthusiastic participatio members in former discus the meetings so successful discussion meetings and o are being planned.

Bananas, a tropical fruit ticularly susceptible to co

*JJJ, always active in extracurricular activities, organizing a meeting at Poly, 1937.*

his victory was tainted. At the same time my discomfort and embarrassment were intense, but because George was my friend I couldn't expose him. Confronted by the age-old challenge of ethical conflict, I failed to meet it.

That was my first exposure to the type of ambition that corrupts. Though I had negative feelings, they were only a passing discomfort then. Only later did I recognize that fierce ambition can often condone dishonesty and, perhaps more important, that the unbridled ambition that countenances dishonesty is likely to end in frustration and failure. Stories in the press notwithstanding, I believe that most businesses are honestly run and that dishonesty leads to many more failures than successes.

George and I spent many hours together in the YMCA pool and, as a result of our friendship, he too went to Brooklyn Tech, though he had no special aptitude for engineering or indeed any intellectual pursuit. He probably was using *me* for a role model. When I think back to my own negative self-image, that seems absurd.

He followed me to college at Brooklyn Polytechnic Institute (he was a year behind me), and I spent hours trying to help him with his studies. In his freshman year he was caught cheating on an important exam and was suspended. The dean, recognizing a disturbed and unintegrated personality, sent him to a psychiatrist. Through George's revelations about what he was finding out about himself, I became intensely interested in psychiatry and, sensing a need in myself, started reading Freud and other writers on the subject.

As many young people do when they go to college, I became rebellious, politically and otherwise. I was eaten with dissatisfaction with myself and my life. I had more questions about myself than I could answer. The field of psychiatry seemed to open infinite possibilities, to give me the tools with which to resolve my inner turmoil and conflicts. I almost envied George. Once after George reported a particularly troublesome session, I called the psychiatrist to offer him help in understanding George. Perhaps I was secretly hoping to be brought into the magic circle. Properly, the psychiatrist told me to butt out and not to interfere with George's therapy!

George ultimately quit engineering school and took a job as an insurance salesman. He was good at it because he was an extremely hard worker, people liked him, and he could be very persuasive. He finally came to terms with himself, though I doubt that he ever quite lost the bitterness of his frustration at not reaching the unrealistic goals he had set. For one as intensely ambitious as I was, then and later, George was a constant reminder that ambition, when not reined in by ethics, can easily lead down unwanted byways.

Rebellion was rising in me. I didn't want to go to Brooklyn Poly, even though it was highly regarded as an engineering school. I yearned to get away from home, but we simply could not afford to send me away to school. I was working 13-hour days, going to school from nine in the morning until three in the afternoon and then working from six in the evening until midnight in a soda fountain. I fell asleep in class more than once, my grades were mediocre, and my discontent was rising. Since my father's death and my brother Ed's defection, my mother adopted the role of head of the family and, with limited resources, ran it with an iron hand.

Another of my Lebanese friends, also named George, had gone to the University of Iowa. That summer he filled me with fascinating stories of life there: a big open campus (Brooklyn Poly was in the center of Brooklyn with a streetcar line for a campus) and lots of dates at a coed school. My imagination ran wild. Could I get a job there? George said yes, he knew the owner of the main restaurant in Iowa City. George also said that I could room with him. Did I dare? This was my chance to break the bonds to my mother, to grow up, to show my independence.

By some machination I converted the check for my annual tuition at Poly to cash and, without any warning to my family, took the bus to Iowa City (a two-day trip). I ran away from home! But I did at least leave a letter. Mom was in hysterics for days, but the others in the family were secretly cheering me on, though they didn't dare belittle my mother's reaction to my deserting her and the family. Evelyn saved that letter. Today I cringe to recall the adolescent, if nonetheless genuine, anguish it projected. The struggle to grow up, to be independent, to cut the apron strings to a strong mother cries out. The whole experience was painful and traumatic at the time, and rereading the letter recreates those emotions even today. But looking back 55 years, I now appreciate this incident as the first step toward emulating my father—toward adventure, and daring, and striking out on my own.

When I got to Iowa, I was looking forward to the freedom I would find there, to rooming with my friend George, and to finding, perhaps, a steady girlfriend—something I'd not had either the opportunity or the time for until then. Two days after I arrived, George moved out to live with a waitress and I was alone. I got the job he had mentioned, but I had a tough time making ends meet. Working as a waiter was no sinecure. I hadn't realized how much my living at home had helped me get along.

Because I was working so hard trying to mature and work out my relationships with girls, my grades were still only average. I never had a steady girl, but had enough contact with them in classes and on the few casual dates I had time for to begin to fight through my shyness.

My Iowa escapade was my first taste of real defeat. At the end of the school year, I was completely broke and almost with relief I yielded to my mother's importunings to come home and return to Poly. I hitched a ride to Buffalo, New York, with a student who dropped me off at my brother Ted's fraternity house at the University of Buffalo. I had exactly 25 cents to my name. Ted, bless him, took me in, gave me a bed, fed me for two days, then loaned me enough for the bus ride back to Brooklyn.

Here I was back home, facing Mom. I had rebelled, made a break for independence and, in my own eyes, had failed. Dejected, I insisted that I wanted no more of college. I would get a full-time job and become independent that way. After all, I had been a mediocre college student. I wasn't sure I was cut out for it. Besides paying tuition was a burden on the family, even though I worked.

My mother would have none of it. I *must* go back to college! I *was* capable! I *could* be something: a successful engineer! There was that stubborn faith again—that certainty that we were better than we believed we were—that had resulted in Evelyn's becoming a famous designer. Mom would not let me accept defeat. Inevitably, I agreed to go back to Poly and got another nighttime job.

That experience had a powerful influence on my life. The humiliation of defeat burned inside me. Defeat cannot be avoided. That is the price of daring. I've had many more serious defeats in my career as I avidly pursued success. Every one of them was painful, but I always fought back. Obviously, the successes outweighed the defeats; hence this book. But, to the extent that the defeats were overcome and conditioned the quality of the successes, their influence on the process of reaching goals reveals the true "anatomy of an entrepreneur," as I hope to tell. As I discovered later, the process is more important than the accomplishment.

FOUR

# *The Boy Becomes a Man and Discovers His Mind*

So it was back to Polytechnic, resigned to the failure of my rebellion; working, studying, and missing the social life that seemed to come so easily to my friends. My academic record as an undergraduate was undistinguished, although it gradually got better in my junior and senior years. I may have expected too much of myself. Working outside as many hours as I did, I had little time for concentrated studying. Though I have been an avid reader all my life (I spent hours reading by flashlight under the covers after my mother had warned me to turn out the lights and go to sleep), my essential learning process, I found to my surprise, is verbal or oral. It is said that people learn best by one of three routes—by listening, by reading, or by writing. I am not a note taker and lack the patience to read long reports. I learn best from an oral briefing at which I can ask questions. So whatever I learned, I learned at lectures—when I was able to stay awake, that is.

For everyone, college is the time of maximum change between adolescence and maturity—a time of questing, of questioning, of developing new role models. It seems preordained that the development of new heroes or idols demands the rejection of those in the family. Mine was no exception. Indeed my search was more intense than that of those who were lucky enough to have a live and vital father as a role model.

There was Professor Ming who taught the simple subject of mechanical drawing—an immaculate, cultured, and ever-gentle Chinese who made even drawing a straight line an expression of meticulousness and elegance. Always dressed in perfect, refined taste, he was a model of culture and style that exposed my own sloppiness, a rebellion against my mother's meticulous habits. Mom wanted me to be neat. Here was someone whose neatness I admired. The precision of his speech, his drawing, his teaching, his self-discipline were a revelation of the power of control and organization of one's talents that represented a new world to me. What I remember most, however, was his dignity. It was impressive to watch someone teaching such an elementary course while radiating dignified composure, born of some inner self-confidence. Perhaps I recognized in him the inherent culture and dignity of my uneducated and illiterate mother.

Surprisingly, there were two teachers who had profound influence upon me who were not engineers at all—they were in the English department. From one I learned to appreciate the value of writing, from the other, the value of speech. James Reid Parker, who in addition to being a teacher was a writer for the *New Yorker*, taught me to write. From him I learned the elegance of the well-turned phrase, the ways in which words could be used to manipulate emotions, and the value of using language clearly. He devoted a whole hour to warning against the use of "nice nellyisms"—calling a prostitute a "woman of easy virtue," an undertaker a "mortician," a boiler stoker a "stationary engineer." The love of the language he imparted stays with me today.

The ability to say what one means is an unusual asset for an engineer, but is essential for the successful entrepreneur. Without an understanding of language, its strength and its weaknesses, it is difficult to run a business of any size. My language ability has been a major asset and has distinguished me clearly from other engineers. I have occasionally wondered if I could have, for instance, operated an advertising business successfully. I think so, but in advertsing my language abilities would not have made as much difference as they have in the engineering business, where the standard of comparison is much lower.

The head of the department of English was S. Marion Tucker, a courtly Southerner who was a dynamic and mesmerizing speaker with an irresistibly captivating and dazzling smile. I had joined the debating society and the public speaking club in high school to help me fight through my shyness. To speak in public, to be able to express oneself well, to be persuasive in argument—these were skills I admired. Hearing Professor Tucker amuse, sway, and hold an audience in the palm of his hand was a revelation. If I could learn to be like that, what could I not accomplish? Would it not be the route to social acceptance and to relationships with women? Words are still a passion with me—an expression of all those internal drives that define the successful entrepreneur.

To this day, public speaking and its derivatives, such as the eloquent defense of an idea or a sales presentation, are among the greatest assets I bring to our company. How many times have I persuaded people working for me to make an extra effort, or to meet high standards of professionalism and ethics, or given them confidence in the future of our company? How many times have I made people feel wanted and appreciated, that their importance to the enterprise is recognized? How many times have I persuaded potential clients to trust us, to depend upon our integrity, to feel that we would leave no stone unturned in the performance of their project? Obviously such eloquence and persuasiveness are meaningless without sincerity and the will to honor our words. But all those basic virtues could easily languish without appropriate projection. Everyone knows that it is *not* true that if you invent a better mousetrap the world will beat a path to your door.

Honor, integrity, and reputation were the keystones of my family's code of behavior. Phony words of promise and the manipulation of emotions without sincerity and integrity get exposed very quickly.

I also learned in those days the seductiveness of words, the manipulative possibilities for good or evil, and understood the reasons for the enormous influence of the media on our lives. To this day I still receive more requests to speak than I can fulfill.

My first class in chemical engineering with Professor Olsen provided a revelation and a shock that influenced me deeply. A legend in his field, he had retired as head of the department of chemical engineering at Poly by the time I met him, but was still teaching. He was a founder and long-time secretary of the American Institute of Chemical Engineers and a pioneer in recognizing that the industrial application of chemical reactions was less a branch of chemistry than it was a branch of engineering.

I'll never forget the first time he asked me to stand up and give the answer to a technical question. After I gave a self-confident answer, he made no comment but merely smiled and asked me another seemingly unrelated question. Again I answered confidently; again Professor Olsen made no comment. Then another question, then another, and on and on for 15 minutes with never a hint from him about how I was doing. Finally he asked one more question and, in replying, I flatly contradicted my very first answer! He had taken me through the circuitous route of questioning, where each answer was allowed to precondition the next one, to this humiliating denouement.

I was furious. I had been made to look like a fool. I shouted, "But you must tell me which answer is right!" He smiled and said, "Why don't *you* decide? Either your first answer was wrong, as you just concluded, or you made a mistake in answering one of the series of questions that led to an incorrect and contradictory conclusion. You find out! Next student, please!" I was shaken to my shoes. One either gave the right answer to a question or the wrong one, and your professor, or your teacher, or your mother immediately told you which.

This was my introduction to the Socratic method. Most of the students hated Dr. Olsen's classes. He made them look like such asses. Here my early influences took over. I would *not* be defeated. I must cope with this or be humiliated publicly, and thus bring shame on myself. (What would Mom say?) So I learned to be analytical, to question all assumptions, to take nothing as a given. I began to enjoy the challenge and became a disciple. A few years later when I was teaching undergraduate classes myself, I took up the style with a vengeance. Then my department head received so many complaints about my "ruthless" teaching style that he reprimanded me. Of course, I had overdone it, probably because the enormous ego satisfaction of the intellectual jousting was too much to resist—especially as my own ego badly needed propping up at the time.

The Socratic method has been a powerful tool for me ever since. I no longer use it to prove that I am smarter than someone else, but to sweep away wishful thinking, to expose underlying weaknesses. For using these methods I'm known as a tough boss, a relentless questioner, and an exposer of phoniness. "Don't give Joe any bull! He'll punch holes in your arguments if they are not supported by facts and facts in depth. Label a guess a guess, or a projection a projection, but don't give unequivocal conclusions without support." That's a common admonition around our office.

Socrates is the god of my analytic ability just as my father and mother are the gods of my synthetic or creative ability. An entrepreneur needs both abilities. Can one be coldly analytic *and* passionately creative? The answer is yes! And entrepreneurship demands it. Not everyone can combine these talents, and the entrepreneur sensitively creates a successful business by hiring and melding people who are dominated by one or the other trait. This is a crucial constituent of the "anatomy of an entrepreneur."

By far the most important influence on me was Don Othmer, who succeeded Professor Olsen as head of the department of chemical engineering. He was not only an excellent chemical engineer, but he was also ambition incarnate. A big farm boy from Nebraska, unsophisticated and unworldly (by New York standards anyway) during those days, he received an early Ph.D. in chemical engineering from the University of Michigan. He had worked for the Eastman Kodak Co. and developed several novel and useful processes there. Why he went into teaching I'll never know. It wasn't a natural talent, yet I learned much from him, little of it in the classroom.

I have never met a harder working person in my life. He had no children and worked every evening and most weekends with a single-mindedness that yielded an outpouring of technical papers, usually coauthored by one or more of his thesis students (I was among them). Their publication in technical journals enhanced his worldwide reputation and brought him a parade of consulting clients.

At school it was said that Don had become a teacher in order to have a free office, free laboratory, and unlimited numbers of assistants (students) for his enormous consulting practice. Though I knew he was receiving generous consulting fees for work I was doing for a pittance, I never resented it. I was so grateful to learn what people in the business world wanted to know about technical problems. It turned out to be quite different from what most professors thought was important. They used the same technical information, but the businessman looked for the pragmatic solution, not the theoretical one the professors usually sought.

What I admired about Don Othmer was his technical salesmanship and his ability to attract consulting clients. He would present new ideas with care and on impeccable scientific and engineering grounds and then make projections and imaginative leaps forward that were clearly speculative. But his sincerity gave those projections much more credence than they deserved. With great skill he used his imposing physical presence, his titles of professor and head of the department, and the enormous number of technical papers he had written. In the profession there was substantial resentment toward him, but most of the criticism came from those who were jealous and less talented. I admired him then, still do, and am grateful for what I learned from him—all outside his classes, for as I have said, he was a mediocre teacher in the classroom but a great one outside.

The teachers I have mentioned are among those from whom I learned more, perhaps, than they thought they were teaching. Because of my working long hours after school and full-time during the summer, I simply did not have the time to get grades that were anything but average. But there was no quitting, either the workload or my studies. I had to succeed so that I could become independent and "go into business for myself"—a drive then hidden deep in my subconscious.

Politically, I moved far to the left, helped form the Liberal Club, read Marx and Engels omnivorously, and flirted seriously with communism, though I never became a party member. Even an archconservative engineering school like Polytechnic had its Marxist contingent, this being the thirties when the Communist party and Marxism, or rather Stalinism, were growing and pervasive forces. I marched in rallies supporting the Lincoln Brigade in Spain. I wrote editorials for the school newspaper castigating the "big" company, Union Carbide, because its miners were developing silicosis. We were such heroes, befriending the underdog and, linking "bigness" with immoral and abusive power, opposing the excesses of "big" business. I put "big" in quotation marks because it is a perfect example of the emotional content of words. That tiny word converts the neutral or even somewhat heroic noun, "business," to something malevolent in most people's minds.

The political rebellion I showed early on was a first step for my slowly developing self-esteem. It made me realize that I had a mind and that I was capable of independent thought. The discipline of engineering and the unrelenting Socratic method allowed me gradually to rationalize that rebellion. My attraction to leftist thought, though relatively brief, was clearly motivated by compassion. I have not lost that compassion. We may have been misguided, but with the stars of certain virtue in our eyes we did not realize that most liberal, or even Marxist, advocates have managed to expropriate compassion as their exclusive province. It is a key to their appeal. The lure of the pseudoscientific rationale of Marxism with compassionate objectives is irresistible to the young seeking their independence. Such laudable motives could easily validate any rebellion we might care to raise against values we learned at home. Only after I had written those stories attacking big business did I recognize the seductiveness of the "nice nellyisms" of Marxist rhetoric. It was even later that I understood how my compassion was subtly corrupted to endorse ideas that had unrecognized and serious hidden consequences that were far from benevolent.

My passionate liberalism in college was accompanied by what I recognize now as an insufferable self-righteousness. I *knew* that my compassion for my suffering fellow man was more intense and more penetrating than that of other college students. They, apparently, just did not care. That is the moral high ground that the liberal left of today commands.

The Socratic method helped me to see through the clichés of Marxist thought. In the thirties, Sidney Hook, the head of the department of philosophy at New York University and a former Marxist, had taken on the Marxist and especially the Stalinist power structure in the intellectual mainstream of the United States. He was the *bête noire* of the Stalinists during the famous Moscow trials. I began to read his surgical attacks on the party and its pseudointellectuals and developed an admiration for his critical analyses of stuffy, intellectual arrogance. My eyes were opened as I saw the corruption of what I considered to be the utopian goal we sensitive college students were so proud of.

Many years later I met Sidney Hook and we became friends. I joined him a number of times in decrying the straitjackets placed upon free thought in universities by the militant left and in exposing the ways in which many well-meaning liberals were being cynically manipulated. We were especially active in the sixties when colleges were being taken over by the radicals, and administrators and faculty were often exposed as weak and spineless. His recent autobiography recounting his jousting with the renowned Marxist intellectuals of the thirties was fascinating to me, though I was only an observer.

In June 1937 I graduated with a bachelor's degree in chemical engineering. Now I would finally get a real job. I would practice my profession! My mother's ambition for me would be justified, and I would finally no longer be dependent upon my family but could contribute to it financially.

I had a rude awakening. The interviews were few and far between in that Depression year. Out of a graduating class of eight chemical engineers, only one of us was offered a job on which to found a career. His salary of $125 a month was considered unusually high, a bonanza. I received only one offer, a job in the analytic laboratory of an electroplating company for $12.50 a week! Hell, I could make twice or three times that as a short-order cook. I might have to work twelve or fourteen hours a day to do it, but I could do it. I despaired.

Then Don Othmer asked me to stay on as a graduate teaching fellow for a stipend of $300 for the year, but with free tuition for the master's degree courses. I was assured that, by teaching in the night school and helping Don with his consulting, I could earn enough to survive. Poly, situated as it was in the heart of metropolitan New York, had a large and active night school with an undergraduate enrollment that was two or three times that of the day school. All of the graduate classes I wanted to attend were given at night too, which would help my scheduling. I had never considered graduate school up to this time because I was anxious to go to work—I wanted so badly to be self-supporting and independent. I had not forgotten the ignominy of my flight to Iowa! But I had little choice. As it happened, I continued graduate work and eventually earned a Ph.D. I tell people today that the only reason I earned that doctor's degree was because I couldn't get a job when I graduated in 1937—a simplification, of course, but largely true. My inability to get a job led me into graduate work and gave me a fortuitous exposure to teaching, which is essentially communication, and the skills I learned in that profession I have used ever since.

Jacobs Engineering is founded upon the chemical engineering knowledge I gained at Poly and its application to the building of process plants. But that is almost incidental. I am convinced that I would have been successful in any field, for the characteristics that make for success in business are only rarely those that arise from specific, narrow, technical knowledge. The real growth of our company was based upon skills and talent quite apart from engineering. In college, because of my heavy courseload, my roving curiosity, my ability to acquire superficial knowledge, and my wide interests were assets. In teaching I found a use for these interests and, in the students and my fellow teachers, the stimulation to challenge myself. I learned to work with people and not just for myself, to find rewards as well in stimulating and challenging others.

# II

# Decisions, Commitment, and a Purpose Unfolds

FIVE

# *Academia or Business?*

The baccalaureate ceremony of the Polytechnic Institute of Brooklyn in June 1937 marked the first measurable and important goal that I attained in my life. As I stepped on the stage, I thought, "There, Mom, I have justified your faith. I did what you insisted that I *must* and could do, and I now have a bachelor's degree in chemical engineering." For her, the degree was proof that she had been right all along. She knew I could do it and so I had. It is not that she considered the achievement unimportant, merely that she, on the one hand, was unsurprised. I, on the other, was. This degree was proof that determination did indeed bring results. I was sure that if I worked hard enough I could do it—but always there was that qualifying if, that acknowledgment that failure might engulf me.

As a graduate assistant at Poly, I taught undergraduate classes and laboratories and, simultaneously, took graduate courses toward a master's degree. Discovering, finally, that I didn't have a mediocre mind, as I had suspected when I was getting average grades, I blossomed intellectually and found that I absolutely gloried in teaching and in being able to stand in front of the class as the "authority," not the learner. In the night school many of the students were considerably older than I was, and that added substantially to the pleasure.

In my graduate courses I made A's easily. In teaching undergraduate classes I polished my language skills and honed my persuasiveness and the ability to simplify apparently difficult concepts. I learned more fundamental chemical engineering by teaching in those few years than I had in the previous four. The fundamental and simple principles I taught carried me through to solutions, in subsequent years, of what appeared to be enormously complex engineering problems.

I lived at home but was now earning enough so as to be no longer a drain on the family's finances. I even had a little spending money and could occasionally see Broadway plays for 50 cents (if I waited until the curtain went up and there were unoccupied seats left). I have fond memories of Lunt and Fontanne, the Mercury Theater's Shakespeare with Orson Welles and Joseph Cotten, Ethel Merman, and others, and my social life started to improve slightly. I had dated enough to feel reasonably comfortable with women—though I would never be the "lover" my friend Michel was.

I had played tennis on the college team, and the game became one of my social entrées. My sister had taught me to dance and I did that reasonably well. So I was a welcome member of the "crowd"—a group of predominantly Lebanese Americans, most older than I was, who met every Sunday. They were bright people and the conversation was witty and stimulating. We played tennis in the early afternoon and then would go to one of our homes for dinner—not much alcohol as I remember—and then would play charades or dance all night. My mother's homemade rolls, ham and baked beans, and other delicious goodies were among the highlights of our weekly itinerary. I liked people to whom intellectuality and clever conversation are important, and though they were older, they appealed to me more than my contemporaries did.

One night we went to Gladys Jabara's house to welcome her younger sister Violet back from Beirut, where she had spent a year with their oldest sister, Florence. Violet had graduated from Wellesley in 1937 and her graduation present was a year's visit to Lebanon.

She was a delight: petite with a pretty, expressive face dominated by the largest dark brown eyes and the longest lashes I'd ever seen. Though not as dark as most, she was the quintessential Lebanese woman. Of course I was attracted to her beauty, but there was something more—a gentleness, a sense of dignity, and above all, intelligence. In those days Lebanese women rarely attended university. They were raised to become wives and mothers. Social graces, cultured conversation, the ability to organize and run a hospitable household were the criteria for success for young Lebanese-American women of our generation—they had no need of higher education.

With her, I discovered new intellectual worlds in the arts, in music, in opera, ballet, and literature. I still am an unabashed Dixieland fan, but because of her I saw another cultural world I'd not known.

One characteristic Vi helped me to crystallize was integrity. My various jobs had exposed me to all sorts of small-time chicanery, exaggeration, and outright misrepresentation—the law of the street. I had been raised to respect pride, honor, and integrity, but it would have been easy for me to be persuaded that in the real world one needed to present a "hollow" ice-cream cone or practice other deceptions in order to survive—especially during those hard days of the Depression. Vi's standards of morality, of integrity, and of almost ruthless honesty were so stubbornly held and close to puritanical that she reinforced and solidified in me the old family standards. I admired her so much, I could not do otherwise.

Obviously Vi has played an indispensable part in my career. Time after time I found that her response to a question, or more likely a request, from me was uncritically supportive. I now see that I took for granted her unhesitating acceptance of any risky or tangential path my restless and discontented drive sent me along. How easily and justifiably she could have asked me to take her wishes or security into account. She never did. How many potential entrepreneurs have been diverted by perfectly reasonable considerations for wife or family?

I was still pretty poor when Vi and I started to go "steady." A Saturday night date often consisted of a subway ride to lower

*Violet Jabara upon graduation from Wellesley College.*

Manhattan, then a ride on the doubledecker Fifth Avenue bus to the northern tip of Manhattan to Fort Tryon Park or the Cloisters, and then return and stop for a cup of coffee. The round trip took two to three hours. Total cost for the evening was one dollar. Conversation, discussion, and dreams—especially dreams: dreams of graduate degrees, of success, of accomplishment, of recognition. With that, the warmth of being together, touching and hugging and sharing—all have continued for almost 50 years, and the memory has been burnished to a rosy hue that binds us together in our later years.

I considered it almost an accident that I was getting a master's degree. I was destined to work and this was just a diversion, but teaching grabbed me. It was such an ego trip! To have students hanging on my words as I dispensed my "wisdom" about chemical engineering made me euphoric. No wonder teaching attracts so many brilliant people with weak egos. The old saw that "those who can, do and those who can't, teach" is not entirely an exaggeration. Many great teachers have the qualities of leadership that would have enabled them to succeed at other professions. They chose the academic life for purer reasons. But many others seem to be motivated by the psychological rewards of the unbridled power they wield in the classroom. Exercised benevolently, as it usually is, this power is a great force, but occasionally it can be used corruptly. Teachers have such enormous power that, when they use it for political manipulation, they can be dangerous. It is so easy for them to bring their uncritical and admiring students under their sway. College students look for new heroes and new role models, often rejecting their traditional family standards, and are frequently gripped by a streak of radicalism. Professors who take advantage of their students' vulnerability and preach political activism instead of examining ideas are guilty of intellectual rape.

To my surprise, I found that teachers as a group can be very narrow-minded and can have rather limited interests. For one who hasn't been on the inside, it may be hard to imagine how petty, childish, envious, and jealous the intellectually brilliant can be. The politicking, maneuvering, and backbiting, under cover of the cultured language and impeccable manners, almost made me long for the directness of the street fights of my youth. Even so, I loved teaching and seriously considered making it my career. But that persistent ring in my ears of the question, "What business are you in?" always haunted me. I must try to make my way in the business world! I must seek adventure and take risks as my father had! Could I tempt failure and win? Was I as good as my mother and family said I could be, or was I as unworthy as I suspected I might be? Should I set the path of my whole life in concrete at the age of 23? Should I settle for the security of something I loved doing and did well? For me, a measure of success was reasonably assured, but my father had found new worlds to explore. Should I do less?

Other than the psychological rewards of teaching, I acquired an asset I carry until this day. In the gamut from the ruthless, penetrating, and agonizing Socratic method to the logical development and simplification of complex concepts that I learned as a teacher, the tools have never grown rusty.

In 1939, toward the end of my two-year stint as a teaching fellow, I selected as my thesis subject the testing of a new process developed by a company, Autoxygen, Inc., that was one of Don Othmer's clients. We built a fairly large pilot plant to test a process that involved the use of an alarmingly large quantity of heated kerosene. The plant caught fire one night at 2:00 A.M. while I was operating it. Don, who had come to see how I was doing, and I finally put it out by using every fire extinguisher we had. I duly completed the thesis and received a master's degree.

Apparently the work I had done was good enough to impress our sponsors. They offered and I accepted a job as a research chemical engineer with them. The salary was modest, but at last I had a full-time job in my profession. Autoxygen, Inc., a small company with five employees and a laboratory in midtown Manhattan, was founded to develop and license new chemical processes dreamed up by one of the two principals, Dr. V. R. Khokatnur. Mr. C. O. Assmus was the president, promoter, entrepreneur, salesman, and manager of the business. Both were caricatures of people I would meet many times in my business career.

Dr. Khokatnur was the technical guru, an Indian who had been educated at Cornell University and had a Ph.D. in chemistry. He had worked for several chemical companies and had obtained some backing to develop a number of new ideas. His routine was to come into the office in the morning, sit at his desk, and start reading a pile of technical journals. He was an omnivorous reader and, as he read, he would spew out ideas: "If this reaction will work here, can it be applied to this other process?" "Here's a new product coming on the market, couldn't it be made by this series of reactions?" and on and on. I don't believe I ever saw him do an actual experiment in the lab. The company employed two chemists to test his ideas, and my job was to assess their economic value or to devise ways to use them commercially.

This was my introduction to the unreconstructed, undiscriminating idea man. To Dr. Khokatnur, every new idea of every new day was as revolutionary and novel as every other idea. He wasted no time on self-evaluation and never doubted the merits of each of his inspirations. Dr. Olsen would have massacred him, but Dr. K. came up with ideas faster than the Socratic method would have had the time to demolish them. And some were good concepts. We developed a number of them and many of the company's patents have my name on them as co-inventor.

In watching Dr. K. develop new ideas from a scrap of information here and a scrap there and then make intuitive leaps to novel conclusions, I learned to emulate his method of "free association." His mind seemed to be a computer bank. As he read, he would scan his memory to see if he could make any connection, no matter how tenuous. Most of us place too many constraints on our minds. He let his roam with abandon. Engineers, especially, are taught to distrust intuition. Ideas, we are taught, must stand up to numerical and quantitative analysis, and until they do they should be treated with suspicion. Not Dr. K.'s. His lack of intellectual discipline and inability to differentiate between flights of fancy and solidly based ideas never gave him pause. Those of us who watched this virtuoso performance learned, in its astounding absence, the virtues of discrimination.

I also discovered the limitations of the Socratic method. Its ruthless examination of underlying assumptions can be sidetracked. If the answer to just one of the questions asked is wrong, the conclusion might also be wrong. Occasionally, when I had "proved" that Dr. K.'s ideas absolutely would not work, he insisted I try. Some did in fact work. He had not been able to counter my arguments, but some long-forgotten observation had supported his "hunch." It didn't happen often, but frequently enough that I no longer dismiss hunches or intuition out of hand. Our brain stores thousands of facts and observations, many buried so deeply in the subconscious that they cannot be brought to the surface easily. Yet somehow they affect the thought process. Can one at the same time be an intuitive thinker and have an analytic mind? I think so.

What did Autoxygen live on? It was supposed to develop processes, license them and collect royalties, and generate great riches. In reality, in the two years I worked there, no process was ever completely commercialized, although several came very close. That's where Cyril Assmus—the consummate salesman (shades of my Uncle Elias)—came in. Tall, distinguished, handsome, with a British accent, he dressed impeccably, wore a

Homburg hat, and carried a walking stick or cane for effect only. He was the soul of urbanity, representing and protecting the funny little Dr. K., who was brilliant and unworldly. He presented Dr. K. as the unpolished diamond whose brilliance would be discovered, burnished, and exploited by those who were asked to sponsor his work. Assmus was able to convince some pretty substantial business people to provide option money to fund Dr. K.'s work. Negotiations always involved the working out of lengthy contracts, detailing all the business arrangements such as market segments, royalties, and so on, just as though the fragments of Dr. K.'s imagination, usually labeled as processes, had already been proven.

The company actually lived on option money for two years. It was a hand-to-mouth existence and often my salary was not paid for a month or more until Assmus made a new deal and found new money. The precarious existence held no particular fears for me. I knew what living from hand to mouth meant. For a potential entrepreneur, my experience at Autoxygen was salutary. That was my first observation of a failed entrepreneurial effort. Assmus, operating with confidence and flair, even on the verge of bankruptcy, made a permanent impression on me. Good ideas are not enough. Good salesmanship is not enough. Seizing opportunity undoubtedly plays a key role in the development of a business, but there must be a focus and there must be discipline: discipline to live within your means, to avoid scattering your energies, and to temper your hopes and dreams with realism. I didn't learn that discipline then but, when I finally started into business, my experience at Autoxygen helped me avoid some of the pitfalls I had seen at first hand.

My job occupied only about 50 hours a week. What to do with all that extra time? After all, rarely had I worked less than 12 hours a day. I had found a logical and easy extension to my work day. I could continue to teach at Polytechnic at night. I spent every night there and, on those nights when I wasn't teaching, took additional graduate courses. Yet, even with that workload, I had no clear-cut intentions at the time of going on to earn a doctorate.

And I was as poor as ever. My oldest brother Ed had divorced, remarried (another "American," Mom fumed again), and started a family. My next brother, Al, and his wife, Emily, finally moved out and they too started a family. Helen was away in China with her husband, and Ted was an intern at Buffalo General Hospital. So there was just my sister Evelyn, the career woman, to support the household. I simply followed the customary routine: I gave all the money I earned to Mom and she doled out an allowance for me. I'd long since suppressed any resentment of the arrangement.

Dates with Vi had to wait for Saturday night or the occasional hour or two squeezed in between work and Poly. Failing that, I'd spend an hour on the phone talking to her. Her father would get furious. "Suppose someone is trying to call us!" he would say. (To this day Vi is uncomfortable on the phone and tends to cut conversations short.) The occasional Thursday nights when her mother served T-bone steaks were luxurious highlights for me.

By the spring of 1941 it was becoming increasingly apparent that Autoxygen, Inc., wasn't going to make it. One evening Don Othmer asked me if I wanted to do some lab experiments in my spare time for another client of his, American Lecithin Co. Lecithin is an emulsifier derived from soybean oil and is used principally in chocolates to prevent the fat from separating out in hot weather. The company believed that one of the oil refiners was using lecithin as an antioxidant in lubricating oils. With Don's introduction, I met the president of American Lecithin and we talked about testing the possibility.

Now I began to synthesize the experience I had been gaining. I sensed an opportunity and went after it aggressively. I suggested that I quit my job at Autoxygen, Inc., go back to Poly, work on the lecithin project full time, and make it the subject of a doctoral thesis. In this, my first presentation of a concept and a program, I outlined an exhaustive study that would allow us to conclude whether lecithin was of any use in lube oils. I managed to express the ideas forcefully without making unrealistic promises.

"How much would this cost?" the president of American Lecithin asked. I boldly asked for $2,000 in salary for the academic year for myself and payment for equipment and expenses. The $2,000 was almost double the usual stipend for a doctoral fellowship. The president agreed; the sale was made. Shades of Uncle Elias, shades of Don Othmer selling a consulting client, and shades of C. O. Assmus selling Dr. K.'s ideas for more rather than less. Finally, shades of my father, the traveling salesman. I had made my first real sale of an idea, of a professional service, of a program rather than a product that you could feel or touch. It was my first step to being an entrepreneur. I had successfully rolled together a salary equal to or better than I could get from a full-time job with the opportunity to produce a doctoral thesis. And I could conveniently continue and even expand my teaching.

When I triumphantly told Don Othmer about it, he smiled and then reminded me that, as my adviser, he had to get a substantial retainer and that the school needed to collect its overhead. I became very angry. I could see my sale being canceled by his aggressiveness. After all, Don didn't know any more about lecithin than I did, and the school had the labs just sitting there. He ignored my indignation, talked to the people at American Lecithin, and easily got what he and the school wanted. Of course, I was dead wrong. The requirements were really reasonable. In truth, I was afraid that my first sale would be negated.

Was academia tugging at me? After all, why else get a doctorate? Doctorates in chemical engineering were rare in those days and their influence on one's success in business was doubtful. A doctorate would make me unusual when seeking a job, but I suspect that I was really "covering my rear" by getting a "union card" for teaching.

I had already received a new and humbling slant on the value of my college education. One summer I went to Cincinnati, Ohio, to work for Vulcan Copper Co., another of Don Othmer's clients and a fabricator of copper equipment for the chemical industry. Ted Wentworth, the oldest son of the founder, had gone to MIT but left after his freshman year to go back to work for his father. Ambitious and hard working, he competed furiously with his autocratic, irascible, and sometimes cruel father. Ted decided that, rather than fabricate vessels to other engineers' designs, he would learn to design them himself—and he did. He further expanded into designing and building whole complicated chemical process plants. Ted Wentworth was one of the smartest and most capable chemical engineers I have ever met. He hired many graduate engineers and could compete with and surpass the best of them. College degrees, it seems, are not much more than an indicator of potential competence; they confer no guarantee of superior knowledge.

In Cincinnati I also learned how tremendously difficult a task it is for a son to work for a forceful, accomplished, and capable father. I watched Mr. Wentworth, the founder of the business, and his son battling constantly as Ted tried to establish his *own* identity. Ted was trying desperately to change the character of the business so it would reflect the result of *his* efforts and not those of his father. It was painful to watch and helped form my very strong aversion to establishing a dynasty or "family business."

Going back to Poly full time in the spring of 1941, I increased my teaching load and worked long hours on my thesis, "The Use of Soy Bean Lecithin in Lubricating Oils." Sometimes I wonder if I exaggerate the long hours I worked, but I have stark memories of night after night spent in that lab and I did, after all, complete that thesis in a little over one year. Most doctoral candidates take two or sometimes three years to complete their theses. It was no profound, fundamental creation. It was a good workmanlike job, filled with masses of data on the way in which lecithin works to prevent lube oils from breaking down and supporting the theory that it improved petroleum lube oils substantially. I believe my studies induced some companies to start adding lecithin to their lube oil. However, its use faded as new synthetic additives proved more effective.

The study of petroleum oils was not something I ever pursued, but the work itself provided invaluable lessons, among them one on the making of first impressions and the subtleties of credibility. Just months before completing my thesis, I was in the lab on Easter day evaporating some samples that I had been preparing for some time. The solvent was petroleum ether, very volatile and flammable. I tipped one of the beakers, the petroleum ether spilled on the hot plate and all the samples went up in flames. Another fire! My samples were ruined. I still remember that as "Black Easter."

I started to reconstruct and repeat my experiments the next day, but was pretty depressed. I went to see my old friend, Dr. Olsen, who was now retired. "Tell me, Dr. Olsen, what the hell am I bothering with this doctor's degree for? What is its value? What does it all mean?"

He chuckled. "I'll tell you, Joe," he said "When you get up on that stage and they read your name and that velvet hood is placed on your shoulders, you'll be mighty proud of yourself—and your family will be too. When you go out in the world, you'll wear a suit with a vest and a watch chain carrying all of your honorary society keys and you'll preen as they call you 'Doctor.' If you go into industry, however, you'll meet or work with people with bachelor's degrees whose engineering knowledge will put yours to shame. You'll even meet people who have no degree who are better engineers than you are [I thought of Ted Wentworth]. Then you'll start to doubt the value of all that education and realize that it says nothing about what you are or what you know. You'll come to the cynical realization that the primary value of a doctor's degree is its 'snob value'." He went on, "Don't you be impressed by your degree, but other people will be, and the impression it makes upon other people is its real value. They will confer upon you knowledge or judgment that you may not have, but that snob value is something you should not decry. Utilize it fully—that's what you are working for! As long as you don't delude yourself, don't be bashful about using its snob value to impress other people. It will get you an audience or give you a stature that you wouldn't get without it." Pretty disillusioning, but absolutely true.

When I started in business in 1947 as a consulting engineer, I remembered that advice and used my academic title unabashedly. Through continued use, the identification of me as "Dr. Jacobs" has continued. In those early, critical days it *was* important—especially because I billed myself as a consultant and the implied expertise was a great asset. Today many consider its use an ostentation, and so it is. Doctorates are so common that most people simply ignore the title except in academia.

In order to enter a doctorate program, one has to pass qualifying exams that are supposed to insure that candidates have some intellectual accomplishments before they embark upon an advanced program. In reality it is an archaic ritual much like a fraternity rite. The exams qualify you as a "pledge." The Ph.D. is the hallmark of the college professor—his "union card"; and the rites of passage into that elite arouse all the power drive and protectiveness that is to be found in the membership of any exclusive club. I had forgotten there were foreign language requirements and only remembered it six months before I was to finish. The doctorate of philosophy implies a broad intellectual education; a qualifying requirement in those days therefore was the ability to read and write two foreign languages. I had taken only two years of German in high school.

Vi turned out to be my savior. At Wellesley her major was French, and she had a facility for foreign languages. She had studied German, Greek, and Latin. So she took me in hand and, in a week of total immersion, worked on my rudimentary German. The French was tougher. I started at ground zero. She spent two weeks on that. Of course I did not really learn either language in that short time and am still a foreign language illiterate—except in Arabic. I'd been around Poly long enough that the professors giving me the language tests were, in a sense, colleagues. They tested me in French and German using technical articles on the subject of my thesis. As I stumbled through, my knowing the technology helped me guess at the translation. To this day, when traveling in France or Germany, I remain mute and Vi takes over.

Vi offered to type my thesis, which was 180 pages long. Eight copies were required and Xerox did not exist. Vi had studied typing and shorthand and gotten a job as a secretary. Not much more was available to women in those days. Looking back, I'm appalled at the waste of intelligence, of knowledge, of ability this represented. It's a running family joke that, because I couldn't afford to pay for the language coaching and the typing services, I settled the debt by marrying her. By this time I had accumulated savings of $800 (after all those years of working) and I spent $300 of that on an engagement ring.

When I finished my thesis, I faced my doctoral committee with shaking knees, even though I knew all of the members and thought I knew my subject well. The worst character flaws in teachers come out when they are holding the "prize" of a doctor's degree. Later, as a member of several such doctoral committees, I saw the ritual from the other side. Years later, when our daughter Linda was preparing for her doctoral exam, I was able to forewarn her. The torture chamber hadn't changed in 30 years.

So on to the peak of my academic achievement and finally life and a career that would enable me, I hoped, to achieve all of those vague, adolescent dreams that had been boiling inside me.

SIX

# *Wartime and Penicillin*

In the space of four days in June 1942, I received a doctorate in chemical engineering, celebrated my twenty-sixth birthday, and married Violet Jabara. Our wedding was in a sense my mother's last hurrah. By all the standards I knew, I was doing everything right and she should be pleased I was marrying not an American, but a beautiful, well-educated Lebanese woman from a fine family. I was confident that I had met all of the criteria demanded of my brothers in previous years.

Mom then raised the question, who would marry us? Vi's folks were ostensibly Eastern rite Orthodox, but she had been raised as a Protestant. Long ago I had given up allegiance to any church. Mom insisted, however, that we should have not only a Catholic wedding, but a Maronite one. Her tears and tantrums intimidated me—I was not yet ready to break the hold completely. Mom had no real allegiance to any Maronite teachings and rarely went to church herself. It was simply a matter of convention, of what was proper. A Lebanese bride *must* follow her husband's religion. She herself had done that and whether or not I considered it important was irrelevant. All that she was after was the symbolism of preserving the appearance so important in our culture, of the dominant male. Interestingly, Vi's parents urged her to acquiesce because they too recognized the cultural conventions. I took her to meet Father Stephen, whom

*Commencement at Polytechnic University, 1942; JJJ earns his Ph.D. in chemical engineering.*

she instantly liked. He was a kind, benevolent man, whom I too remember fondly, though he would constantly scold me about not going to church. The last time I met him, he was in his middle nineties and had come to honor me as a contributor to a retirement home for elderly Lebanese in Brooklyn. Bent over, he shook his finger at me and said, "Joseph, you should go to church!" Then he kissed me on the cheek. I was in my sixties at the time. It brought the house down.

Vi, in a rare act of defiance, refused to take instruction to convert to Catholicism herself. I admired her courage. The cultural pressures, especially when exerted by my mother, were strong indeed. Father Stephen agreed to marry us in her house, since we were not allowed to be married in church. The Maronite ritual is full of a symbolism that is mostly beyond my knowledge, but I do recall that orange blossom crowns were placed upon our heads. They symbolized that we were the "king" and "queen" of a new family to be formed. During the ceremony the crowns were passed back and forth between us three times to denote the interchangeability of our dominion over our future family. The ritual was colorful and impressive, with its chanting and incense and ancient Aramiac prayers, but I noticed it hardly at all. I shudder

*JJJ, Vi, and Emily Jacobs (Albert's wife) at Joe and Vi's wedding, June 14, 1942.*

to think what would happen if we tried to impose such cultural burdens upon our daughters today.

After a two-week honeymoon in the White Mountains of New Hampshire, I started to work for Merck & Co., a manufacturer of pharmaceuticals in Rahway, New Jersey. Even in 1942, Merck was an impressive company housed in handsome brick, colonial-style buildings in a setting that made it look more like a university than a manufacturing concern.

We rented a fourth-floor walk-up apartment in Brooklyn Heights, at that time a genteel, but modestly priced neighborhood. Today it's been "gentrified," is known as Cobble Hill, and the real estate prices are outrageous. Brooklyn Heights had some romanticism for us; I had proposed to Vi while we were strolling near the "Penny Bridge," a local landmark. Why did we decide to live there? Both of our families were living in Brooklyn and I had decided to continue teaching in the night school at Poly, which was within walking distance.

But what a commute to work! I can retrace my steps still. Down four flights of steps, walk four blocks to the subway, go down the longest set of steps and escalators in the world (that station was the last stop before the subway entered the tunnel under the East River), go one stop to Chambers Street, get out, walk one block to the H & M tubes (now known as the PATH train), go two stops underneath the Hudson River to Jersey City, then outside to board the Pennsylvania Railroad train for the 40-minute ride to the North Rahway station, and walk three blocks to the Merck offices; 1 hour and 15 or 20 minutes each way. Ever since, I have made a fetish of living as close as possible to where I work.

We had been at war since the previous December 7. The tension was high, there was worry, and fear, and urgency in the air. I debated whether I should volunteer when I received a draft notice. I did not request exemption, but when I went for my physical examination, I was rejected because I was so nearsighted. When my boss at Merck found out that I hadn't requested exemption, he was furious. He felt my work was more important for the war effort. As senior chemical engineer I was thrown into process development and pilot-plant activity right away. My hands-on practical training at Poly gave me an immediate advantage. My first project was to develop a process for the recovery of butylene glycol from a fermentation broth. This was my first contact with fermentation, a field that became a specialty of mine and, later, of the Jacobs Engineering Group. Butylene glycol was of interest as a raw material to make butadiene, a constituent of synthetic rubber. (Imports of natural rubber had been cut off.) The main problem was recovering the butylene glycol from the fermentation broth. I devised a simple extraction technique and then built special laboratory glassware (I even blew the glassware myself) to test my process.

Despite the wartime atmosphere, I was buoyant and life had its light moments. Just two recollections: There was another fellow from Merck who was foolish enough to continue living in Brooklyn, as I did. His name, too, was Joe. We'd meet on the train in the morning and I'd settle down to read my newspaper or grade papers for my classes; Joe would hit the seat and fall asleep immediately. Finally one day I said, "Hell, Joe, you just got out of bed, how can you fall asleep at 7:30 in the morning?" He yawned a little and said to me, "Joe, you don't realize it, but I'm a very slow sleeper. Most of you guys sleep 8 hours and get 8 hours sleep, but I'm such a slow sleeper that I only get 6½ hours' sleep when I sleep 8 hours." I laughed all the way to Rahway.

Another time I was in the hall outside my lab at Merck talking to Tom Cleary, an associate and a mischievous wit. Inside the lab was my new assistant, a young Chinese from MIT. He was a brilliant fellow, but had no manual dexterity at all. Tom and I were smoking (I smoked heavily in those days) and suddenly we heard glassware crashing on the floor in my lab. We looked in and there was my poor assistant in a pile of broken flasks, beakers, etc. Tom looked at me and said, "Did you ever see a Chinaman in a bull shop?"

I believe that my cultural influences and my willingness to try new ideas contributed to my ability to generate more new ideas than most of my colleagues at Merck. In addition, my work with Don Othmer, who was constantly searching for new ideas about which he could publish papers, and with Dr. K. at Autoxygen, the ultimate idea generator, gave me an unusual breadth of training.

Something else happened at Merck that is of historical interest and demonstrates how intuitive thought can produce remarkable results. Many of us in the research and pilot plant group brought our lunch to work. Some would play bridge for the rest of the hour, and others would simply have a bull session about our work, about sex, or about broad scientific or engineering subjects.

One day I asked if anyone had seen the big ads in the *New York Times* for a company called Kellex Corp. They had noticed them, and recalling that the advertisements were seeking metallurgists, inorganic chemists, physicists with isotope separation experience, spectroscopists, chemical engineers, and so on, we wondered what the company was working on. I mentioned what I knew: that Kellex had been formed as a separate company by M. W. Kellogg, then a process engineering and construction firm in New York, that some of my students at Poly were working for the company—and that the work was "secret."

Kellex, I had heard, had designed a plant in Tennessee, where the security was heavy. The company town was reported to be enclosed by barbed wire. I related also what my friend Ted Wentworth had told me: that his company, Vulcan Copper, had received orders for a large number of distillation towers, which were shipped to Knoxville, Tennessee. The mystery intrigued us. We kept trying to unravel the puzzle until someone said, "I'll bet they are working on a uranium isotope." It was an intuitive leap, but as we looked at the kinds of people they were recruiting, it began to seem a reasonable guess.

We recalled reading that Niels Bohr, the great atomic physicist, had predicted that if anyone could isolate the U-235 isotope (contained as a small percentage in natural uranium), bring a critical mass together, get sustained fission, and release its energy under control, one pound could take a battleship around the world. We concluded that was probably what they were doing down in Tennessee—recovering U-235 for use as a fuel. Our guess about the use of the product was wrong, but I have always been amazed that four or five engineers, without any special knowledge of nuclear physics, could deduce so much from just those scraps of information. The town near Knoxville, entirely enclosed by a fence, was later identified as Oak Ridge.

That very night I jokingly asked one of my students, whom I knew to be working for Kellex, "How's the U-235 plant coming?" I still remember watching the blood drain from his face. "How did you know?" he blurted out. I told him, smugly, that I had just guessed. The next day I was summoned urgently to the office of the director of research and then questioned in a private room by two men from Army Intelligence. Somewhat accusingly, they repeated my conversation with the student and asked how I had come to the knowledge I implied. My heart sank as I realized that we had stumbled upon something important and classified. After I repeated the whole story, they talked individually to each of the fellows in the group, finally deciding that our conclusion was only fortuitous and that we had no malevolent motives. They never acknowledged that we were correct, but warned us all in stark and threatening tones not to mention U-235 again in any conversation. This was more than two years before Hiroshima.

At about the same time, I received a call from my boss who, after swearing me to secrecy, introduced me to Dr. Howard Florey from England. I was told that a man by the name of Alexander Fleming had discovered a mold in one of his laboratory petri dishes, later identified as *Penicillium notatum*, that exuded something that killed bacteria. Somewhat later Dr. Florey and a Dr. Chain set about trying to isolate and purify the material released by the mold. They had succeeded and had come to Merck for help in establishing the commercial production of what they called "penicillin." This had occurred some time before I met Florey, and Merck was producing small quantities of the material in the laboratory. The names Fleming and Florey will be recognizable as winners of the Nobel Prize in 1945 for the discovery and isolation of penicillin, a new antibiotic and the wonder drug that saved so many lives during and after World War II.

Penicillin was a new word to me, and my association with it marked, in many ways, a fateful crossroads in my life. In the basement of the Merck research building were rack after rack of odd-shaped flasks lying on their sides. In each was a shallow pool of golden colored liquid, covered by a blue-green mold. I was told there were over two acres of these flasks from which minute quantities of the new wonder drug were being recovered in the laboratory. The flat flasks exposed the maximum surface of the mold to the air it needed in order to grow. (Such organisms are classified as "aerobic" that is, they require air to grow.) Essentially though, Merck was duplicating the laboratory techniques of Florey and Chain.

My assignment was to find out how to grow the mold in large quantities and to develop the equipment to recover the product efficiently in a large-scale plant. Starting with a 50-gallon glass-lined vessel, I put in an agitator and then inserted a nozzle "sparger," as it was known, to blow air in and disperse it finely over the growing mold in the "broth." This vessel was the progenitor of the deep-tank aerobic fermenter. Eventually, we built several of 10,000-gallon capacity at Merck, and today 50,000-gallon or larger units are common in antibiotic manufacturing plants. I'm simplifying a lot; there were myriad problems with sterility of the air and preventing strange organisms from contaminating the batches, but we solved them. Recovery of the penicillin was difficult. Evaporation of the water by heating, as would be normal, caused the penicillin to decompose. So we developed the process of "freeze-drying," adapting a laboratory curiosity to commercial-scale equipment. Ice will evaporate under a high vacuum, so we froze the penicillin concentrate solid and kept it under a high vacuum until all the ice was gone and only the yellow penicillin powder was left behind. As far as I know, this was the first use of freeze-drying on a large scale. Little did I dream that it would eventually be used for anything as mundane as instant coffee. Subsequently, many engineers at Merck worked on the penicillin process, but I like to think I was responsible for the basic approaches to the production of penicillin in the large quantities needed during World War II. Justified or not, I take pride in my own contribution to this great forerunner of the antibiotics that have saved so many lives.

Then something untoward happened to me. In the spring of 1943 I came down with a fever that I first assumed was just the flu. But I couldn't shake it and it kept getting worse. Finally they put me into a local hospital and gave me sulfa drugs, the "wonder drug" of those days. After a week there was no visible improvement and I was having alternate bouts of chills and fever. By this time everyone, including me, was worried about my fever. My brother Ted, a physician and a major in the army, was particularly concerned. I finally asked my doctor if he knew about penicillin. He'd never heard of it and couldn't find any reference to it in the library. I should have known better: It was a highly classified project and product. Vi, however, called Dr. Joe Stevens, my boss at Merck, who arranged for a consultation with Dr. D. W. Richards of Columbia University Medical School, who was Merck's consultant and in charge of testing the new drug. Dr. Richards was a world-renowned physician with a doctorate in bacteriology. Several years later he too won the Nobel Prize. How many people are lucky enough to work with or be treated by a Nobel laureate?

Dr. Richards was understanding, compassionate, and concerned. After moving me to the Harkness Pavilion at Columbia

University Hospital, Dr. Richards had batteries of laboratory people trying to culture and identify the bacteria causing my septicemia, but with no success.

One night my temperature reached an unbelievable 106.8 degrees and I became delirious, though I do remember nurses bathing me all night with ice water. Vi reports that my brother came out of my room crying and involuntarily she cried out, "He's not going to die. I know he won't die." Although his hands were tied by red tape because *all* penicillin was on allocation to the Army Medical Corps for controlled experiments, finally, Dr. Richards, bless him, said to Vi and to my brother, "This guy's worth saving and to hell with the regulations, I'm going to try penicillin." They injected me with 50,000 units of the new wonder drug (no doctor would give less than ten times that now, because most organisms have developed penicillin-resistant strains). The dose was repeated four times a day for three days and my temperature came down to 99 degrees. I often wonder what compelled Dr. Richards to think I was worth saving and sometimes think that some of the decent things I've done during my life have been prompted by a need to justify his faith in me. Though he had spent nights and days looking after me, he refused any fee!

While I was so ill I spent many nights awake, either burning up with fever or suffering chills through chattering teeth. Making sure that no one was there, I would repeat out loud, almost shouting, "I'm not going to die! I'm not going to die! I'm not going to die." I formed an opinion then, and in subsequent illnesses that opinion hardened into a belief. I became convinced that my determination had some effect that was added to the penicillin. I give all credit to that miracle drug, but I won't minimize the effect of grim determination and what it added to my recovery process.

I never related this to anyone at the time because so mystical a belief was entirely contrary to my self-image of the hard-headed, pragmatic, and cynical scientist. Many years later I read *Anatomy of an Illness* by Norman Cousins and subsequently many other articles that provided a scientific basis for such beliefs. The claim was made that the brain can be stimulated to secrete powerful chemicals, such as endorphins, with remarkable healing properties and the ability to stimulate the immune system. A mystical and intuitive belief now seems to have scientific support.

After a month's recuperation, I went back to Merck. The small group of people who had been helping me when I started the penicillin work had by then grown into a full team. I pitched in, helping to translate the results from our pilot plant to detailed designs from which a full-scale plant could be built. This was my first complete "plant design" and that's the business that Jacobs Engineering Group is in today.

I place great store in the intuitive leap, but it can be costly too. While we were working night and day designing an enormous plant to make penicillin microbiologically (by fermentation), a group led by world-renowned Dr. Karl Folkers, one of the great synthetic organic chemists at Merck, was attempting to identify the chemical composition of the active ingredient of penicillin with the objective of synthesizing it. The Army Medical Corps had offered Merck an open-ended supply contract and asked the company to build the first fermentation plant to produce penicillin. Technically, Merck was far ahead of other pharmaceutical companies that had more recently been asked to work on this new drug. But, during the fateful meeting to decide whether we would build the plant, Dr. Folkers announced that his group was within weeks of identifying the structure of penicillin and from there, a synthetic route would inevitably come and thus make the fermentation method obsolete! So Merck decided to delay building a plant. It turned out that Folkers was wrong and Merck lost its lead in penicillin manufacture. Folkers had every right to make such a prediction and the Merck management had no reason to be skeptical of his statements, but we must all live with such fallibility. It was many years before penicillin was synthesized, and even then the process couldn't compete with fermentation. To this day it is still made by fermentation methods.

I was given another interesting, and secret, project to spearhead. In 1860 a Swiss chemist wrote a rudimentary description of the reactions necessary to produce a chemical called dichlorodiphenyl trichloroethane, a name we ultimately shortened to DDT, and I was asked to see if I could duplicate those reactions in the laboratory. If I could, I was to work out how to produce the chemical in large quantities. Merck had been given this assignment because it was the only pharmaceutical company that knew how to make chloral hydrate, one of the raw materials necessary in this reaction. Chloral hydrate was an old-fashioned but well-known sedative—the original "knockout drops" that bartenders would put into a boisterous customer's drink. Merck was making the chloral hydrate in a 50-year-old plant in stoneware pots tended by an operator who had been there for years and knew the process like the back of his hand. When we redesigned the process and transferred it into a modern plant, the operator, confronted with the new, highly sophisticated plant, decided to retire. We had taken his baby away from him!

I managed to make small quantities of DDT in the lab, commandeered a 500-gallon glass-lined reactor in our pilot plant, and started to produce it in larger quantities. In developing the process, I had some difficulty removing the solvent from the product. One night I left an operator in charge of a large glass vessel from which the solvent was slowly evaporating and went upstairs in the pilot plant building around 10:00 P.M. to try to get a nap. (It wasn't unusual for me to work all night on a critical project.) During the evening, Dr. Max Tishler, who happened to be working that night, came along and told my operator to stop the evaporation because so little solvent was coming off. When I came back, I was more than annoyed. I tested the product and, of course, there was much too much solvent in it.

Dr. Tishler was practically an idol at Merck. A brilliant and inventive chemist, trained at Harvard, he was high in the hierarchy of the company and one of the giants of the pharmaceutical industry. Nevertheless the next morning I called him on the phone, told him to keep his hands off my experiments, and not to give my operators orders before checking with me! He was taken aback and apologized. Everybody in the lab who heard me talking to the great Max Tishler in that way was appalled. Apparently he didn't bear a grudge. Later, when I decided to leave Merck, Max Tishler tried to persuade me to change my mind.

In the final push to make what I believe was the first commercial production of DDT in the United States, I worked 48 hours around the clock. During the night a valve on the bottom of one of the vessels was opened by mistake while I was standing under it. I was completely covered with hot DDT in a solvent. When it dried, I had DDT an inch thick all over me—in my hair, in my ears, and in my mouth and nose. I took off my clothes, showered, and scrubbed, but probably ingested more DDT during that one incident than is today considered safe to absorb over many years.

The first 500 pounds of DDT that I made was picked up the next morning by an army truck. The following week we received a telegram that, as I remember it, said, "President Roosevelt has asked me to thank the people at Merck for producing the 500 pounds of DDT so quickly. It was shipped to Italy by air where it was used to stop a typhus epidemic in our army. It is estimated that 5,000 lives were probably saved by destroying the typhus-carrying body lice infesting our soldiers." It was signed by the surgeon general. I was pretty proud.

There is a postscript to that story. Many years later, we were having dinner with our three adult daughters, and one of them was decrying that terrible chemical, DDT, that was being used to kill the tussock moth despoiling Douglas fir trees in the Northwest. It had been found that DDT acted to thin the shells of certain birds' eggs, and the environmentalists were in full cry to have DDT banned completely. When I heard them excoriate DDT, I bellowed in full fury: "Listen, young ladies, I will not apologize to you or anyone else for having produced DDT." I told them about the lives it saved in Italy and said, "In addition, do you know how many lives have been spared from malaria because DDT eradicates the anopheles mosquito, the carrier of malaria? Sure, I agree that DDT is not a benign chemical and its use should be carefully controlled, but banning it completely is insane! It has been a great benefit to man—far outweighing its admitted harmful effects! You'll get no apology from me!" I still feel that way! I think that environmentalists, in their elitist arrogance, often do more harm than good. I have never seen the harmful effects of

DDT compared with the enormous good it has done and could still do. But I was a voice crying in the wilderness.

Despite my miraculous recovery and my exciting work, I felt an underlying dissatisfaction and even unhappiness that I ascribed to uncertainty about the future and a continuing uncertainty about my own worth. On the face of it, I should have been a contented man: I had earned a Ph.D., I enjoyed teaching, I was happily married and working at an outstanding company on very exciting projects. I was well regarded, even admired, by my colleagues and bosses. I no longer worried about money, though I was far from flush. I had many of the things I missed when growing up and a clear-cut path for the future either in industry or in teaching. Yet I was as discontented as ever—but in a different way. I could no longer attribute my malaise to fear—after all, I had almost died but survived. Why was I so dissatisfied and so discontented? It took me many years to rationalize and understand the somber, brooding gnawing in me that was almost overwhelming.

Although my work at Merck was exciting, the juices were boiling. The discontent, the drive to get ahead, to "succeed," was almost eating me up. I remember in a conversation with a Dr. Engels, the number two man in the Merck hierarchy, expressing my discontent that I hadn't progressed in responsibility at Merck as much as I thought I should. He looked at me kindly and said, "Look, Joe, you've been here less than two years. We consider you one of our most promising young people. Be patient. Do you expect to become a vice president so quickly?" My irreverent and unforgivably arrogant answer was, "If I'm capable enough, why not?"

I became interested in California. The frontier was luring me. Would my discontent be diminished there? I wasn't willing to wait 20 years or even 10 years to become a vice president at Merck. In my superficial, impatient view, the paths to the top were too rigid, too tightly structured. Hidden somewhere, but unrecognized, was a longing for adventure, for risk, for attacking the unknown—a legacy from my parents.

Then one of those amazing coincidences happened. Vi was at her parents' home for dinner one night (I was teaching at Poly) when a former neighbor dropped in to see them. He was a produce wholesaler who dealt with many growers and marketers in California. He claimed to have originated the idea of having the unemployed sell apples on the street during the Depression. People who came to his office could get a case of apples on credit to sell on the street, and he hadn't been cheated once. When he found that Vi was married, he asked about me and, hearing that I was a chemical engineer, expressed an interest in meeting me. When we subsequently did meet, he told me he had an old friend in the chemical business in California who was always interested in bright young men for his company. "Was I interested in meeting him?" The answer was, "Of course!"

About a month later I received a call from Mr. E. E. Luther, identifying himself as the old friend of Vi's neighbor and asking me to meet him at the Waldorf-Astoria Hotel. There he told me about his company, Chemurgic Corp., in Richmond, California (near San Francisco). Most of its production was war materiel. Before the war, he had made his fortune in the insecticide business and his eyes lit up when I told him about my experience with DDT. He saw it as a potential agricultural insecticide. After the interview he said he wanted to talk to his son, who was president of the company, and he would then be in touch.

The next day he called to tell me that they wanted to hire me as technical vice president (!!) at a substantial raise over my salary at Merck. He described the job and some of the things he wanted me to do. I said "hold on" and, still holding the phone, I turned to Vi and said, "Honey, I've been offered a job in California. Do you want to go?" Without hesitating, she said, "If you want to go, of course I will." To this day I marvel at that almost instinctive reaction of love, of faith in me, of self-abnegation, of making her proximity to family and friends and any fear of the unknown completely secondary to what I obviously wanted to do. With unquestioning and unselfish support from the woman in my life, I had a start on my adventure.

SEVEN

# *Go West, Young Man*

My father crossed an ocean. I crossed only a continent. Objectively, my adventure was much less risky than his, but the exhilarating challenge and understandable fear were heady. I took a certain amount of delight in telling my bosses at Merck that I was going to be a vice president of a chemical company in California. Several of them tried to dissuade me, painting a rosy picture of my future at Merck.

Chemurgic Corp. and E. E. Luther, its venerable chairman, were important to my development as a businessman. A brilliant and bitter man, he was a legend in California's agricultural chemical circles. In the early 1920s he started a company called California Spray Chemical, which prospered selling insecticides. The brand name was Ortho, still a leading brand of garden and commercial insecticides. In the mid-thirties Luther was courted by Standard Oil of California and sold his company to them. Among the inducements was the promise of a vice presidency in that large and prestigious company. It was a short honeymoon. E. E. Luther simply didn't fit in. Despite his brilliance and exceptional ability, he had run into that phenomenon called "company culture." He just didn't fit the mold. His resignation was followed by a long and costly lawsuit. Luther obtained a substantial financial settlement and a release from his noncompetition clause. Though wealthy enough, with the sale price of his company and the legal settlement, he still emerged a bitter man.

He started a new business with two clearly defined motives. One was to compete with and get back at his "betrayers" at Standard Oil. The other was to establish a business for his three grown sons. Its name, Chemurgic Corp., was an attempt to characterize a company that produces chemicals *for* agriculture. Actually it was a misuse of a word then in common use for a branch of science devoted to producing chemicals *from* agricultural products.

Just before the outbreak of World War II, Luther had built a modern, reinforced concrete office and laboratory, intending to go into the insecticide business to compete with Standard Oil. When war broke out, the company had to find new business. Most of the original key employees were members of the Luther family and their friends, among them Tom Ready, who had spearheaded a move into defense contracts that saved the company. (He subsequently had a meteoric career with, and became chairman and chief executive officer of Kaiser Aluminum & Chemical Co. during its heyday.)

The oldest son, Everett Luther, was president of the company, and other assorted relatives and family friends were in key positions. The vice president of production, for instance, was a brother-in-law who, I believe, had run a garage and auto parts store before joining Chemurgic. It was a humming, bustling business when I arrived.

At the time, the company was making practice ammunition products based upon the pyrotechnic formulations that are used to produce fireworks. A separate factory produced the bodies and flammable materials for incendiary bombs. Originally these consisted of clusters of tubes of powdered magnesium that ignited on impact. The burning magnesium would spread fire on the target. Later on we filled the same tubes with a jellied gasoline that had the dubious "advantage" of sticking to any surface. That jellied gasoline was napalm, as terrible a weapon then as it was in Vietnam.

The DC-3 I boarded for my trip west took 13 hours and made innumerable stops between New York and San Francisco. It was my first airplane trip and, of the millions of miles I've traveled since, is still the most vivid. Having flown through the night, the pilot, as pilots often did in those days, spontaneously decided to fly a couple of lazy circles only a few hundred feet above the rim of the Grand Canyon. The brilliant early morning sun against the western canyon walls and the blue-black color of the walls in the shadows provided a spectacular introduction to the overpowering and awesome scenery that characterizes the West. This was the great adventure! Shades of my father's journey. For a kid raised on the streets of Brooklyn, going west was scary and exhilarating at the same time.

The San Francisco Bay Area and Berkeley, where I was lucky to get a hotel room, were a revelation. Shipyard workers, soldiers, sailors, Japanese bombing scares, and one night the explosion of an ammunition ship at Port Chicago 40 miles away brought the war much closer. But what really astonished me was to find myself looking out of the window of my hotel room at swaying palm trees and nearly freezing to death! In my movie image of California, the swaying palms came with bright sunshine, beautiful beaches, and hot weather. Of course that was a depiction of Southern California and the Bay Area is quite different. I also found out that simply by driving 10 miles, through a tunnel in the Berkeley hills into the hot, dry Walnut Creek farming area, I could experience a 20 or 30 degree rise in temperature. Such extremes of temperature and weather were a revelation to an Easterner.

It was almost impossible to find housing in the Bay Area. Chemurgic's office and plant were in Richmond, which was also the site of the enormous Kaiser shipyards, where the famous Liberty ships were built. It took a couple of months before I found a small apartment in an old three-story wooden house in Berkeley. That modest little apartment was a happy place to relax and enjoy the headiness of a new exciting job.

When I called Vi to tell her about the apartment, she responded with more good news—that she was pregnant. Her doctor agreed that she could drive to California with me. I flew back to Brooklyn and bought a used five-year-old Dodge—my first car. My mother insisted upon coming back with us to help Vi through her first pregnancy and to help keep house for us.

Our small kitchen faced west and we had dinner every night at a table from which we could see the San Francisco Bay *and* the spectacular sunset behind the Golden Gate Bridge.

Chemurgic was wholly owned by the Luther family, and the board consisted only of insiders. This was my first time as a board member, and I began to learn the dynamics of that institution. Out of that experience I developed a strong antipathy to "inside" boards. At Chemurgic, board meetings were little more than a formality, ratifying actions already made in hallway conferences, in bull sessions, and by executive fiat.

As an outsider who had been given the title of vice president and a position on the board of directors, I aroused some jealousy, especially among employees who were not members of the family and who, perhaps, saw their own positions threatened. I had to learn how to cope with jealousy and the sometimes subtle, but often overt, attempts to undercut a new player who is perceived to be threatening.

E. E. Luther was a radical in many ways. There were no private offices. All of our desks, and those of our secretaries too, were in a large open office, an arrangement that worked well in facilitating the interchange of ideas. But the inevitable distractions, noise, and inhibition of confidential conversations were difficult to endure.

My first assignment was to work on the plant operations, suggesting improvements, increasing efficiency, and providing much-needed technical support to the vice president of production—a nice guy who had his job because he was Mr. Luther's brother-in-law. Still determined to be in the insecticide business to beat out Standard Oil, Mr. Luther urged me to make some experimental quantities of DDT in the laboratory. The end of the war was coming and he wanted to prepare to go back into the business he knew so well. We made some substantial quantities in the laboratory and even began designing a plant to make DDT. We tested the product on a number of insects, one of which was the grape leafhopper.

Luther knew everybody in agriculture and arranged for us to visit the Beaulieu Vineyard in Napa Valley, which was owned at the time by the De Latour family. Hélène, the daughter of the founder, who was married to a Frenchman, the Marquis de Pins, controlled the operation, and they lived the luxurious life in a beautiful house on the property. We were invited to lunch one time. The main course was rack of venison and there was plenty of wine. The marquis presided at the table imperiously, and when everyone finished he simply opened a newspaper and started reading it. Being inexperienced, I assumed that such incredible rudeness was permissible for the aristocracy.

Our DDT powder did a spectacular job on the leafhoppers and we returned several times to repeat the spraying. The most memorable part of those visits was meeting André Tchelistcheff, the young and brilliant enologist at Beaulieu. Of Russian extraction, he was born, raised, and trained in France. In the years since then he has become recognized as the dean of California winemakers, the man who set the standard for the superb California wines and, particularly, for those of the Napa Valley.

I had drunk little wine in those days, but had heard of the superiority of French wines, the existence of vintage years, and other aspects of the industry. We spent many hours sitting on the dusty hillsides as the vines were being sprayed, and Tchelistcheff would answer all my questions about wines—why, for instance, vintage years, important for French wines, were much less important for California wines. He explained the reasons in technical terms relating to the physiology of grape viticulture. He predicted then that the wines of California would ultimately surpass the best French wines.

Before the end of the war, I had been given the assignment of planning for a civilian business. Of course it was to be the insecticide business and our market would be the agricultural industry. I developed a series of formulations for insecticides, many based on DDT, some based on hexachlorbenzene, parathion, and other new products that had emerged from the war effort. We contemplated making the DDT raw material, but so many plants had been built during the war that building new capacity didn't make sense. We concentrated on formulating end products and set up a mixing plant to make bulk insecticides for use on farms.

We also decided to develop a series of consumer products. Garden insecticides were an obvious choice, and we also developed various others. Because we had neither the money nor the experience to test the market, we were guided entirely by instinct. I believed that I knew what the consumer wanted and, if I liked a product or it appealed to me as a buyer, that was good enough. How wrong I was! Distribution for the retail market is so multilayered, and so many products are trying to enter the market that the entire business is a jungle I have since learned to avoid. However, before I understood the marketing problems, I developed a product that I naively thought would be a winner—a tarnish remover for silver. The process was simplicity itself. The tarnished silver was immersed in boiling water in an enamel pan. A measured amount of washing soda (the conductor) was added and, when a piece of aluminum was dropped in to complete the electrolytic circuit, the tarnish disappeared as if by magic, removed by electrolytic reduction of the oxides of silver (tarnish) when the aluminum completed the electrolytic action. The chemistry was well known. My "clever" idea was to design a package made from recently developed aluminum foil that would contain the proper amount of washing soda. One would heat water in an enamel pan, open the foil package, dump in the soda, and then throw in the package and the tarnished silver! It really worked well and I was sure it would be an instant success. It was not. We sold it to a number of stores but very few people bought it. We had no idea how to draw the consumers into the store where they could *ask* for our marvelous products.

My other misadventure into the consumer market was much more expensive for me, personally. The partners in our advertising agency were about to launch a new project—the large-scale manufacturing and marketing of the "Bannanza," a perfectly delicious ice-cream confection consisting of a banana on a stick embedded in ice cream and coated with chocolate. One taste and, with my surefire instinct for the retail market, I was sold. I invested $1,400 and persuaded my mother-in-law to do the same. I was even ready to abandon my career in chemical engineering and take on the distributorship in Southern California. The fatal flaw surfaced just as the $400,000 Bannanza plant was about to go into production. The company that owned the franchises for all the similar products on the market—Eskimo Pies, Popsicles, and so on—also owned the freezer boxes in the stores. The stores were therefore unable to store the frozen Bannanza, and the great product could not get to the consumer. My mother-in-law said never a word in reproach, and I was completely disillusioned with my "instinct" for the consumer market.

Chemurgic searched for new products and ventured into the fertilizer business, which had many similarities to the insecticide business, and the marketing channels were the same. The active ingredients in fertilizers were made by large chemical companies, but the final product was blended, packaged, and sold to the farmer by "mixers. We decided to set up a mixing operation at our idle plant in Turlock, California. We hired a consultant, a retired executive from a major fertilizer company, who served us very well in working out formulations and helping us design the plant. I supervised the design and start-up of this plant, as well as the others we built.

Everett Luther, the oldest son and president of the company, had an old friend heading up the sales effort. By the time we had the production facilities going, our sales were not keeping up. The company was losing money rapidly and I complained about our inept sales effort at board meetings and almost daily to E. E. and Everett. "Okay," they said, "you become vice president of sales." Seeing how little headway we were making, I reduced the sales staff for the consumer product line and concentrated on agricultural sales. The lines of distribution were much shorter and we had to deal only with the local warehouse, or "store," where the bags of fertilizer and insecticide were stored and from which they were delivered to, or picked up by, the farmer. Even in this market we had to "move the product off the shelves" so we had a small sales force call on farmers to help them decide what kind of fertilizer to buy or what insecticides to use. I spent a year traveling over virtually every square inch of California. There's hardly a valley or hamlet where crops are planted that I haven't visited at one time or another. (I often wonder how many of the millions of people who have migrated to California since World War II, and who live in the metropolitan areas, have any conception of this enormous and infinitely diverse state. California is larger than many countries and has a "gross national product" greater than all but six countries of the world.)

During my year or so as vice president of sales for Chemurgic, our sales increased substantially. But to my dismay, the company was still losing money. I concluded that the corporate overhead—inherited from wartime operations, was too high. Everett Luther agreed that costs needed to be cut, but very little happened. In argument after argument Everett tried to prove to me that it was only a matter of time before our increasing sales would cover the overhead. "But," I countered, "meanwhile we are losing money." He was concerned that many of the people working for the company would encounter hardship if they lost their jobs. I promised to *try* to increase sales to cover the overhead. Sales did increase, but I was never able to generate enough to compensate for Everett's compassion!

The situation, and the way Everett Luther reacted to it, epitomized the conflicting pressures a leader in business must bear. Everett was an absolutely fine, decent, highly intelligent, and sensitive person. I can best sum up his personality by telling you that later on, after I left, when Chemurgic got into predictable financial trouble and the banks asked Everett to leave, he became an ordained minister! He was constitutionally unable to reconcile his sensitivity and compassion for the people who would have to be fired and his responsibility as the president of the company to have it survive. Although he avoided the anguish of firing a few people, the jobs of many more were eliminated when the company went out of business. It is so gut wrenching to ask people you know and like to leave their jobs that it's no wonder that we all delay too long or look for other events to solve our problems for us. Most of us come to realize, over time, that we have no right to make life easy for ourselves by avoiding the issue and thus imperil the survival of the enterprise. Do we have the right to put the jobs and livelihood of 90 percent of the employees of the company at risk in order to avoid the unpleasantness of firing someone? Everett never did face that question. Perhaps he never asked it. Many times I have had to remind myself, and people working for me, that we do not have the luxury of being caring and compassionate to some if it is at the expense of the rest of the employees, all of whom depend on the survival of the company and depend on managers to make the tough decisions. I've slipped on that moral ground more than once and faced the identical dilemma many years later when Jacobs Engineering Group suffered substantial losses.

EIGHT

# A Family Business?

People invariably ask if any of my children are in the business. When I answer with an emphatic no, they take note that we have three daughters and no sons and think that explains my position. Not so! All of our daughters have the intelligence and the independent minds to have been at least candidates for responsible positions within any corporation. They all chose other careers, with, I am proud to say, no parental pressure at all.

My observations at Chemurgic had hardened a growing conviction. I was determined to avoid a "family business" well before we knew how many children we would have or what their sex would be. In concluding that mine would not be a family business, I had to counter a strong Lebanese tradition and break decisively with my background. In the male-oriented family or tribal culture of the Lebanese, the establishment of a family business is almost sacrosanct, a traditional aspiration as important as being in business for oneself.

At Chemurgic, when I had begun to see that the company's problems of mismanagement were intensified because of the underlying flaw of its being a "family company," I recalled hearing in my youth story after story about conflict in family businesses in the Lebanese community. Even in my father's business, the family was in evidence. Models of razors were named "My

Edward" for my oldest brother, "Prince Albert" for another brother, and "Junior" (a short-bladed model) for me.

When Helene Lingerie was established, it was assumed that Ed, as the oldest son, would go into that business and would eventually inherit the mantle of the patriarch. Ed had been a good athlete in high school, playing football when size didn't count so much, and ice hockey, at which he excelled. He also showed some artistic talent, which I remember in his prolific production of handpainted posters for various high school functions. In his later years Ed developed into quite an artist. Like my friend Michel, Ed had many talents, and though he did become a successful businessman, he never quite realized the full potential of his abilities. After high school he joined Helene Lingerie, ostensibly to take over as my father's successor. Even though Helen was at the core of the business because of her designing ability and it benefited from her excellent business instinct, the family assumed that she would eventually marry and that Ed would carry on. But Ed was not behaving according to form. His succession of American girlfriends didn't meet with my mother's approval. His attitude at work was unsettling—he alternated between arrogance, arguing with my father's way of doing things, and diffidence. I suspect now that Ed was rejecting his role as the oldest son and all that that implied in a Lebanese family. Though I knew none of the details, I could sense the tension around the house. When Helene Lingerie began having financial difficulties, he left amid much anger and recrimination and took a job as a sales clerk at Macy's department store. When he met and married an attractive assistant buyer (an American) he became a virtual outcast from the family. The marriage lasted only a few years. He divorced and came home again. Then he married another American, a wonderful woman, had three children, and made his own career. He "went into business for himself," opened a high-fashion retail store in Buffalo, New York, and operated it successfully until he retired. He had made his rebellion stick, in spite of the emotional toll.

Throughout the Lebanese-American community, I saw similar dramas enacted. There were exceptions, of course, but many of the sons became either weak shadows of their strong fathers or lived lives of rebellious conflict.

Like so many other Lebanese immigrants, my father-in-law, F. M. Jabara, started as a peddler with a suitcase, learned the language, saved his money, and finally went into business for himself, importing fancy, hand-embroidered linens, first from Italy and later from Madeira and China where he built factories.

Shortly after establishing his business, he brought two of his brothers to the United States. In a typical family gesture, he simply gave each brother a third of the business, which he called F. M. Jabara and Brothers. They prospered mightily during the twenties and even during the early years of the Depression. One of the brothers was a good salesman; the other was dubbed the "string saver"—his self-appointed function was to avoid extravagance. During the years of prosperity they divided the profits equally, although the contributions of the partners were not by any means equal.

When the business started to deteriorate during the Depression, hidden resentments began to surface—resentments arising from the fact that their contribution to the business had not been equal. But an open disagreement among the brothers would bring "shame" on the Jabara name within the community, so my father-in-law virtually gave away the business to one of his brothers. Eventually that brother also left to strike out on his own. So, during the war, while Vi's two brothers were in the service, their father kept what was left of the business going by himself until they returned. Raymond, the older of the two and a graduate of Princeton and the University of Pennsylvania's Wharton School, had been shot down over Germany when he was flying as a bombardier in a B-17. He spent 14 months in a prison camp and came back emaciated and dispirited. Will, the younger brother, who had been wounded in the infantry, decided he did not want to go back to college. Neither of them really liked the business, but the pressure of tradition was too great. My brothers-in-law have never told me how they felt during this period, but I can imagine the emotional burden of being the sons of, and working for, such an imposing, accomplished, and overwhelming father,

*Peggy, Val, and Linda, Joe and Vi's daughters, 1953.*

one of the patriarchs of the Lebanese community. Their relations with their father were not particularly strained, though there were periodic outbursts. After Vi's father died in 1949, they continued the business for a few years, but their hearts were not in it and they finally liquidated it. The accepted wisdom in the community was that those boys were lucky to have an established business to go into. No one recognized that it also was a devastating trap.

The family business has some distinct disadvantages. Apart from being a trap for reluctant, uninterested, family members, it offers no real opportunities to outsiders. The glass ceiling was in place, in family businesses at least, long before women went into the corporate world and found it there. I hit it at Chemurgic.

Because my name wasn't Luther, my progress in the company would be limited. My ability would always be secondary. I thought I was a better executive than Everett Luther was, yet I knew I would never get his job. Whether my appraisal of our comparative abilities was realistic matters not at all. The second element of the equation was true, so our respective qualifications were irrelevant. In a family business, the law of succession skews relationships and motivations throughout the company, simply because merit and individual worth are not the final arbiters of success. All companies generate their own politics, and the ability to handle them is an important part of leadership. But when the rewards of leadership clearly depend on who you are and not on what you can do, the politics become unhealthy, the ends become perverted, and the rewards go to the manipulative.

From the sidelines, and insulated by the presence of three independent-minded daughters, I have observed many non-family or outsider employees in family businesses. There is the sycophant who fawns all over the heir apparent, currying favor. This sort of behavior demeans the employee and feeds the natural self-doubt of the heir. "Is this guy being nice to me because I'm the boss's son (or daughter) or does he really like me?" With insecurity like that, it is no wonder that so many heirs turn out to be either weak or imperious.

Then there is the persecutor, who works on the principle that "this S.O.B. only has this job because he's the founder's son. I'll show him!" and does everything he can to expose the poor man's weaknesses, especially in the father's presence. No neophyte's mistake goes unnoticed. The father, who usually is bound and determined not to show favoritism to his heir, overreacts violently, and the young son is crushed in between.

And what of the boss? The reactions of parents in such situations vary from intolerance and the imposition of impossible standards to overprotection, and the pressures that evoke those reactions are intensified because the arena is public. For many, the strictures of society ("What will people say?") are as influential as any other consideration. There is another agenda.

In Cincinnati, at the Vulcan Copper Co., I watched the clashes between Ted Wentworth and his father. The loud, vitriolic arguments embarrassed all of us who heard them and must have been hell for both of them. E. E. Luther took a different tack with his son Everett. He had vowed that he would not interfere—that he would let Everett learn by making his own mistakes. It was almost tragic to watch as the father sat opposite his son, seeing his mistakes in judgment, made out of naïveté or indecision or lack of resolve or whatever, and lifting not a finger. I know how he felt because Mr. Luther used me as a sounding board and a conduit to transmit his criticisms. He would always ask my opinion on controversial issues and I usually agreed with him. Though he never asked me directly to talk to Everett, he knew that somehow I'd put in a comment or two during a meeting, reflecting some of his thoughts, and he would benignly remark to Everett that maybe I had a point.

Eventually, I felt I knew the old man well enough to ask him why he dealt with Everett in this roundabout way. After all, I made my share of mistakes too, and Mr. Luther would not hesitate to tell me about them either, kindly most of the time, or angrily when I deserved it. He told me of his resolve to let Everett learn by making his own mistakes. To me it was obvious that, as Everett was failing, so was the company, but there was that mysterious blood connection between father and son that demanded different rules of conduct. I concluded that it simply was not possible for a man to have the same business relations with his son that he did with others in the company.

With rare exception, every interaction between father and son that I've seen has dimensions and dynamics different from those of normal interactions. Everything is distorted. The dictatorial intolerant boss will be twice as hard on his son as he is on others. The fatherly, patient teacher-type of boss will be more tolerant of his son. Even worse, he will sometimes be intolerant of his son when ordinarily tolerant of other people, just to show that he is not playing favorites. The rebellious son will most often rebel violently, not just go get another job as anyone else would. The son who is determined to outperform his father, to show the world that he is *not* in his father's shadow, is one of the most driven men in the business world.

A successful business is hard enough to sustain without being weighed down by emotional baggage. For the son coming into an established business, this baggage has the effect of tying one hand behind his back. The fight is not fair. The son who competes with his father and comes up short finds his self-esteem shattered. The son who wins and far outstrips his father's accomplishments finds his victory tainted. Could he have done it by himself as his father had? Did the head start given him make it possible? There are always people around, not the least of whom may be his father, to remind him in subtle ways of the advantages he started with.

Mr. Luther had what was described as a nervous breakdown. It was heartbreaking to see such a vital, intelligent, and capable man reduced to periods of depression and melancholy—all because of his generous and natural desire to bequeath his business to his son. E. E. Luther had deluded himself that, by holding his anger in and sticking to an unrealistic vow, he would let his son "make his own mistakes," he would groom a competent manager. How wrong he was.

So many family companies have been established that the species is obviously not doomed to failure. The successes have in common a son who did *not* try to emulate his father, a son who was allowed to develop his own personal style. Yet I still wonder, how many family companies actually last more than a few generations?

My other quarrel with the family company is about the concealed motives of the founder. We all strive for immortality in one way or another. For those who are deeply religious, the prospect of life after death in heaven or in God's arms answers that need satisfactorily and completely. For those who are not, the possibility of life after death may not be enough. But a form of immortality is there for us after all—in the people we've met in our lives, the people we've touched and influenced, the people who have borrowed some trait of ours, some gesture, some ethic, or some measure of integrity. Those who make charitable gifts may have a building or two named after them. That's another form of immortality. But the most direct line to immortality is through our children. Much of what I have accomplished and much of what I am today I derive from my family, by inherited genes, by example, and by environmental influence. Much of what our daughters accomplish today and in the future has been influenced, I am sure, by their genetic heritage and by their association with Vi and me. Is it any wonder then that the drive to establish a family business is so common? It is a bid for immortality. The dream of a vital, throbbing business with your name on it thriving in future generations must be more exciting than having your name on a building. Nevertheless, the immortality projected for a family company is mostly an unfulfilled dream, a chimera, an idealistic view rarely realized.

So many fathers say, "I worked hard to establish this business. I built it up from nothing. I want my family to have the fruits of all that effort. I do not want my son to have to go through the same struggle, the same uncertainties that I did. I have built something here of value and I want my children to have it!" This attitude is natural, and generosity to one's heirs is hardly a crime—but in it are the seeds of destruction. As I observed at Chemurgic, relationships among family members are colored by apparent irrelevancies; sons find themselves failing or perhaps even succeeding at great cost to themselves. Generosity is a two-edged sword. Indeed, generosity can be devastating if not handled with care because generosity begets obligation and from obligation can sprout the seeds of resentment.

When there is more than one heir sibling rivalry becomes an issue. Which of the heirs will lead the business? Must the father choose, or will they decide among themselves? I've seen many parents torn between their desire to be fair to all the children and their knowledge that one is more qualified to run the family business. We have all read the screaming headlines about bitter rivalries between brothers and sisters over family businesses and family fortunes. Good intentions are not enough.

Success in business brings with it a measure of power. In a family business that power is used, albeit unconsciously, to order our children's lives. For the sake of that sacred entity, the family business, they have to do thus and so; they are deprived of the joy and pleasure of making whatever they want to make of themselves on their own. They are trapped by a selfish bid for immortality by founders willing to sacrifice the individuality of their children in order to preserve their own self-esteem.

From adolescence our daughters have known my feelings about family companies. Not making a place in the company for them did not mean that chemical engineering as a career was closed to them. Jacobs Engineering Group is not the only chemical engineering and construction company in the world. It did mean that they were under no obligation to do anything other than make their own careers as they chose. Our children take from us only what they choose to take in shaping their lives. Sooner or later, consciously or unconsciously, they will reject what is forced upon them.

Everett Luther never had that choice and unfortunately did not measure up. I saw little prospect that he would undertake the tough measures necessary to return the business to profitability. Was this the time to go into business for myself? Or was it too much risk? I was 31 years old, married, with one child and another coming. We had saved some money because Vi and I lived very simply, and Vi was a careful manager. I shared my dreams with Vi and tried to assess the risks. She understood that I was thinking about taking the plunge so that I could, at last, answer the eternal, haunting question out of my past, "What business are you in?"

What to do now? I had made the radical move from a large, structured company to a smaller one. I had more varied experience than most people my age had. I felt well rounded and ready to go into business, but where, how, and what would my product be? I pondered that many evenings. Vi, as she has done almost every time we've had a decision to make, expressed simple and unrestrained confidence in whatever I wanted to do. She has never urged me to take any particular step in my career, nor has she ever opposed any step because of its effect on her life. Having seen the careers of hundreds of men altered, hindered, or just as often helped by the emotional needs of their wives, I appreciate Vi's unwavering support. I am sure she had misgivings because she tends to be conservative and is not a risk taker. But she has a deep sense of loyalty, derived partly from her Lebanese upbringing; it is also an aspect of her own personality. She says that she always had a lot of faith in me. Usually she is somewhat shy and can get astonishingly (to me, anyway) upset about trivial annoyances. But when it counts, she has enormous courage and resources, a steel core that enables her to weather major crises. Perhaps her faith in me was counterbalanced by an inherent faith in herself. Failure was something that she knew she could draw strength from, not something that she feared would break her. Perhaps it was Vi's Lebanese heritage or just her deep sense of loyalty. Whatever the source, her absolute equanimity and unquestioning support have allowed me to undertake venture after venture with little fear that she would be worried or concerned, or that she did not have the strength to adapt if I were to fail. I simply cannot place a price on it, nor can I estimate how much her attitude has contributed to my success as an entrepreneur, but it has been profound.

NINE

# *The Fateful Step*

I considered many possibilities, quickly ruling out any manufacturing operation because of the capital requirements. I felt particularly effective at selling ideas, so becoming a consultant appeared to be a prime possibility.

I had good academic credentials as well as a quick and fertile mind capable of spewing out innovative technical ideas. I had integrity and the courage to give direct and honest opinions. Thanks to Dr. Olsen and the Socratic method, I had the ability to cut through to the essence of problems and to look at them with a critical eye.

I had deficiencies too. I lacked gray hair. Traditionally consultants are men with long years of experience—their curriculum vitae is their primary sales tool. I had no particular technical specialty in which I might have had a recognized reputation, although I reasoned that I was better rounded, by far, than most chemical engineers I knew; if sold properly, that could be a greater strength than depth of knowledge in a very narrow area.

The most difficult question to answer was how long it would take to build up a clientele large enough to support my family. I knew we could live for a year without any income. Was that enough time to build a consulting practice? Uncertain, at best. Then I hit upon another idea. Why not become a manufacturers' representative?

During my stint at Merck and also at Chemurgic, I had been visited by many manufacturers' representatives, commission agents who sold lines of equipment used in chemical plants—heat exchangers, fired heaters, pumps, flow meters, and other equipment. Most of those whom I met were typical sales types—hail-fellows-well-met, personable, fun to be with, but often not too knowledgeable about the design and finer details of the equipment they were selling. "I'll check with the factory," was their usual rejoinder when asked a technical question.

Could someone with a Ph.D. become a successful "peddler"? Doctorates were rare enough in those days so that some would think it beneath one's dignity to become a commission salesman. Also, with some justification, many engineers looked down their nose at salesmen and peddlers.

Indeed, selling did tend to attract the less studious and less knowledgeable engineers whose idea of salesmanship revolved around personality or being liked. Remember, this was 40 years ago, and those characteristics were common enough to justify the derogation, "typical sales type." Today that uncomplimentary image is no longer applicable. Good sales people must have as much professional integrity and knowledge as their engineer clients. There is as much added value to be gained from good salesmanship as there is from good engineering. I tell everyone who will listen that the greatest single asset I bring to our business is my salesmanship. I sometimes take perverse pride in calling myself a peddler, thus defying the derogatory stigma. I cannot forget my father's carrying a suitcase containing razors, knives, and scissors from door to door. My "suitcase" is somewhat larger and the doors I knock on are more elaborate, but I have come full circle. He was a role model for me, and I wear the title of peddler proudly.

I believed that if I could get good lines of equipment that already had acceptance in the marketplace, I would find selling a much surer and certainly a quicker way to generate income. But why must I choose between being a consultant and being a manufacturers' representative? Could I do both? As far as I knew, no one had carried on both businesses simultaneously, so I had no experience to guide me.

The key question was that of a potential conflict of interest. A consultant must be always objective and have no ax to grind, whereas the sale of a given piece of equipment requires a narrow focus of advocacy. I finally decided, against most advice, that it could be done, provided I was absolutely honest with my clients when facing any potential conflict. The fact that it had never been done before gave me pause, but my entrepreneurial instincts made me dare to defy conventional wisdom. (In the 15 years that I operated the two businesses side by side, not once did a conflict arise, nor was my independent judgment ever questioned by my clients. My instincts served me well. Unfailing honesty and directness are the most effective sales tools one can use.)

Having decided on this dual approach, I should have had a business plan. Not knowing any better, I simply flew by the seat of my pants. I approached a company in Alameda, California, called Pacific Coast Engineering Co. (Paceco), fabricators of tanks, agitated vessels, and other equipment. I had bought equipment from them for many of the small plants I built at Chemurgic. They gave me a small retainer against future sales commissions to open a sales office in Southern California. On the consulting side, I persuaded a small start-up company in the liquid fertilizer business (a relatively new product in those days) to retain me.

Where to establish my new business venture? With a push from the Paceco offer, I decided to move to Southern California where I judged the market for consulting services would be better. There were more small to medium-sized chemical companies in Southern California. Very large companies need much less consulting help because they have large in-house staffs. The industrial base was growing faster in Southern California than it was in the Bay Area, thus also offering more opportunity for sales of equipment.

There were other subtle, unspoken reasons too. Vi and I had broken contact with our families rather abruptly, and even though they came to visit occasionally, I could see that Vi missed her family. We had made friends in the Bay Area, of course, but they were new ones and the limitation of our social contacts was exacerbated by the remoteness of our home in a rural area. Vi had a dear, sweet aunt (her mother's sister) who lived in Los Angeles. She and her husband were at the center of a large Lebanese-American community in Los Angeles. But it wasn't just Vi. I felt a strong pull too, even though Aunt Abla and Uncle George were not my direct family. Family and familiar culture drew us southward.

So I took the fateful step—I would set up a business in Los Angeles. Vi's Uncle George was in the real estate business, and he kindly offered me the use of a desk in his office. Because I had a consulting contract in the Bay Area with the liquid fertilizer company, and my principal sales account, Paceco, was also there, I commuted by car between Los Angeles and the Bay Area every week for four months. Vi stayed in the north until I found a house for us to live in. After spending a week in the Bay Area, I would leave midday Sunday, drive to Los Angeles, and stay at Vi's aunt's house until Friday, then go north again.

Housing was short in 1947. Uncle George, however, was the sales agent for a new development built in Altadena, a suburb of Pasadena, in the foothills of the San Gabriel mountains. The site was an abandoned grape vineyard at an elevation of about 1,200 feet. The houses were typical tract houses of about 1,100 square feet, and we paid $11,500 for the house with FHA financing. That was in December 1947, and we have lived in the Altadena and Pasadena area ever since.

My first office, after we got settled and the commute to Uncle George's real estate office got too rough, was with a laboratory supply store in Whittier. At Merck, I had learned to blow technical glassware and would often make my own glass equipment. Once when I needed to control the vacuum in a system rather precisely, I devised a special vacuum regulator out of glass that I later called a Cartesian Diver vacuum regulator. The principles were not new and I'm not sure something similar hadn't been built by others, but my design was compact and workable. A laboratory supply house salesman saw it and asked if his company could manufacture it for sale. I agreed, and they eventually sold thousands of them to laboratories all over the world. It never occurred to me to ask for any royalty or payment for the use of my design. It was not the last time I had "cast my bread on the waters."

Much later, the owner of the laboratory supply house bought a store in Los Angeles in partnership with a thermometer manufacturer from Brooklyn. When he found out that I was starting a business in Los Angeles, he asked if I would make my office at his new place in Whittier, California. It was a good deal for me—no office rent, the use of a secretary, only 35 minutes by car from my home in Altadena—and I got a small salary. I was to supply technical back-up to the rather mediocre management they had, but I think also that the owners were looking for my business judgment and perhaps even for me to be their resident eyes and ears. It took some time for me to overcome the local management's suspicion of me as a "spy."

That arrangement lasted about a year and a half. Meanwhile, consulting clients were few and far between. The business was even slower than I had feared. Within six or eight months after I started, the liquid fertilizer manufacturer got into a financial bind and canceled my retainer fee, which was the major part of my consulting income. It was a pretty scary time because my assured source of income had virtually disappeared, and with it my sense of security. So I concentrated on my manufacturers' representation business. I took on the representation of more companies and sold equipment from morning to night, driving many miles in the suburban sprawl of Los Angeles.

Finally I was ready for my own office. I rented a small suite of two offices and a reception area in the Subway Terminal Building at 417 South Hill Street in Los Angeles. I bought used furniture and moved in. Vi was my part-time secretary until she became pregnant with our third daughter, who was born in 1950. I advertised for a part-time secretary and hired Alta Wall, who was married to a Los Angeles policeman and had one child at the time. She'd get her young boy off to school, come to work for me, and then go home in time for his return from school. With time out to have another child and some other interruptions, Alta worked for me from 1950 until she retired from Jacobs Engineering Group in 1979 after her husband had retired from the police force. She is a wonderful person who was of inestimable help throughout my early career.

When I moved to Hill Street I was earning a pretty good living selling equipment and doing a modest amount of consulting. My decision to defy convention and be a representative while simultaneously attempting to establish myself as a consultant was fortuitous. I doubt whether I'd have survived with just the consulting work I did during the first years.

One of the owners of the laboratory supply house where I made my first office has stuck in my memory as a caricature of one type of successful businessman. Relatively uneducated, from the slums of the Brownsville section of Brooklyn, he started work as a bookkeeper for a German thermometer maker. He worked hard, saved his money, and when the owner died, bought the company from the widow. He invested in other businesses and acquired quite a bit of money (by my standards in those days, anyway). He was one of the most parsimonious men I ever met. His office at his factory was a ramshackle desk in the corner of the shop. He wore work clothes all the time. Surprisingly, he did not have the sour disposition one usually associates with misers. He was a good storyteller and could be fun to be with. But he had two obsessive traits. Making money was one and not spending money was the other. He was especially proud of the latter trait. He boasted that he would not forget his origins, that he would not let money spoil him. What everyone else regarded as miserly, he spoke about with pride and as a virtue. He would remain what he had always been, a poor kid from Brownsville. He was still living in the slum apartment that he had rented when he first married. Once he drove his wife and children to California in a rusty old car that barely made it across the country. I remonstrated with him about the safety of his family, but he was almost boastful that he hadn't succumbed to the temptation to get a new car—not even a five-year-old one. Although he claimed his niggardly spending habits were a virtue, he was probably just covering up his fear of being poor again. I've observed that the single-minded pursuit of money can be an obsession as addictive as drugs.

He was on one end of the scale of poor kids who had "made it" that I've observed over the years. The definition of "making it" varied considerably with each individual, but in all of them the condition has recognizable characteristics and symptoms. On the other end of the scale were the other poor kids who had "made it," who spent money lavishly, ostentatiously, and almost obscenely on cars, mansions, yachts, and so on.

My second employee was Harry Vinock. I hired him to help me with sales work. That was about the end of 1950, and by that time I had a number of other accounts to represent. Harry was a chemical engineer working for a heat exchanger manufacturer as a salesman. He was aggressive (though with a quiet voice), sensitive, and easily hurt, and had an intelligence he never stopped flaunting. He had apparently had the highest I.Q. in Texas when he was in high school and pulled out the yellowed newspaper article proving it at the drop of a hat. That article had turned into a terrible burden for him as he kept trying to live up to its promise.

It was a big decision to hire someone to work for me, because there were some clear advantages to being alone. There was, of course, the independence—not being answerable to anyone but my own conscience and my sense of responsibility. I could work as much or as little as I wanted. But I couldn't help thinking, "What happens if I get sick or disabled?" At the same time, my ambition was such that the slow, almost patterned and programmed acquisition of worldly goods seemed to mark the abandonment of challenge. It was somewhat analogous to my decision not to remain in teaching. What's out there? What challenges do I need to meet? Sure, I'd gone into business for myself, something that had been a major objective all my life. I'd certainly reached that important goal I'd set for myself. Now it wasn't enough. I had to reach for new goals, didn't I? For those not cursed (or blessed) with driving ambition, that may seem a silly question. Others will understand. I am not sure I used the phrase "delayed gratification" in those days, but that was my instinctive leaning. Those years of hard work and the decisions, time after time, *not* to cash in on each small achievement but to reinvest my time and energy in trying for a new goal had become a pattern or life-style.

Was it in my genes? Was it from family influence? Was it from a mother's ambitious drive for her family? Or was it an acquired habit such as smoking or brushing my teeth? It wasn't until later that I was able to resolve some of those motivations, but at the time, the instinct to reinvest in the future was overwhelming. That has been my style every since. Reinvest for future growth!

I had demonstrated two characteristics of all entrepreneurs. One was a willingness to risk failure; the other an inherent need to push things further, when the average person would have been satisfied to rest on his laurels. I may have adopted these characteristics for the wrong reasons, but I believe my instincts were the right ones because, whatever the emotional motivation, they made economic and moral sense. The morality derives from a perceived obligation to contribute all one can to the growth of an enterprise because those who depend upon that enterprise for their sustenance deserve it. So I decided to chance it, hired Harry Vinock, and started the pattern of reinvesting in growth that is a hallmark of my entrepreneurial style.

The next person I hired, Jim Sublett, was not a professional salesman but a process engineer who thought he'd like to try sales. I trained him to sell as I did, with lots of technical input, to become a sort of consultant to the customer about the best and most efficient use of the equipment we were trying to sell. So the equipment representation business continued to grow and prosper until it had five full-time sales engineers representing about six companies and pretty well covered the process and power industries in California.

In the early 1960s, when our engineering consulting business had grown to a significant size, I had long since been separated from the day-to-day management of the equipment representation business. I was distributing most of the profits to the employees and drawing only modest amounts from that business for myself. I decided to sell it to the employees, led by Jim Sublett. It went on to become quite successful, and Jacobs Engineering became one of its prized customers.

During those early days I had a number of small consulting assignments that were primarily techno-economic ones. I provided technical know-how, but the inherent business orientation of my culture made me valuable in judging the business prospects of technical innovation.

One day someone from Kaiser Engineers called from Oakland to ask if I were available for a consulting assignment. Was I *ever!* Kaiser Engineers was the foundation of the famous Kaiser empire. At that time it was one of the largest engineering and construction companies in the country. Henry J. Kaiser, a renowned entrepreneur, had started in the construction business and used it to launch his empire. His was one of the six companies that built the Hoover Dam during the thirties. The "six companies" won that contract because Henry Kaiser had the courage to defy the "cement trust." That colossal dam would use enormous quantities of cement. The cement producers quoted exorbitant prices to all the contractors bidding on the project. Kaiser hired his own engineers and decided that he could design and build a new cement plant in record time. Even with all the capital required, his cost for cement would be far below that of the cement companies. That gutsy gamble by this exemplary entrepreneur helped win the contract. Kaiser Engineers and Constructors was the base upon which Henry Kaiser built an enormous empire in cement, aluminum, magnesium, steel, coal, shipbuilding, automobiles, and on, and on.

In those days Kaiser Engineers did the engineering work for the whole stable of Kaiser companies. Why did they contact me? The director of research for Kaiser Aluminum and Chemical Co. was Dr. Al Byrnes, whom I had met in the Bay Area. After I moved south, I called on him occasionally, probably to sell equipment, but I also mentioned my consulting activities, I'm sure. We had become good business friends and he recommended that Kaiser Engineers contact me. What was the assignment? Kaiser Aluminum had obtained the rights to a series of salt brine wells in the Ohio Valley that contained high concentrations of bromine. Kaiser Engineers asked me to estimate the cost of building a plant to recover the bromine. They had no expertise in this area.

My consulting fee in those days was $100 per day. I flew up to Oakland, got the details, and promised to give them a report in three days. Because I had visited the bromine recovery plant run by American Potash Co. at Searles Lake, I knew the approximate size of the stoneware towers used to recover bromine. I understood the recovery process pretty well and was able to construct a flowsheet (a graphic representation of all the chemical equipment needed to make the product). From that I did a plant-cost estimate. I may have charged $300, but I certainly spent a lot more than 24 hours preparing that report.

Kaiser Engineers and Kaiser Aluminum were impressed with the practical answers I supplied. They then revealed to me that they had hired the Arthur D. Little Co., the foremost chemical consultants in the country, to perform the same assignment. Little's charge was $2,800 and the report had been prepared by a junior engineer who had simply abstracted some articles in the literature. My report was based on actual industrial practice and the contrast was stark.

As a result of this study, Kaiser Engineers put me on a retainer of $100 per month and began calling upon me regularly to do one- or two-day spot assignments. So I was on my way in the consulting business. Many things grew out of that original contract and the impression made with that $300 report.

TEN

# *A Precious Freedom and the Second Battle of Vicksburg*

We who live in a democracy are properly proud of our freedoms. We endlessly recite the Bill of Rights and all other codified expressions of our pride in our wonderful political system. But there is one freedom, often unrecognized, that I consider to be one of the most precious. That is the freedom to fail! No one reveres that freedom more than an entrepreneur.

It is hard for a compassionate person to accept that the freedom to fail should be revered. Failure involves the trauma of defeat, anguish, and a diminishment of self-esteem. But without the freedom to fail, there can be no freedom to succeed. One can only measure success against the consequences of failure. Indeed, the prospect of failure is itself a goad to success. If there's little chance for failure, the success attained has little value. Exalting the freedom to fail necessarily carries with it the willingness to accept the consequences of failure, for only then can the success be properly evaluated. If we cherish our freedoms, we must cherish this one with great fervor. The tendency in our society to protect and cushion every person from every possibility of failure is reprehensible even if compassionate. Is it possible for a compassionate act to be at the same time reprehensible? Of course it is.

For an illustration of the societal paradox at an everyday level we need only point to the thoroughly spoiled child who becomes a miserable and unhappy adult as a result of compassion taken to misguided limits. The overprotected child who has been insulated from failure and grows into a whining adult is a monument to compassion grown corrosive. Thus compassion, as admirable as it is, can undermine a society's fiber when carried beyond tolerable limits.

I find it hard to decide whether to trace the history of Jacobs Engineering as a series of successes attained or a series of failures avoided or overcome. My early life was a constant series of obstacles to be overcome, so I think my tendency is to look at events mostly as defeats to be avoided.

This viewpoint is pertinent because the first real step toward the establishment of Jacobs Engineering as a viable entity involved an enormous risk, a project that could have easily resulted in failure. I look back at it now and wonder at our daring. I confess quickly that ignorance and naïveté may have given me more courage than prudence. But the story of the progress and growth of the business is replete with risk taking and the courting of failure. Of course not every risk we took was successfully overcome—we've had many spectacular failures—but most of the successes were a result of exercising that freedom to fail that I consider such an essential part of our economic and political system. Underlying all the risk assessments was the recurring picture of my teenaged immigrant father sailing from Lebanon to the United States. My risk taking will always pale in comparison.

The consulting side of the business consisted mostly of minor assignments for Kaiser Engineers and for other much smaller companies. One day in 1953 I received a call from Aubrey Smith, the assistant general manager of Southwest Potash Co. of Carlsbad, New Mexico. I had been enthusiastically recommended to him by my friend Dr. Al Byrnes of Kaiser. (The $300 consulting job I had done for Kaiser really paid off.) I went to Carlsbad and was quickly retained as a consultant for Southwest Potash. That was my first contact with potash mining and recovery. The volume of consulting work for Southwest Potash grew substantially during the next few years. Though my technical consultation was impressive to them, my pragmatic and instinctive business judgment turned out to be even more valuable to their management.

In 1955, with the consulting work taking virtually all of my time, I hired Stan Krugman, who was a senior process engineer with C. F. Braun and Co., a large engineering construction company. Having previously worked for Merck & Co., he had heard about me and came west to work for Braun with introductions from a number of my old friends.

As a manufacturers' representative, I regularly called on all the larger engineering-construction companies. I admired C. F. Braun for its professionalism, ethics, and meticulous engineering and for the way its employees, its clients, and even its vendors were treated. Carl Braun, the founder, was a legend in the industry, a master salesman, a superb organizer, and a rabid defender of the professionalism of engineers. To its clients the company was known as the Cadillac of the engineering-construction business.

Stan started by helping me with the continuing consulting for Southwest Potash and occasionally on work for Kaiser Engineers. In late 1955 or early 1956 the president of Kaiser Engineers asked me to come to Oakland for a meeting. Stan came with me. Kaiser Aluminum Co. had just commissioned Kaiser Engineers to build an $80 million plant to refine bauxite (an ore containing aluminum) into purified alumina, from which aluminum metal is made in electrolytic cells. The new facility was to include a plant to produce the 100 tons of caustic soda per day needed in the refining process. The technical people at Kaiser Aluminum, claiming that Kaiser Engineers knew nothing about chemical processes, wanted to award the work to another engineering company in the east. In order to keep the work in house, Kaiser Engineers invoked my name as their chemical process expert. When we arrived, the president of Kaiser Engineers came to the point. "Joe, can you do the process work and the detailed design of a 100-ton-per-day caustic chlorine plant."?

"Yes."

"OK. Write us a proposal."

My knowledge of the design of such a plant was practically nonexistent and at that point we had no technical staff—just Stan and me. Fortunately, I was never asked if we could assemble the staff, where they'd come from, or any other key questions. Could he have had that much confidence in me to accept my simple yes? Apparently he did.

Because I was experiencing some emotional turmoil at the time, I think I needed a tough, concrete goal to go after. After all, the drive for those tough goals was what gave my life purpose. I couldn't retreat into fear now. If anything, I must take a very big risk to bolster my eroding self-confidence and to rivet my attention. I had used the aggressive pursuit of goals as a crutch all my life and it provided a focus for me in business during those days, even while I was exploring the dark corners of my feelings outside.

In retrospect, the enormity of the risk that I took appalls me. To the layman a caustic soda plant looks as complicated as the inside of a submarine; even to chemical engineers it's a real technical challenge. I had studied the basics of the operation in college courses and had visited a few such plants in the past, but that was all—a far cry from being able to design every nut and bolt in such a plant. Yet I had said yes! An entrepreneur courts failure!

Stan and I hit the library and studied the literature. I wrote a commercial proposal quoting competitive rates for our people (yet to be hired), and Kaiser gave us the go-ahead. We proceeded to recruit about 30 engineers and designers. My years of "peddling" to engineering companies paid off—I knew every bright engineer working for the major companies. Because I admired them so much and because Stan knew them too, most of our engineers came from C. F. Braun. To this day I use the C. F. Braun of those days as our professional role model. I tell our people to copy the company's high standards and to project its pride, cautioning them, however, not to develop the arrogance that Braun ultimately displayed. (One of the mottoes of our company, "pride without arrogance," reflects that admonition.)

To provide us with the detailed knowledge that we lacked, we found a retired chief engineer from Hooker Electrochemical Co. who had spent his whole life designing caustic chlorine plants and hired him as our technical guru. Our new team went to work in a second-story loft we had rented and furnished sparsely with a few desks and drafting boards. That was the foundation of the business that exists today as Jacobs Engineering Group.

Over the years I have drawn some hard conclusions about our business that I think apply to other businesses as well—conclusions that were influenced by some of the things that happened on this first important project. I don't remember what we paid the expert from Hooker, but it was minuscule in relation to the overall cost of the project or the profit we earned on it. Yet that man knew more details about a caustic chlorine plant than Stan or I could ever know. He had spent a lifetime at it and consequently he kept us out of trouble. I had been taught to revere technical knowledge in college and was a pretty good engineer myself. Yet the sad truth is that detailed technical knowledge is a relatively cheap commodity. What the client really pays for is the ability to collect, organize, and direct such specialists to produce something useful to the buyer. We call it "management."

We did the detailed design and Kaiser took the responsibility for the construction of this plant as part of the whole alumina plant facility built in Geismar, Louisiana. While the plant was being built Stan and I spent a lot of time at the site inspecting, interpreting drawings, answering questions, and so on. Bone weary, we often relaxed in the French Quarter of New Orleans, listening to Dixieland jazz. Many people in Kaiser Aluminum were skeptical of our ability to design such a facility, as well they should have been, and we were all pretty nervous when the start-up was scheduled. Though there were some minor hitches, they were remarkably few considering the complexity of the plant. Did we do a good job? The plant was completed in 1957, and thirteen years later, when Kaiser Aluminum decided to triple in size, they came back to us to design the expansion. The rewards of doing good honest work are obvious, but what a challenge met and what a clear-cut risk of failure averted!

In 1959 we were given a small engineering job by Kerr-McGee Corp. for a metallurgical project in New Mexico. As we were completing the engineering, they asked if we could handle the construction. That was a dilemma for me. When I started consulting, I had rather fatuously proclaimed that we would not go into construction, because it would sully our professionalism. I had the mistaken impression that the construction business was venal and that somehow construction people, dealing with craftsmen, could not be professional. But we couldn't turn down a good client. My opinions about construction turned out to be absolutely wrong—construction can be, and is, every bit as professional a service as engineering. People make the difference—if their attitude and approach are professional, it doesn't matter whether they are doing engineering or construction. Our company has provided both engineering and construction as professional services ever since.

We took an even greater risk with our other major client, Southwest Potash Co. When the crystallization process we had been studying for them had turned out to be uneconomical, we studied two alternatives. One was the relatively straightforward expansion of the existing refining plant to increase efficiency and capacity. The other was a radical new process that I had recommended and that the company enthusiastically supported. We followed both paths simultaneously.

Early in 1960, Southwest Potash decided to implement our first recommendation to modify and expand the standard flotation refining plant rather than build the originally contemplated crystallization plant. Though we had a modest staff of 50 or 60 people by then, the largest design project we had done was that of the Kaiser caustic chlorine plant, and our construction capability was brand new.

Our process consulting for Southwest Potash was admired by most of the people there, but when it came to awarding the total expansion project to us, many of them were quite properly nervous. The personal reputation I had established with the management finally tipped the scales in our favor. Indeed I remember vividly, lying in bed recuperating from my first heart attack in 1960, talking on the phone with Fred Stewart, the general manager of Southwest Potash. The gist of my message was, "Trust me, Fred, we can do this project and it's so important to us that I simply will not let anything go wrong." A reputation for honesty is an indisputable asset for an entrepreneur.

The other path we took with Southwest Potash reflected Joe Jacobs at his best or worst, depending upon the viewpoint. I became a reincarnation of Dr. K. of Autoxygen and Don Othmer of Poly. With a bold intuitive leap, I went way out on a limb recommending a radical and brand new idea. An understanding of the nuances of the enormous risks we were taking requires some technical discussion.

The standard potash used in fertilizer is potassium chloride, just as common table salt is sodium chloride. In agriculture it had been found that chlorides, derived from potassium chloride, were harmful to some crops—tobacco was one noteworthy example. For those crops the material of choice was potassium sulfate, which contained no chlorides. Southwest wanted to produce potassium sulfate, and our investigation of the economics of producing it showed a marginal return on investment.

Finally I remembered an obscure chemical reaction I had read about somewhere and did enough literature research to confirm that the reaction worked in the laboratory, though no one had ever attempted to build a commercial plant. This process involved the reaction of potassium chloride with very strong nitric acid to produce potassium *nitrate* and chlorine gas as a byproduct. If the process could be made to work commercially, Southwest Potash believed that the product would have substantial marketing advantages over potassium sulfate.

But the reaction I proposed was fraught with problems. First, it had only been carried out in the laboratory. Second, the conditions of the reaction were such that the intermediate products were as corrosive as anything known in chemistry. One is *aqua regia* (the "water of kings"), which is the only known chemical that will actually dissolve gold. Could that fearsome product be contained in any commercial equipment? If so, how much would the plant cost? If we made the product, how much would it sell for? Would it replace the existing market for sulfate of potash and would the new product find other uses? Though I was proposing a very daring technical leap, I was cautious enough to recommend that Southwest Potash build a small model or pilot plant first.

The company asked us to help implement an experimental program at the Colorado School of Mines Research Foundation in Golden, Colorado. This started in 1957 and continued into early 1961. The length of time is an indication of the number of problems we had to solve. (One of the young chemical engineers assigned to our project at the School of Mines was Noel Watson, who is now the president and chief operating officer of Jacobs Engineering Group Inc.)

In order to make the process economic, we had to make it "continuous." The costs of production would be astronomical if we made the product in batches, as was done in the laboratory. We needed to be able to feed in raw materials continuously and withdraw the product from some yet-to-be-devised equipment. In the pilot plant we successfully put together the equipment to carry out the reaction continuously. But could we design a large plant that would operate for days or weeks on end? Experts from all over warned us and Southwest Potash that we'd never be able to handle such reactive and dangerous chemicals in the tonnages we were contemplating. The predictions of the doomsayers just goaded us on. There was that urge to hurdle obstacles, to do things others said couldn't be done. That urge, as often as not, can lead to disaster or failure but is at the same time an indispensable characteristic of an entrepreneur as a risk taker.

Finally we were commissioned to start preliminary design work on a plant to produce 60,000 tons per year of this revolutionary new product. I won't recite all of the design alternatives we studied—all I can say is that we used every new and exotic construction material known or being proposed. For instance, the plant we finally built used the largest amount of titanium metal sheet that had ever been used to that time.

Previously we had studied potential plant locations and had finally decided to build the plant in Vicksburg, Mississippi. Construction began in early 1961 and was completed in the spring of 1962. Our experiences in Vicksburg stay in my memory, and I can relate many stories about that city and our long stay there, be-

*Potassium nitrate plant, Vicksburg, Mississippi, 1962.*

cause the start-up of this plant was the toughest and longest of any I've ever experienced. The doomsayers were *almost* right. Though the comparison is not valid in scale, I still refer to it as the second battle of Vicksburg!

You've heard many stories about the South but let me tell you that Vicksburg, Mississippi, was really the *deep* South. For people from New York City, even having adapted to the easy style of Southern California, the friendliness, courtesy, and good manners of southern hospitality were a revelation. The shopkeepers' greetings—"You all come back, hear?"—though just pleasantries, were a welcome relief from our daily pressures.

To put that in proper perspective, I tell a story about Noel Watson. One morning after a tough night at the plant, we met as usual for breakfast at the Magnolia Motor Hotel, our home away from home in Vicksburg. Noel was grumbling and grousing about how he hated the recalcitrant plant that wouldn't start up and how he hated Vicksburg. I said soothingly, "Come on, Noel, at least you've got to admit that the people here are nice. They are cheerful and hospitable and seem to welcome us. It could be worse you know!" Reflecting the pressure and his frustrations, he shot back, "That's the trouble. When you first come here you are so impressed with their hospitality and charm. Then disillusionment sets in when you find out that they really are no damned good just like everyone else from other parts of the country!" True enough, they have the same human motivations and frailties of all of us, but the veneer still makes life much more bearable there than it is in junglelike New York. The irony of that story is that Noel met and later married a local Vicksburg girl, Phyllis Herring, whose charm and friendliness are as genuine as his momentary cynicism was an aberration.

The plant we built was impressive. I need only look at old pictures of that plant to recreate the thrill I had in 1962. This was my creation. I had conceived the idea. I had brought it from dream to reality. What a monument it was, dominated by the 160-foot high central structure. This ten-story tower contained the continuous reactor at its core. It had an outside elevator and an emergency evacuation slide for operators to use in case of a blowout of the dangerous chemicals in the reactor. Around it were numerous alloy vessels with orderly piping in neat racks above the roadways.

During that spring, the plant kept starting up and shutting down for seemingly simple reasons. The operators, it later turned out, were trying to push the start-up too fast. Later, when we were reviewing the history of this most difficult start-up, I concluded that I had made one very serious mistake. No one in the management of Southwest Potash or its parent company, American Metal Climax Co., had any experience in the chemical industry, and I had not prepared them for the potential problems. I should have warned the management that we were plowing new, innovative ground, that the start-up would take time, and that patience was needed. To be sure, we made lots of technical errors and some bad judgment calls, and I must admit that the start-up was even more difficult than I had ever imagined or could have predicted. But the top management at American Metal Climax was totally unprepared for what we were going through.

Vi and I had gone away for our twentieth anniversary and when we returned, I got a phone call from Tom Childs, president of Southwest Potash and board member of American Metal Climax Co. He was the epitome of the polished business executive. Tall, handsome, a graduate of Princeton, and a former Rhodes scholar, he spoke with the slight overlay of a British accent and was as urbane, sophisticated, and usually unruffled as the stereotypical high executive. Uncharacteristically, he said, "Goddamn it, Joe, you got us into this project. It was your idea and we put a lot of money behind it and it's not working! You'd better get off your ass and do something about it." This was backed up by more than one call from John Payne, the executive vice president of Southwest in New York and Fred Stewart's direct superior. John's language was a lot saltier than Tom's. John was a tough, brilliant, geologist and mining engineer who was a terror to deal with when he was mad—and he was mad then. We eventually became good friends, but he was on my tail. I found out later that he appreciated the fact that I didn't run away from the seemingly overwhelming problems. Can you see my mother's influence here? You don't quit! Face the music!

So, in the summer of 1962, I went to Vicksburg and spent most of the next six months living there at the Magnolia Motor Motel, going home on occasional weekends. Stan Krugman took over the day-to-day operation of the company, though I was constantly on the phone with him. Even though we were not given the direct authority, we virtually took over the start-up, moving my guys, Noel Watson, John Buehler, Chuck Scott, and Bill Day, into direct control of the shifts of operators. We manned the plant around the clock.

There were many ups and downs as we solved some problems and new ones appeared. Finally, around Christmas at about 1:00 A.M. we all stood in the large warehouse designed to store 25,000 tons of potassium nitrate, watching with fascination as the crystals cascaded down the conveyor belt onto the warehouse floor. We had made product! It took several months to get the plant up to its operating capacity, but eventually, by tinkering and redesigning pieces of equipment, that plant was regularly producing 100,000 tons per year—two-thirds more than it had been designed to produce.

I remember that the thrilling moment when we saw the first production was around Christmas because the whole family was in Vicksburg with me. I had known we were reaching a critical time in our start-up, so had asked Vi to bring our three girls, then between the ages of 12 and 17, to spend Christmas with me. There is a story behind that too. I have talked proudly about my Lebanese heritage and remarked on the number of successful Lebanese businessmen in this country and, indeed, all over the world. A few weeks after I arrived in Vicksburg, I returned late one night to the Magnolia Motor Hotel and found a message asking me to call somebody whose name I didn't recognize. Nor can I remember it now. I did that the next morning and a heavily accented voice that I instantly recognized as Lebanese said, "How dare you come to town without calling your cousins! I just heard you were here and I am related to your wife and I am coming to see you. Furthermore, you must come to my house and have dinner!" On and on he went—all in good fun. So we met.

Over the next few months, I was introduced to the Lebanese-American colony in Vicksburg, about 100 strong. What a revelation and surprise! With names such as Jabour and Abraham and Nasser, they owned clothing stores, supermarkets, real estate, and cotton farms. As I got to know them better, I realized that these Lebanese "cousins" owned literally half of Vicksburg. As a group, their business acumen was spectacular. They would all have given varied but positive answers to the question, "What business are you in?" Most of them were first-generation Lebanese Americans, their fathers and mothers having emigrated in the early 1900s. They were all either related or from one of two small towns in northern Lebanon, one of which was a town near Tripoli, where Vi's mother was born.

They told us the probably apocryphal story that the original émigré of one of the families had boarded a flatboat somewhere upstream on the Ohio River and asked to be dropped off at Pittsburgh, where he might find work. The ship's crew misunderstood his accented English and took him down the Ohio to the

Mississippi and dropped him off in Vicksburg, where he prospered. He sent to Lebanon for a wife, and subsequently his relatives and hers from the nearby town in the "old country" came to Vicksburg to be helped, taken care of, and encouraged by the patriarch to go into their own businesses. My father's story repeated in this remote small town!

The people I met were well educated and intelligent, and most had taken over their fathers' businesses. They were a close-knit, ingrown, ethnic enclave, and though they had been there 50 years or more were still looked down upon by the upper class in Vicksburg. Because the Lebanese were outsiders, in pure jealousy or envy the old "aristocracy" resented their economic power in the town. Just a year earlier the Vicksburg Country Club had accepted its first member from the Lebanese group. He was wealthy, a good golfer, and had been a football star at Ol' Miss, but he was a dark-skinned "foreigner." His admission into the country club was the equivalent of breaking the color barrier.

My new friends had the well-known natural hospitality of the Lebanese and an overlay of southern hospitality that made them almost smother me with attention during my stay. They insisted that I bring Vi and the three girls down for Christmas and they put us through a round of parties that was overwhelming. I reveled in nostalgia as I relived my youth with these, my people. They were a throwback to the Lebanese-Americans I knew as a child. They were still entertaining and keeping up the old Lebanese customs, as my parents had done. They had *maherjan*, the Arabic word for big festive parties. They roasted whole, stuffed lambs over coals (in Arabic called an *oozey*) and danced the *debky*, a happy, stomping dance with waving handkerchiefs, not unlike the Greek dances. Even the second-generation children joined in and jokingly called the dance the "Kibby Stomp." (*Kibby* is a Lebanese dish made from pounded raw lamb meat and cracked wheat.) Their relative isolation in a culture that was already insulated from the mainstream of America and their classification by the locals as "foreigners" caused them to preserve the old country values and style for much longer than those of us raised in cosmopolitan New York. I must say that their warmth and hospitality made my stressful tenure in Vicksburg much easier to bear.

The climax of this bold and risky project that I considered to be "my baby" came in 1963 when Southwest Potash Co. was named the recipient of the Kirkpatrick Award by *Chemical Engineering* magazine. This award, named after the long-time editor of the magazine, recognizes the exceptional achievement of the most innovative new chemical process brought to commercialization during that year. A satisfying ending to a daring adventure that for a long time looked as if it would be a disaster.

The two risks we took with Kaiser and Southwest Potash illustrate my point about the value of the freedom to fail. I'd like to claim that we succeeded in both these cases because we were smart. Maybe we were, but I know that, without the specter of failure and without being keenly aware of the consequences of failure, we probably would not have worked so hard or pushed ourselves to the extent that we did. If I had had a wealthy father to start me in business again if I failed, would we have tried as hard? I doubt it, except for one factor that must always be coupled with the fear of failure—pride. Pride is that intangible motivator that is the antidote to the fear of failure, for the crushing of pride or self-esteem is the worst consequence of failure for all of us entrepreneurs.

ELEVEN

# The Edge of Darkness

Clearly, my venture was beginning to take shape and the prospects for success were bright. At the same time, I was beginning to experience physical and emotional problems that, though they were submerged during business hours, were affecting me and my family. Can constant brushes with death affect the development of an entrepreneur? Does an understanding of one's drives and the rationale for one's ambition improve one's chances for a successful business career? In my case, the answer to these questions is an emphatic yes!

I am not at all sure that there is any common lesson to be learned from my experiences, because they involve my body, my genetic heritage, my environment, my mind, and my psyche. Even though they are unique, I daresay somewhat different trauma, somewhat different psychological influences, and somewhat different deeply affecting events might have provided the dynamics and motivating forces of similar intensity for other entrepreneurs. They are such an important part of the anatomy of this entrepreneur that, as painful and distressing as it is to recall those events, they must be recorded if that anatomy is to have a throbbing pulse.

My ordeals, both mental and physical, escalated from what should have been only a minor incident. One Sunday in 1951 we came in from Altadena to visit Vi's Aunt Abla and Uncle George in Los Angeles. Uncle George Fuleihan came from a well-known Lebanese family, all talented, intelligent, and well educated. He was handsome, irresistibly charming, and one of the best extemporaneous speakers, in either flawless English or Arabic, that I had ever met. He and Aunt Abla had moved to California in the mid-1920s and he became an insurance and real-estate salesman. He was the center and the darling of the considerable Lebanese colony in Los Angeles. But he was irresponsible. He gambled. He spent more than he made. I found out later that he had borrowed to the limit against every life insurance policy he had.

That afternoon he had taken a nap and Aunt Abla asked me to wake him up for dinner. I tried to arouse him to no avail, and we called the paramedics. He had died of a heart attack. The event was traumatic for us all, but it was earth shattering for me. It brought back many painful memories: my father's heart attack; his five years of angina pain and his death; my oldest sister's sad death from ulcerative colitis (before they knew about colectomies); my mother's death from painful colon cancer in 1949.

As the man in the family, I took care of arrangements. I tried to straighten out Uncle George's chaotic affairs. It was depressing. This was at the end of 1951 when it appeared certain that I had established a business that would not only provide a living, but also was capable of growing. We had moved to a larger house in Altadena. We also joined a small country club so that by any of my previous standards or any of my youthful fantasies, I had "arrived." Why was I depressed?

Sometime after Uncle George died, I felt an alarming pain down my left arm and pressure on my chest. Scared, I went to the young internist who was our doctor then. He examined me thoroughly, took an EKG, and told me I was fine—physically. Psychosomatic illness was in vogue with young physicians at that time and especially with him. He concluded that there was a relationship between my perceived pain and the trauma of Uncle George's death—and indeed there was.

Though his diagnosis was superficial, I was satisfied with his explanation of my hypochondria. But I found myself visiting this doctor frequently over the next four years with all sorts of ailments—

gastrointestinal pain, arthritis, lower back pain, shortness of breath, and so on. This was when my business was beginning to show healthy signs of growth. We had obtained our first big project from Kaiser Engineers and yet I was getting more and more depressed and anxious, though I concealed it well in my daily contacts.

Things were deteriorating at home as well. I was picking fights with Vi and yelling at the children intolerantly. Talking to the doctor helped a lot but he was too much like me. He needed to dominate, to make me dependent upon him, and it wasn't working. He was finally perceptive enough to suggest that I seek professional help. "Not me," I thought, "not with my strength, my intellect, my willpower." But I became tense enough and anxious enough to be worried, especially as my family was obviously unhappy and I was getting very little satisfaction from the excellent growth of the business. I then remembered my friend George from my adolescence, and his therapy sessions. I recalled my unspoken curiosity. During the intervening years I knew I was driven, but there were always goals to be attained, new hurdles to surmount. The questions came back. What made me tick? It was not as simple as working hard and achieving. For I had done both and was still unfulfilled and unhappy. Why? Because there was no rationality to my depression, I finally sought help.

Over a period of four years I spent an hour a week talking, letting out my anger, resentment, and dissatisfaction. I'm sure that my verbal orientation helped enormously in exposing and recalling all the childhood hurts, the unrealistic expectations of myself, and the unconscious drive to please my dead mother. Fortunately also, I had a core of tough fiber that prevented me from reestablishing the dependency of childhood, or from wallowing in self-pity. Eventually, I recognized that I had learned a process, and I felt confident enough now to rationalize my feelings and behavior on my own. I'm not foolish enough to think that my insights and understanding are by any means complete or even right, but whatever they are, I have accepted them and I live with them comfortably, with only a healthy amount of self-doubt.

Subsequently, I began to understand the roots of my ambition, the role models, good or bad, that I was using. My understanding came most rapidly in the first few years and was intensified again as I repeatedly went through real physical health trauma. What did I find out about myself?

The most obvious relationship I had to resolve was that with my mother, the dominant figure in my turbulent adolescence. Which was she, idol or menace; object of love and softness or a resented, stern, and forbidding taskmaster? The answer is simple and obvious. She was both! That was the situation that could not be undone. Acceptance of that was the first and most difficult step. The second step was equally important. Why should I feel guilty and disparage myself because my feelings toward my mother were so ambivalent? Only in fairy tales are mother and child blessed with pure, unadulterated, saccharine love. I had every right to hate her for pushing me and for withholding her love when I didn't perform to her high standards. My drive to perform and to meet her standards, as I sought her approval and love, was natural and perfectly understandable.

The second conclusion I drew was, if anything, more important. I have already said that Vi and I were going through some turbulent times. She was confused, hurt, and resentful as she saw me troubled, angry and withdrawn, and rejecting her and the children. My conclusion about my relationship with Vi was so simple and so obvious now. I finally realized that Vi wasn't my mother! A simple statement and a profound fact. My not understanding that was a difficult emotional burden for her and also drained a great deal of my energy.

It was only when the business was clearly established and it appeared that I had reached the goals I had set for myself over the years that the emotional impact hit me. As I reached each goal, I kept looking to Vi for the accolades that I would expect from my mother. I kept looking for aggressive urgings to go on, to expand, to do better. I kept looking for a bit of preening, a bit of the grand lady, a projected and visible pride, even for a bit of discreet boasting about me. If my mother had been alive, she would have done all that. After all, wasn't that one of the reasons I had worked so hard, had driven myself to meet my mother's high standards of performance—so she could shine in reflected glory?

But Vi needed none of these things. She was modest. She shunned ostentation. She was content to live with me as my wife, whether I was a tycoon or working behind a soda fountain. Her faith, pride in me, and respect for me were not something to be trumpeted. They were a given—taken for granted and not tied to any level of achievement. More important, they were not something to be withheld if I didn't succeed. Did Vi take for granted that I would be successful? Of course she did, but her high regard and love for me were not dependent upon material measures of success or upon admiration in the community. Her need for recognition was minimal almost to a fault. Pride, reputation, and integrity were important, but for her they had a meaning very different from the one I had been taught.

The simple realization that Vi wasn't my mother led to the resolution of an enormous number of conflicts. I could accept Vi for herself. I could admire and love her for what *she* was. I learned not to confuse her needs with my mother's. Without that resolution of my feelings for Vi and the elimination of the deep conflicts in me, I am certain that my success in business would have been limited or, if not limited, not at all satisfying. It is not a necessary condition, but a relaxed, understanding, and tension-free family life adds immeasurably to an entrepreneur's arsenal.

That is not to say that warped personalities cannot be successful entrepreneurs, but an understanding of one's own motives and therefore an understanding of others can make the process easier and, most important, enhance the satisfaction. My old friend Socrates said, "if you would know others, you must first know yourself."

The more difficult emotions to analyze and to rationalize were those motivating my ambition. Obviously, much of the original motivation was provided by my mother's drive, her ambition, her need to overcome her illiteracy and to become, through me as a surrogate, the "classy lady" she yearned to be. But having concluded that, and having removed it as the prime motivating force, what was left? Should I abandon my striving? Should I leave my business and go back to teaching? Were my ambition and drive and accomplishment unnecessary or worthless because I no longer had to prove something to my mother? I finally concluded that there were other independent forces that went into my makeup. I don't know if it was my genes, other environmental influences, positive and negative role models during my early days, or simply an inner strength of ego of unknown origin that demanded worthy targets. In any case, in my middle thirties, the path I had set was obviously the path to be followed. Rejecting it all to "find myself," would have been senseless; a neurotic overreaction merely to demonstrate that I had completely rejected my mother's influence. It would be just another adolescent rebellion. The surprising discovery that I had an inner need to excel was, in fact, entirely independent of the influence of my mother.

Here I wish to make a disclaimer: Despite my experience, I am no rabid Freudian. Many of Freud's theories are fantasies and the sexual connections are tortured, to say the least. But my major criticism is that he essentially studied only abnormality. His was a morbid view of man's psyche. Though Freudian techniques will expose origins and causes, that's only part of the job. They clear the foundation to build a new emotional structure. But how does one do that? Other psychologists, such as Abraham Maslow, recognized this underlying fault of Freudianism and have developed a psychology based upon the study of successful and relatively happy people in contrast to abnormal and unhappy people. It was years later that I read Maslow and his theories of "self-actualization." I found that I had inadvertently organized my own restructuring along similar lines. I found that it was possible to build a life-style of ambition, achievement, and accomplishment based upon deliberate adult decisions made for positive reasons rather than upon compensation for neurotic stimuli received in childhood. Maslow loosely described "self-actualization" as "the full use and exploitation of talent, capacities, potentialities, etc. Such people seem to be fulfilling themselves and doing the best that they are capable of doing."

Now that I had finally removed the neurotic goads to success, what would guide me as I pursued my career? I had looked forward to feeling an enormous satisfaction from each goal achieved as I was growing up, graduating from college, getting a doctorate, getting a job with Merck, moving west, working at Chemurgic, and finally going into business for myself. As I achieved those goals, they turned out to be much less satisfying than I had fantasized. Indeed, that was the point of my dissatisfaction, my anxiety, my seeking to understand my ambition and my drive. In establishing a business, I had reached another important goal and I was *still* dissatisfied. If attainment of these goals was unsatisfactory, why strive? For the accumulation of money? Certainly not!

For what purpose? To be able to look at profit numbers on a financial statement? In our economic system, in our capitalist world, that is a well-recognized method of keeping score. I know that, for many people, those numbers on a financial statement are the be all and end all of ambitious striving. Of the many measures of a man's accomplishments, his monetary worth is one of the few that can be quantified—unlike artistic or musical talent, or even simple goodness. Because it can be expressed in numbers, the accumulation of money is often overrated as a measure of a man's value to society.

No doubt there are many driving and driven people for whom money is the *only* measure of success—either on a balance sheet or as expressed in things, such as a fancy car or a palatial home. I do not admire such people. I have found, however, that most successful people I know, financially and otherwise, have other, less obvious goals, such as the simple need to excel.

Here I was also influenced by Vi and her standards. In sharp contrast to my mother, Vi does not find "things" important. My mother would have strived for larger and larger houses, jewelry, and fancy cars. Not Vi though. Oh, we lived well and we raised our daughters in a pleasant environment, but thanks to Vi, they were unspoiled. Vi was so easily satisfied that it was no longer possible for me to be self-satisfied about whatever material success I was attaining. With Vi as a mentor, I gradually learned that material things weren't that important to me either. Neither of us wanted to emulate my friend who lived in the same old apartment he started in, and who drove a 15-year-old car, but there was a finite and relatively low limit to the pleasure we derived from possessions.

Then how was I to rationalize my ambition and my energetic drive? The answer came from two sources. A series of illnesses, some almost fatal, impelled me not to waste my life indulgently or to pursue only self-gratification. A growing realization that results and goals attained were much less important than the process or methodology of attaining them gave me a justification for my drive. This realization crystallized much later when my daughter Linda found a delightful paperback by Samuel C. Florman called *The Existential Pleasures of Engineering* (Griffin Books, 1976). This book, by an intellectual and reflective engineer, expressed almost all of the things that I had already rationalized in my mind.

I have not read much of Jean-Paul Sartre's own writings, but I had read enough about him and his philosophy to develop a rather simplistic view of existentialism. The essence of life and the real accomplishments of man are not in attaining goals or objectives, but rather in the *process* and energy invested in attaining those goals. The caricature of that philosophy is the "me generation" of the 1980s. But the "me generation" forgot that there can be pleasure in delaying gratification if that delay is conceived as *part* of a process. I think that, to become a hedonist, to live only for momentary sensations, is a corruption of existentialism (at least of my interpretation of it). The philosophic *core* of celebrating the journey rather than the arrival is not a new thought, but I made it mine.

The very title of that book by Florman jumped out at me, not only because it accurately reflected my own internally generated ideas, but also because of the massive contradiction projected in those few words. Is there any profession or business that is as results-oriented or objective as engineering? We design a bridge because we want a bridge! There it is in steel and concrete, and trains and cars roll over it. We design a chemical plant to produce chemicals and so it does. When we are in school, our whole objective is to get the "answer in the back of the book." We engineers are only taught the process or methodology for designing that bridge or that chemical plant as a means to an end. Our mentors teach us these processes almost as a necessary evil, needed only to achieve the final result, though occasionally you'd hear a reference to an "elegant solution." The idea, new to me, that the process was *more* important than the result was revolutionary for someone with my background. Here in a marvelous little book by another engineer was a rationalization of my ambition. Life is not an aimless wandering, a search for sensation. There must be a target, and one needs goals in order to experience the pleasure of devising the process for attaining them. The emphasis, for me, however, had shifted from the goal to the process. I had already discovered how little pleasure there was to be derived from the goal alone.

I cherish this little quote from Florman:

> My proposition is that the nature of engineering has been misconceived. Analysis, rationality, materialism, and practical creativity do not preclude emotional fulfillment; they are pathways to such fulfillment. They do not "reduce" experience, as is so often claimed; they expand it. Engineering is superficial only to those who view it superficially. At the heart of engineering lies existential joy.

How did this existentialist view of my life help me rationalize my own ambition and drive? It was simply that I no longer expected, or perhaps even needed, gratification from the accomplishment of given goals. Indeed, I pragmatically accepted that the attainment of those goals, whatever they might be, would *never* provide the gratification equal to my childish expectations. It would be foolish to deny that the attainment of the goal did not result in some pleasure. But with my new view, goals were necessary primarily because they challenged my ability to develop a process to attain them. Most important, the pleasure in the process was immediate and not rooted in the future. The process was indeed the stuff of life and life is important to me. And, because of my many brushes with death, I could be cut short before I reached those goals, so why not concentrate on the pleasures of doing? I did not want to die a disappointed man.

The observation that life is important to me may be fatuous in the extreme, but I have special reasons for making it. As the title of this chapter suggests, my several encounters with death have had a profound influence upon me. Although my various illnesses may be tedious or even unpleasant to read about, the anatomy of this entrepreneur would not be complete without an account of them. For I am convinced that the characteristics of courage, of daring, of swinging for the fences, of tempting fate, of risking failure, and finally of refusing to give up when faced with potential defeat, though mainly culturally derived, were substantially enhanced by my medical trials.

I have already related the story of my severe septicemia in 1943 and my miraculous good fortune to be cured by penicillin. My gritty determination not to die then is the type of character molding that I have benefited from time and time again. Actually that was not my first serious illness or brush with death. I was just five years old when I had my first experience. Did I have any concept of death or did I know that my life was in jeopardy at that age? Of course not, but I heard so much about this illness while I was growing up that my mind has created a vivid memory of it.

At that time our family was affluent, and we lived in a luxurious brownstone house near Prospect Park in Brooklyn. I was kept at home in a large bedroom, and for five months I had a sore throat, a fever, and round-the-clock nurses. Our doctor, a Lebanese, was known as a "heart specialist," though what that meant in the 1920s I don't know. He had diagnosed my illness as rheumatic fever. The doctor said that X-rays revealed I had "a pus sack over my heart as big as a silver dollar." Though I carried the diagnosis of rheumatic fever with me for years, doctors who examined me later marveled that I showed no signs of heart valve damage—a usual consequence of that disease.

Now go fast-forward 54 years to 1975; I lay in the intensive-care ward after open-heart surgery for a coronary bypass. I had been diagnosed as having 90 percent of the three main coronary arteries blocked. The surgeon told me that he had been able to do only a double bypass rather than the triple that had been planned. He explained that when he tried to bypass the circumflex artery he found my heart bound tightly to the pericardium (the thin membrane that separates the lung cavity from the heart) by very old scar tissue. He didn't want to take a chance by cutting through that, so decided not to bypass the circumflex artery, which goes behind the heart. When I told him the story of my so-called rheumatic fever at the age of five, he concluded that I had been misdiagnosed and that I had really had bacterial pericarditis, an infection of the pericardium, rather than of the heart valves, as in rheumatic fever. That explained the shadow on the X-ray plate in 1921. A diagnosis delayed more than half a century!

That childhood illness left an impression, as I repeatedly heard about my lucky escape from death. By itself, it may not have been too important, but it was the start of a series of illnesses that gave me a special view of the value of life.

In 1960 I developed some chest pain and pressure. The doctor said that there was not much change in the EKG and concluded again that the pain was psychosomatic. I felt rotten for a week, and after I played golf one day the pains returned. I suffered through the weekend in bed and visited the doctor again on Monday. My EKG then showed a depression of the "S and T" waves. This was a real heart attack and I'd probably had it for a week. Into the hospital I went. I was given heparin to thin the blood and morphine to kill the pain that had become excruciating. I had a second attack in the hospital about five days later. Then came bed rest and a period of introspection, depression, inactivity, reflection, and finally, acceptance. I describe these emotions matter of factly now, but, as anyone who has had a heart attack knows, it was overwhelmingly frightening.

When I want to be lighthearted about this, I say I had this heart attack because I *stopped* smoking, which in a perverse way is true. I had smoked since adolescence and was a heavy smoker until 1959 when I abruptly quit. (Had I learned less dependency?) Because my appetite increased enormously, I gained 25 pounds in that one year. I was told that my sudden gain in weight had placed an extra strain on my cardiovascular system, which could have precipitated the attack.

I was 44 years old, in the middle of building a successful business, and I might have died. Commonly, the overwhelming emotion after a heart attack is a stark confrontation with one's mortality. I had had two previous close calls, but a heart attack is so much more dramatic. Everyone expects to die and knows he will someday, but it's always something that will happen in the future and by rationalization, in the *distant* future. Depression is therefore a common aftermath of a heart attack. Cardiologists say that, after a period of introspection, most people have one of three different reactions. One group rejects the idea of a heart attack, blocks out the idea that one has really occurred, and continues to smoke, overeat, and enjoy life to the fullest. Much more common is the "cardiac cripple" who severely limits his activities and generally lives a fearful life trying to prevent another attack. Then there are the fortunate ones who modify their life-style somewhat, but go on living a full life. Luckily, I had been prepared by previous illnesses, and my newly acquired, or perhaps newly rediscovered, inner strength helped me enormously to live a nearly normal life.

Fifteen years later in 1975, I started having angina pains (shades of my father!). An angiogram showed severe blockage of the major arteries feeding blood to my heart. I was offered the alternative of leading a restricted life on medication or risking open-heart surgery. As scary as the prospect was, there was no hesitation in my choice. Despite the surgeon's being able to bypass only two of the diseased arteries, I recovered quite well and played nine holes of golf five weeks after surgery. Though a bypass operation can be routine, it is still a traumatic experience and thoughts of death are not far away as one enters the operating room.

The saga of my heart problems didn't end there. Coronary bypasses made with veins taken from one's legs have a limited life, often estimated to be between 10 and 15 years. Modern operations done by an experienced surgeon may last longer. In 1982 I began having angina pains again and the X-rays showed that my seven-year-old bypasses had clogged up with plaque (a mixture of cholesterol and fibrin). Again the choice was there—medication and an invalid's life or another operation. Second bypasses are rare because the scar tissue from the first operation makes the second one technically much more difficult. My case was further complicated by the old scar tissue from my childhood illness. The heart team in Pasadena who had done the first operation, though extremely competent and well regarded professionally, felt that the risks were too great and declined to operate, an honest decision that I respected. Still, that decision wasn't very reassuring.

I turned down the choice of living an invalid's restricted life and went to the Cleveland Clinic to have a second bypass. The coronary bypass operation was developed there and Dr. Floyd Loop was world renowned for performing difficult open-heart surgery. He had done over 500 second bypasses—more than any other surgeon. As any doctor will tell you, surgery is a technical and mechanical skill—the more operations a surgeon does, the better he becomes. This time Dr. Loop and his team were able to perform a quadruple bypass—two on the circumflex and two new bypasses on the clogged old bypasses. A damaged phrenic nerve reduced the capacity of my left lung, but otherwise my recovery was uneventful and another risk was taken and overcome. So I am living on borrowed time until the next bypass or the next heart attack.

My almost 30 years of cardiac difficulties have led me to understand the process pretty well. It appears that I inherited not only some admirable traits from my father, but also a bad cardiovascular system. Knowing that inherited factors are much more important than all the diet, smoking, and other behavior patterns that we hear about has helped me avoid much of the guilt that heart patients have. "What did I do wrong?" Genetic predisposition is a far greater contributor to heart problems than is life-style—though that should not be an excuse for ignoring moderation.

The other major illness that has affected my life and in a perverse way enhanced some of my abilities as an entrepreneur was probably inherited with my mother's genes. In 1949 she died of cancer of the bowel. My oldest sister, Margaret, died in 1933, about six months after the death of my father, as a result of ulcerative colitis. I remember that when she came down from Buffalo for my father's funeral, she looked terrible—gaunt and emaciated. Later I learned that she had been having diarrhea and bloody discharge for almost a year but had been too ashamed to go to a doctor. Finally, she was hospitalized; because the doctors were unable to stop the bleeding, she died.

In 1961 I had taken the first of innumerable trips to the Middle East, where I had a bad attack of what is known over there as "Gyppy tummy." There are similar names for it in Mexico and other undeveloped countries where sanitation is minimal. Though the water is a common cause, no precautions I took were able to prevent repeated attacks. In the late sixties I began to see blood occasionally, but it would go away. It came back, however, with increasing frequency, and finally a gastroenterologist diagnosed ulcerative colitis.

This disease is one of the autoimmune diseases, which include rheumatoid arthritis, lupus, early-onset diabetes, and others. The immune system, which normally attacks external pathogens, for some unexplained reason turns on the body itself and attacks the body's own tissue as if it were a foreign body. In ulcerative colitis, the bowel wall is attacked, causing ulceration and bleeding. It is usually a cyclical disease with patients going through periods of remission. It appears to be mostly genetically predisposed and is often triggered by repeated bouts of diarrhea or other physical attacks on the colon. Unfortunately, I had very few periods of remission and it got steadily worse.

The six years or so that I suffered with it were the most stressful of my life. Not only was it physically debilitating, but it is a most humiliating disease. The loss of control of bodily functions led to many embarrassing incidents. I had every gas station restroom spotted in the four miles between my home in Altadena and my office. Time after time, during a conference with clients or with my business associates, I would arise abruptly, sometimes in midsentence, and excuse myself. I must say everyone was extremely kind and pretended not to notice. During this period, I did not have any feeling of impending death similar to that induced during a heart attack, but the daily stress was severe. I was traveling constantly, and every time I visited somebody's office I would locate the restrooms before my meeting. Thereafter, no business loss or defeat, though painful, could ever be as important or as embarrassing. Finally in the early 1970s the scar tissue on my colon was so severe that it had lost all flexibility—it was virtually a straight, narrow, inflexible tube. There was no alternative; I had to face "the operation."

Since the days of my sister's illness, a radical operation had been developed known as a total colectomy or an iliostomy, in which the whole colon, from the ilium or the end of the small bowel to the rectum, is removed. The end of the ilium is brought through an incision in the lower abdomen, folded back, and sewn on the outside of the abdomen. This protrusion is known as a stoma. By various methods, which have improved over the years, an appliance or pouch is secured over this outlet to collect wastes. One can imagine how psychologically scarring this operation can be—so much so that people who've had the operation regularly volunteer to help patients go through the postoperative depression that often occurs. I adapted to it quite well though and have worn an appliance for more than 20 years. Scarcely anybody knows it, and it has not slowed me down one bit.

Those life-threatening illnesses may also be a clue to my focusing on an existential viewpoint. For, if life may end at any time, what of those unattained goals? Will I be deprived of the pleasure of attaining them? Overlay that viewpoint with the discovery that the goals themselves turned out to be not as pleasurable as I had fantasized, and the focus on process begins to make sense.

An airplane crash, a heart attack, some other form of failure, and the ultimate failure of death face us always. And all entrepreneurs face failure almost daily. There isn't one I know of who's had an unbroken string of victories. In the end, the success of an entrepreneur is the integrated sum of how he faces, handles, and finally overcomes the threat of failure. Thus, one begins to understand that success can only be measured against the possibility of failure. Having faced the ultimate failure of death, I consider no potential failure in my business life nearly so daunting.

TWELVE

# A Company's Character Is Formed

In 1957, what had been a sole proprietorship was incorporated as Jacobs Engineering Co. Bob Barton, who prepared the documentation for incorporation, became our attorney. Bob handled our legal affairs and also became my confidant and friend, as well as a member of the new corporation board, along with Vi. Almost every major decision I've made since then has been made with Bob's counsel—and always with Vi's unquestioning support.

In the 1960s we grew steadily in the western U.S. market from our Pasadena location. We took advantage of our smaller size and sold ourselves as professional, fast on our feet, and with lower overhead than the well-known companies in our business. This was when we began to form our management team and to develop the management style that has characterized our company.

One of our projects during the mid-1960s was for Merck & Co., who had acquired a plant on San Francisco Bay to recover magnesium products from sea water. Merck, my old "alma mater," liked our work and hinted that, if we had an office back East, we would be considered for other projects, but made no firm commitment. We were unwilling to gamble on opening an office without more insurance than that.

Soon an opportunity to open an eastern office did arise. The plant we had designed for Merck involved the recovery of magnesium hydroxide from sea water for conversion to milk of magnesia, the laxative. Shortly thereafter a promoter came to us, asking us to design a plant to recover magnesium hydroxide from sea water at a site in the province of Newfoundland, Canada. He was primarily interested in using the magnesium product not as a laxative, but to manufacture a special brick that is used in steel plants. The processes by which the white powder of magnesium hydroxide is made are the same as those used in the Merck plant, but this plant added a step to calcine the magnesium hydroxide by heating it to high temperatures, creating magnesium oxide from which the hard firebricks are made.

The promoter was financed by funds from the provincial government of Newfoundland. Because the plant site was so far away from Southern California, he was easily persuaded to let us do the project in the East. In 1967 we opened an office in Linden, New Jersey, in an empty furniture store. We sent Jim Klohr back to run the operation and Noel Watson to be project manager. That project went all the way through design but was never built because we could not verify the economics projected by the promoter. Once established on the East Coast, we did get a small project from Merck and then a larger one from Squibb, the design of pharmaceutical plants to be built in Puerto Rico. To this day, we retain an office in New Jersey. This series of events demonstrates the combination of caution and quick response to the market that is a hallmark of our company.

During the sixties our staff continued to grow, and most of the people moving into management positions were from the original crew that had worked on the Kaiser project. Stan Krugman was the clear-cut choice for managing the production or operations end of the business as well as directing the performance of our engineers. Under Stan Krugman's direction, our production staff and project managers were developing into a solid core of reliable professionals. Stan was a vital part of the growth of our business in those early days. Stan is tall, handsome, and projects great self-confidence, though in fact he was very shy in social situations. What self-confidence he projected was primarily rooted in his excellent technical knowledge and a very logical and analytical mind. It was Stan who set the standards of performance, hired the people, rode herd on the engineers, and got the projects done on time and on budget.

But there was a serious flaw in his relationship with the people working for him. The remark I heard frequently was, "Everybody respects and admires Stan, but nobody likes him." That is, of course, grossly overstated because nobody's feelings were that black and white. They didn't dislike him, but there was little warmth exhibited in his relationships.

He ran his business from behind his desk, calling innumerable meetings, at which between three and seven people sat around answering his penetrating questions. He was good, make no mistake about it, but I found myself, more often than not, soothing bruised feelings after Stan had ridden roughshod over his people. Though the differences between a manager and a leader are extremely complex, here was a narrow example of one of the differences. Stan was a good manager in that he knew what people should do, but did not know how to tell them what to do, or how to inspire them to want to do it for reasons other than fear of his criticism.

I am not a rabid fan of so-called theory Y management, the theory that promotes the use of only positive rewards for performance. Theory X management, which deals with fear as a motivator, is not my cup of tea either. Still, fear of failure is inevitably a force that cannot be ignored. Part of my reverence for the freedom to fail is the impetus it gives people to succeed. Recognizing its importance does not diminish the fact that the more positive rewards of success should be used in substantial ways too and as much as possible. We all would like to use inviolable formulas; but like most things in life, the true answer is somewhere in between. The skillful manager tends to shade toward theory X; the successful leader tends to shade toward theory Y.

Unlike Stan, I was an early devotee of what later became known as "management by walking around." My use of this technique predated any writing about it that I was aware of. It was not intellectually conceived, but purely instinctive with me. I felt good doing it and people felt good when I did it. Indeed, until 1974, when we became too geographically dispersed, I handed out the paychecks to everyone twice a month. I must confess that I had the payroll department help me by stacking the paycheck envelopes in the order in which the desks were arranged so that I could address each person by name as I handed him his check—a bit of fakery, but it was flattering to the person nevertheless. Some of our staff who were around then still remind me of those days. Occasionally I'd stop for a couple of minutes to chat and frequently discovered little tidbits about different projects going on in our office. I was careful not to direct or tell anyone what to do; I would just listen sympathetically if they had a problem, or admiringly when they boasted about something they had done. Frequently I would go back to Stan and ask him if he knew that we were having "this kind of a problem on such and such a project." He was always amazed at my intelligence gathering. He never did appreciate how my sensitive antennae picked up information as I handed out those checks. I am still a passionate advocate of management by walking around" and still spend more time in other people's offices than I do in my own.

The catchword of today, and one I've heard throughout my business career, is "systems." That word describes a wide gamut of methodology—from computer software to elaborate methods for paper shuffling. What it represents is a desperate search for a panacea to overcome the imperfections of man. To deny that those imperfections exist and that they need to be guarded against would be myopic, but I'm afraid that reverence for the "system" is likely to obscure the purpose. Too often we are beguiled into thinking that "the system is the solution."

When carrying out projects our company has voluminous records and highly developed procedures that presumably highlight problem areas gleaned from thousands of projects we've done; still, though, the experienced project manager is more valuable than any standardized procedures. Systems are a tool, but they do not make up for experience.

One of my rather acerbic comments about stylized management tools is that they teach "management by history." Voluminous reports tell you what happened yesterday! In contrast, the good manager senses what may be about to happen tomorrow and moves to prevent it from happening. Theoretically a well-constructed report may tell what went wrong and thus prevent its happening again. But how many of those reports, after the novelty has worn off, are shuffled directly from the "in" basket to the "out" basket? Of such stuff is the mountain of paper in American business constructed. Even under the best conditions, there is a finite lag between event and report. This is the clear advantage of managing by walking around.

Voluminous reports have another disadvantage that their devotees do not appreciate. Reports and systems sometimes act as a narcotic. A manager can be beguiled into believing that the system will automatically tell him he's got a problem and ring an alarm bell. By the time it gets into the report, it is often too late—the fire is raging.

I never could get Stan to hand out the paychecks. He felt secure behind that big desk of his. It was the picture of Stan sitting behind his desk with his minions arrayed on the other side that made me reflect upon office furnishings. Some 25 years ago I decided that a desk was an anachronism. After all, desks came into use when people wrote things out in longhand (using quill pens, of course!). In analyzing what I did in my office, and out of it, during a typical day, I found that 95 percent of my time was spent talking or listening on the telephone, to my associates, to clients, to visitors, and of course to my secretary. Did I need that large desk to sign my letters or documents? Of course not. It has been remarked that a desk is a symbol of power for the man sitting behind it and that those sitting on the other side are supplicants. A manager who is also a leader must listen as well as instruct. In the interplay between people, a relaxed atmosphere is the best stimulant I know of in which to gain and give out information. What finally convinced me to get rid of the desk was the realization that I spent more time, by far, at my business than I did at home. I didn't sit at a desk at home when people visited me, why do so at the office? Why shouldn't my office be as comfortable and friendly as my living room at home? And so it is.

The main piece of furniture is a long couch in a tweedy fabric over which is draped a colorful crocheted afghan knitted by my

*JJJ in his current office at JEG headquarters. Left to right: JJJ; Noel G. Watson, president; James E. Berkley, executive vice president; John W. Prosser, senior vice president.*

92-year-old, nearly blind mother-in-law just before she died. I sit in a low upholstered armchair with an ottoman upon which I prop my feet. I don't hesitate to lean back for a 15-minute snooze periodically. A small octagonal table at arm height, decorated with calendar, clock, and a picture of Vi, is used for incoming mail and miscellaneous stuff to be read, or decided upon, later. The table is so small that Betty, my recently retired "right hand," would get impatient with its untidiness pretty quickly, at which point she exercised her preeminent right to make me feel guilty for all of the things I had left undone. I love my office and enjoy having visitors. When I first furnished my office this way, it was considered radical. Today many executives have adopted a similar style.

Now I have a most serious confession to make. After all my protests about the eighteenth-century habit of writing, I wrote the manuscript for this book in longhand! I have never learned to type, and although I have had a long list of skills that "I am going to acquire someday," none of which I've gotten to yet, typing has always been low on that list. Much higher on my list, for instance, would be to learn to play jazz on the piano, and I've not yet gotten around to that either. For most correspondence I can construct grammatical and reasonably fluid sentences and paragraphs in my mind as I speak. But for speeches and papers, and especially this autobiography, I find that by writing in longhand I can do some self-editing as I go along. In one corner of my office I have a leather-topped table about the size of a bridge table that I use for my occasional scribbling and the rare occasions on which I need to spread out plans or drawings.

I've taken time to describe my office because it epitomizes the importance I place upon communication and the role it plays in successful entrepreneurship. "My door is always open," is a cliché honored more in the breach. Although I can be an overwhelming talker on many occasions, I know that even the sometimes brutal Socratic method would not be effective if Socrates did not listen!

I wish I could point to a well-defined outline of how we operated our business in the sixties. It would be nice to tell you that we had a clear-cut vision of where we wanted to go and that we followed a well thought out business plan. But in fact we had no planned growth and were content to be unabashed opportunists. We did not grow on a steep curve, but went through a series of flat spots in our business. I believe we had fewer than 100 permanent staff members in 1960 and close to 400 by 1970. Our earnings were climbing at a satisfactory rate, though unevenly.

Though the stepwise growth was mostly inadvertent, I argue that a business cannot grow healthily on a continuous rising curve. Whether fortuitously, which is more often the case, or by design, a business needs a period of consolidation after a period of growth. Having seen our business grow from a one-man operation to one with almost 5,000 permanent staff today (with our craftsman labor, we have over 10,000 employees), I am thankful for that pattern of stairstep growth. An organization needs to learn to adopt new management styles at different stages in its growth. A 1,000-employee business requires a different management style and technique from that of a 100-person company. That's why meteoric entrepreneurial growth often results in companies that outgrow their founders. Apple Computer is an example of a business that grew faster than its founder, Steve Jobs, was able to change his style to fit it. The collegial style that he and the cofounders of Apple Computer found so effective would not work when the company grew enormously within a few years. Jobs's style was right for the founding and John Sculley's style is right for the company today. Compare the meteoric growth of Apple Computer with that of its next-door neighbor, Hewlett-Packard, a business that was started in a garage by two bright young engineers, but grew in more of a stepwise fashion that allowed the development of a management capable of handling each step of the growth.

Many times I have wished that we had the open comradeship and quick decision-making ability of our youthful company. But those steps in our growth taught me that changes in management style were dictated by forces beyond my control—by sheer numbers, for instance, if for no other reason. I still get twinges of disbelief and even some regrets as I see reams of reports, computer printouts, and other bureaucratic procedures inundating our people, but I have learned to accept the inevitable. Fortunately, at this stage I can afford to ignore it all, but I must honestly admit that our business could not run without it. My style hasn't changed that much, but my influence on what is done has diminished—and that's as it should be. I guess, in all fairness, I do act as a moderator because everyone knows of my antipathy to "paper" and "systems."

Is the work we produce at our current size therefore worse? No, it is not. Over the years we developed methods and procedures to support and help decision making instead of depending upon impromptu or freewheeling decision making, as we did in the early days. The sheer force of numbers is what generates paperwork in companies. Without having developed these methods, our company would not be able to perform as well as it has in recent years.

During that period of our growth in the sixties, and especially during the flat periods when I had the opportunity to reflect upon the new managers we were developing, it became apparent that I must do something positive to motivate and reward our hard-working people. Though financial reward is not the most important motivation for engineers, it nevertheless is a measure of the esteem in which they are held. Something in addition to professional pride is needed to make engineers feel that they are worthy.

As we grew and made profits, I started to pay bonuses. It was purely arbitrary and, as I sadly came to recognize, somewhat paternalistic. Uncomfortable with arbitrary bonus allocations, I really anguished over the decisions. Was this fellow twice as good as that fellow?. Was I treating this one unfairly? The bonus scheme worked for a while, yet the idea of encouraging key people to own shares in the business kept arising. But there were pitfalls to be avoided.

I developed a set of criteria that I used as a guide. These were distilled from observations of other companies and their policies and from my own conclusions about human nature and motivation. The latter, no doubt, arose from my own understanding of what motivated me and the importance I had placed upon self-esteem and human dignity. The first was that I would not "give" any ownership in the company to key employees. This decision was not based upon greed or lack of generosity. It was more fundamental.

There is an old but true adage that things are only worth what you pay for them. These people deserved reward for their contributions to the growth of the company, but in my view those rewards were properly made through salary and bonuses or profit sharing. But isn't ownership profit sharing? No it isn't, because ownership is different in a very important way. Ownership involves risk! Ask some of the disappointed employees of companies whose Employee Stock Option Plan (ESOP) funds were used in unsuccessful leveraged buyouts. Even though people may say they want ownership, it is often more an emotional than a well-considered choice. I was adamant that our key people make a conscious choice to accept risk and that they make a considered judgment that the risk of buying stock in our company was worth it.

I considered what would happen if one of these now valued employees decided to quit, or if I decided to fire him. Who would he sell his stock to if we were a private company and at what price? There was only one buyer, me (or the company), and I would have an unfair advantage. I know there are partnerships in which "buy and sell" agreements are made, but I've rarely heard them described enthusiastically. There are some justifications for "golden handcuffs," but they are still handcuffs. Having that kind of power over a person's free choice was unappealing to me. I didn't want to place an economic shackle on a fellow's ability to tell me to "go stuff it," if he should quit in anger.

We finally decided to hire an outside consultant to study and reconcile the conflicting requirements and then recommend what we should do. John Lovelace, Sr., was well respected in financial circles and we felt that his small company, Capital Research Corp., could give an unbiased view. (That firm is now one of the largest fund managers in Southern California.) Its carefully prepared report made an unequivocal recommendation that we take the company public by making an initial stock offering through an underwriter.

THIRTEEN

# *Going Public—The Company Grows*

The conclusion of the Capital Research group that we should offer shares to the public made eminent sense, primarily because it provided a suitable method for our key employees to share in the company's future growth through stock options. There was no real need on my part to "cash out" a part of my ownership, nor was there a need for a cash infusion to the company, the usual reasons for an equity offering. Our aim was to create a public market so that stock options would have an unbiased pricing mechanism. Options therefore would meet all of my criteria for offering equity to employees:

- Options do not take any cash out of the pockets of the employees; they would buy the stock only at some future date, when its value had, we hoped, been enhanced as a result of their efforts. If the stock did not rise in value, they were not forced to buy it. There was, therefore, no risk of loss.

- A public market would place a value on the employees' stock if they wanted to sell, and they would not have to contend with some arbitrary valuation dictated by me.

- According to the rules in effect then, there would be no tax consequences, even after the options were exercised, until the stock was finally sold. This consideration no longer holds; the IRS has changed its rulings.

- Employees could calculate the value of their stock simply by reading the paper in the morning. And I hoped that stock ownership would become a source of pride and motivation for them.

This last assumption turned out to be questionable. People often ascribe to the stock market a wisdom that it simply doesn't possess, except in the crudest way. In fact, my observation of the opinion makers on Wall Street is that, rather than being logical analysts of values, they are more often ruled by emotion and the herd instinct. The wave of interest in and the fluctuation in price-earnings ratios for various stocks seem often to follow childish impulse rather than rational analysis.

Stock options are still a useful tool, but many of the tax advantages have been negated. Some politicians classify these tax changes as "closing loopholes"; demagogues classify them as "closing loopholes that benefit the rich." In reality they represent a political decision to change the social agenda. The populist view in those days was that employee ownership of businesses was a good social goal, because "people should own the means of production." That inspired the tax concession on stock options. But populist viewpoints are notoriously fickle. Because of explainable differences in objectives, the more highly paid employees took advantage of stock options; the lower paid ones tended not to. This was viewed with horror by those who regarded the income tax system as a vehicle for social engineering—not, as originally intended, simply as a method of raising money to run the government—and the rules were changed. They keep changing periodically as the demagogues promote ever-shifting goals of "fairness," a subjective criterion if there ever was one!

An interesting but obscure book that treats the subject exhaustively is *Envy, A Theory of Social Behavior* by Helmut Schoeck, an Austrian sociologist. His thesis is that envy is an essential ingredient of human nature and that no political or social system that does not take this into account can survive. Herodotus said,

"Envy is born with man from the start." Schoeck distinguishes envy from jealousy. The jealous person says, "I wish I had what he has"; the envious person adds, "and if I can't have it, I don't want him to have it either." The book is replete with deeply researched data on all types of tribal and other social systems in which envy has to be reckoned with. His evidence is strong and disquieting. It is a pretty shocking conclusion for all of us idealists who believe in the perfectibility of man. If it's true, the utopian society we all fantasize about will never be a reality. I find it interesting that Schoeck cites the graduated income tax in the United States as the ultimate expression of the political force of envy. This dismal Hobbesian view of man cannot easily be dismissed no matter how depressing.

Schoeck examines Sweden's requirement for public disclosure of all income tax returns over $3,600 (which predates our Freedom of Information Act). The disclosure is touted to promote honesty in tax returns, but is more likely to cater to envy. How many exposés that are justified as being for the public good are in reality pandering to the feelings of envy? Putting it succinctly, he says, "Social life would be impossible if cultures did not succeed, within reason, in forcing those who have real cause for envy to cooperate. For after all, a society in which there was never cause for envy, a society of total and constant equality, would not be workable even as a theoretical experiment." The scholar Michael Novak has voiced similar views in many of his writings. The populist idea of absolute equality is a stygian nightmare—not a utopian dream.

All entrepreneurs and business people who aspire to leadership must heed this caution. The best way to blunt envy is to help those who have cause for envy to consider themselves part of the enterprise. Remember, "*We* are succeeding," not "*I* am succeeding." All kinds of emotional turmoil can be resolved by carrying out that simple dictum in our daily actions!

It's ironic that many of the socially driven (or envy-driven, if one were to be more cynical) tax provisions go awry. The stock options that I advocated enthusiastically are a good example. I started by giving options widely through the company—as few as 100 shares each to secretaries and others. That was a futile gesture. It was meaningless to most recipients and had no effect on their identification with the company or on their work habits. I thought that ownership would add an extra dimension to the employees' work, but it didn't for 90 percent of ours. Those small options produced no visible positive effect; nor was there any adverse reaction when we stopped giving them so widely. A few people—perhaps 10 percent at most—understood stock options, appreciated their value, and were aware that investment involved risk. But that 10 percent aroused the envy factor in government. "Only a certain 'elite' benefited from the stock options," the social planners said. So they changed the tax rules, declaring them to be discriminatory, contradicting their initial assumption that the offering would spread ownership, and without acknowledging that an opportunity offered to all only became "discriminatory" because of the free choice of those who decided not to participate. In case after case, tax statutes designed to spread benefits or wealth turned out to benefit a small percentage of the population and so became the target of another new "tax fix." Will we ever learn?

The Capital Research group made several other recommendations. One was that, when we became a public company, we should have a board dominated by outside members. That made sense to me. Inside boards are a travesty, as I had learned at Chemurgic. Another recommendation was that I invite onto the board people who were my friends but were not beholden to me financially or otherwise. "Friends will not be obstructive and, at the same time, they'll fight to keep you out of trouble." Because they have a fiduciary responsibility to the shareholders, board members must be persons of principle and integrity. I have never regretted following this advice.

Our first board of directors consisted of Bob Barton, our outside counsel and company secretary; Hugo Riemer, a former president of Pacific Coast Borax; Barney Bannan, chairman of Western Gear; Stan Krugman; and myself.

I'm very proud of the caliber of the boards of our company over the years. What I'm proudest of, though, is that I have never once invoked my dominating shareholder's position to force through something that I proposed. Indeed, it is a matter of procedural style with me that I will readily abandon a proposal that evokes any strong opposition from even one board member. If other board members choose to argue the case, that's okay, but I won't. Consequently, almost all actions taken by our board are unanimous. Superficially, this may look as if the board is a "rubber stamp," but that's far from true. In fact, lively discussions, and even heated arguments, are a staple at our meetings. We have never kept count of the thousands of proposals that I or our management made that were never taken to vote because of active and vocal opposition from one or more board members. My ego says, "If I cannot persuade these friends of mine through the sheer logic of my arguments, then the use of the voting power of my stock position to carry the suggestion is a confession of abject weakness on my part."

Finally, even though our earnings would probably be toward the low end of a desirable stock offering, the Capital Research people insisted that we contact one of the eight or nine top-ranked investment bankers at that time. Just as in the selection of accountants, they said, "go first class."

Among those I contacted was White Weld Co., a leading underwriter at the time. Frank Kiernan, the legendary head of White Weld who had arranged financing for most of the major pipelines built in the United States after World War II, came to our company apartment along with his right-hand man, Paul Hallingby. (Because I traveled to New York frequently and had tired of hotels and their cost, Jacobs Engineering had rented a modest apartment that everyone in the company used.) I showed them our figures and projections, and before they left, they committed themselves to underwrite our offering. Their quick responses, their penetrating questions, and their decisiveness made the company stand head and shoulders above the other major firms I had talked to. Paul, who has since become a good friend, was a graduate engineer who had chosen finance for a career. He managed our offering and within a few years succeeded Frank Kiernan. White Weld subsequently merged with another firm.

So, based upon our audited year-end results of September 30, 1970, we went public in November 1970—an event of great

*Jacobs Engineering Co.'s first headquarters building, in Pasadena, California, 1962.*

significance financially and psychologically. Our original prospectus was extremely simple compared with the documents the Securities and Exchange Commission (SEC) requires these days. We offered a total of 320,000 shares at $12 per share. The proceeds from 150,000 shares went to the company and the proceeds from 170,000 shares came to me. I then sold 20,000 of my shares to key employees at the offering price with no underwriting commission. We were traded on the over-the-counter (OTC) market for the first six months and then transferred to the American Stock Exchange (AMEX). The prospectus referred to "previously granted stock options of 30,000 shares at an option price of $5.00 per share." In the section of the prospectus entitled "Use of Proceeds," the company said it would buy our headquarters building on South Fair Oaks Avenue from me for $1,050,000, as appraised by the American Appraisal Co.

There is an interesting story behind this. In 1962, as we were beginning to grow, we needed new space. Because we were a corporation, and because of the current varying and high tax

*Current headquarters of Jacobs Engineering Group, in Pasadena.*

rates, depreciation on real property was more useful to an individual than to a company. I decided to build a headquarters building and rent it to the company. I found an empty lot in southwest Pasadena in a rough area of machine shops and warehouses, bought it for 50 cents a square foot, and built a two-story frame and stucco building on it. The company rented it at rates that I made certain were competitive with anything we could find in Pasadena.

This was the start of a whole series of real estate transactions that I made on behalf of our company and that became an important source of income over the years—at one time preventing the company's possible collapse. After we became a public company, all of my real-estate dealings were made on behalf of the company except for a few investments that had nothing to do with the company's needs.

I had stumbled upon a hidden asset of our engineering business. We employed a lot of people—highly desirable, well-educated people—and housing them could be the basis of important real estate transactions. We did not need a "downtown" address for reasons of prestige, but the mere presence of our professional staff would immediately increase the value of any neighborhood we moved to. We had the means, therefore, to upgrade real property substantially. That first building was a prime example of the value of our need for space. Many people advised against the purchase of that land, as cheap as it was, and the siting of an office building there in such a rundown, industrial neighborhood. The property that I paid 50 cents a square foot for in 1962 is probably worth $40 or $50 a square foot today, though we no longer own it. We sold it in a complicated real estate transaction in 1974.

*Opportunity* has been a recurrent theme in the life of this entrepreneur. That's a word that implies a fortuitous encounter but is, in fact, a strongly energizing mechanism for an entrepreneur. For isn't the first requirement of an entrepreneur the recognition of opportunity? And isn't the second requirement the willingness to take risk? And isn't the third the ability to exploit that opportunity so as to minimize the risk or maximize the gain, remembering always that risk and reward are invariably interlocked? The recognition and exploitation of opportunities may be the primary acts that differentiate entrepreneurs from other people in business.

Our stock offering became effective on December 10, 1970, and it was well received. For the first time the public, my friends, and my family were fully aware of what our business was, what our profits were, and other facts about what I had been doing over the previous 20 years. The financial "strip tease" required by a public offering affected my life profoundly. Now that we were public, we were able to concentrate on building a healthy company. The strong drive to grow and excel was undiminished, but now I had an external motivator that stimulated me even more.

Cynics rarely believe me, but with the sale of that stock, I took upon my shoulders a personal obligation to stockholders. Many of my friends bought stock at that initial offering, so I tended to characterize all stockholders as "my friends." Therefore, my

*PROSPECTUS*

# 320,000 Shares

# JACOBS ENGINEERING CO.

## Common Stock

(Without Par Value)

Of the shares being offered, 150,000 are being sold by the Company and 170,000 are being sold by the stockholder named under "Principal and Selling Stockholder". Of the shares being sold by the Selling Stockholder, 20,000 are being offered to employees of the Company as set forth under "Offering to Employees". The Company will not receive any of the proceeds from the sale of Common Stock by the Selling Stockholder.

Prior to this offering there has been no public market for the Common Stock of the Company. The offering price has been determined by agreement among the Company, the Selling Stockholder and the Underwriters. The Company intends to apply for the listing of its Common Stock on the American Stock Exchange as soon as practicable following completion of this offering.

**THESE SECURITIES HAVE NOT BEEN APPROVED OR DISAPPROVED BY THE SECURITIES AND EXCHANGE COMMISSION NOR HAS THE COMMISSION PASSED UPON THE ACCURACY OR ADEQUACY OF THIS PROSPECTUS. ANY REPRESENTATION TO THE CONTRARY IS A CRIMINAL OFFENSE.**

| Shares To Be Offered by the Underwriters | Price to Public | Underwriting Discounts | Proceeds to Company (1) | Proceeds to Selling Stockholder (1) |
|---|---|---|---|---|
| Per Share ........................ | $12.00 | $ .90 | $11.10 | $11.10 |
| Total ........................... | $3,600,000 | $270,000 | $1,665,000 | $1,665,000 |

| Shares To Be Offered to Employees | Price to Employees | Underwriting Discounts | Proceeds to Selling Stockholder (1) (2) |
|---|---|---|---|
| Per Share .................................. | $12.00 | None | $12.00 |
| Total ....................................... | $240,000 | None | $240,000 |

(1) Before deducting expenses estimated at $52,166 payable by the Company and $50,337 payable by the Selling Stockholder.

(2) Assuming sale to employees of all 20,000 shares offered. No representation is made, however, that all or any specified portion of such shares will be sold.

These shares are offered by the several Underwriters named herein, subject to prior sale, when, as and if delivered to and accepted by such Underwriters, subject to the approval of certain legal matters by Voegelin, Barton & Callister, counsel for the Company and the Selling Stockholder, and Gibson, Dunn & Crutcher, counsel for the Underwriters, and subject to certain other conditions.

## White, Weld & Co.

The date of this Prospectus is December 10, 1970

*Prospectus of initial stock offering, 1970. Today (mid-1991) the value of each share would be worth close to $200.*

drive to grow and succeed was enhanced by my need to be sure I didn't let my friends down. Did I have an unwarranted need for approval? Perhaps, but I've never claimed to be able to make completely dispassionate decisions.

With publicly traded shares, we began to make a series of small acquisitions of professional service businesses that had special market niches. Most were of companies employing between 10 and 40 people, primarily architects, with a desirable geographic presence. Some brought special know-how, such as Pridgen Engineering, whose phosphate technology is the basis of our current position as world leaders in this field. Most of the rest were of indifferent caliber, some bad and some reasonably good, but of minor consequence in our growth.

The major benefit resulting from our having a public stock available was the merger we consummated with The Pace Companies of Houston, Texas, in 1974. The Gulf Coast area had become a large and expanding center for the process industries. Texas and Louisiana had, over the years, turned from being producers of crude oil and gas (shipping those natural resources to refineries in the Northeast) to becoming important refining centers. Because of cheap energy and relatively low labor rates, the region was quickly becoming the petrochemical center of the United States.

The Pace Companies started as a partnership of four chemical engineers who had left Exxon (then called Esso, Standard Oil of New Jersey) to open a consulting practice. They went through the usual struggles: one partner left and was replaced by another, then one was added. By 1974 there were four senior partners, Warren Askey, Dick Kruger, Bill Service, and Bill Broyles. The company's growth somewhat paralleled that of Jacobs Engineering, though on a smaller scale. Starting with pure process studies and reports, it progressed to doing detailed process calculations, then detailed design packages, and became known as a highly professional firm of consultants and technologists. Some two years before we came along, the partners had felt the pressure to become a completely rounded company (they had watched our progress with a bit of jealousy, I found out later), so they acquired the Hydrocarbon Construction Co. of Houston and the H. E. Wiese Co. of Baton Rouge, Louisiana. Both were construction companies, each founded and run by a tough, risk-taking construction man. Though both of the acquired companies lived primarily on competitive fixed-price bids, Wiese had fortunately started to diversify into contract maintenance. The latter is a high-revenue, but low-margin and low-risk business that is now an important part of our company's revenues.

For several years before our approach, the Pace group had taken substantial financial losses as a result of fixed-price competitive bids. By the time I came along to talk to Warren Askey, they had been pretty badly bruised, but had survived and were profitable again. The partners had considered going public, but their bad experiences with construction had sidetracked them. Because we were already a public company and had survived the two depression years of 1972 and 1973 with only a slight diminishment of profits, we were an alternative to be considered seriously.

I visited Warren Askey in Houston and broached the subject of a merger. To my pleasant surprise, he was receptive. I hadn't realized how shaken the partners had been by their flirtation with serious financial loss. We were obviously a much sounder company financially, and because we were only about twice their size, they felt that they weren't being swallowed up by a giant. I was sincere in selling the concept that we would merge, not just financially, but managerially as well. We would let the cream of both managements rise to the top. I can be forgiven if I secretly felt that our people would probably prevail, but I accepted the possibility that I could be wrong.

After my initial meeting with Pace, I took Stan Krugman with me to subsequent meetings, as I valued his analytical appraisal of The Pace Companies' business and how it would fit with ours. At some stage in our negotiations it became clear that Stan's personality was a potential stumbling block to my hope of homogenizing the management styles of both companies. Warren Askey finally said that if we merged he would not report to Stan Krugman. I explained the situation to Stan, who understood but naturally was disappointed.

I proposed that Warren Askey become president and chief operating officer of the company, move to Pasadena, and join our board. Warren reluctantly agreed. He liked Houston and I think he felt uncomfortable living outside that special culture. But clearly he felt an obligation to his people. He would be their representative and protector up there in, perhaps hostile, Pasadena.

In a long heart-to-heart talk with Stan, I explained that, in my opinion, he had more talent than anyone in either company, but because the Pace people didn't automatically accept him, he had to earn the leadership. "Stan," I said, "if you have the ability I think you have, you should be able to demonstrate to them that you are the one they will look to for operating management. If I force you on them, their resentment will sink you. You must make them want you! Warren Askey will be president and chief operating officer of the combined company to symbolize that it is a true merger and not an acquisition. I will suggest that you be elected executive vice president of the combined company, report to him, and have the responsibility for integrating the two companies. Get an apartment in Houston and spend half your time there and half your time here in Pasadena. That will give you the opportunity to get to know them and to demonstrate your talents to the people in Houston. Make yourself indispensable to Warren, because you know so much about the details of operating an engineering and construction company that he will learn to lean upon you!" I sent him off to that assignment with great hopes that he would meet the challenge.

Stan and his new wife went to Houston where the Pace people gave a big party for them, Texas-style, which was a disaster! It was followed by other strained social occasions. When Stan sensed the resentment, he became increasingly morose and withdrawn, and though he stayed with our company for an additional six years and remained effective with the Jacobs Engineering people, his impact on the company's growth was much less than it had been in the early years. He did not achieve what I hoped for him and what he yearned for. Partly because Stan was not able to bridge the gap, for years there was a division between the "Pace people" and the "Jacobs people" that I had to work hard to eliminate. It was not

*JJJ and Vi Jacobs about 1970.*

a happy time for Stan. He realized that he hadn't met the challenge. It was also an unhappy time for me because I had to acknowledge my own failure to help Stan grow to the position he clearly deserved. I have since concluded that I was probably asking too much of Stan—and of myself—under the conditions that prevailed then.

Although I only dimly recognized it at the time, there was, in fact, a vast cultural difference between the Pace people and ours that took years to reconcile and delayed for many years the synergy or even the melding of the managements that I had hoped for. Pace had started as a partnership and we had started as a sole proprietorship—that difference alone was profound. All of the partners of Pace took great care to tell me that Warren Askey was the "first among equals" though, in my opinion, he was clearly the most qualified to be president of the group. They had a collegial style, exaggerated substantially by a Texas "good old boy" network. We were a more monolithic company and there was little doubt that I was the boss, even though I did not run the company imperiously. My name on the door and my clear majority ownership had a subtle but profound effect upon our working style.

Another difference was in our social lives. The Pace people and their wives did a lot of socializing together in the friendly fashion typical of Texas. We did that a lot less. I confess readily that this was a personal prejudice of mine and a style I had set. Oh, Vi was an indefatigable and gracious hostess. When we had couples from the office to our house for dinner everyone was completely taken by Vi's unassuming friendliness. In the early years we had the employee Christmas party at our house. Vi prepared all the food and washed all the dishes when our guests left. But I had seen enough of excessive socializing at the executive level in other companies to be cautious of the spillover of social pressures onto business decisions. I didn't want an added dimension in the daily relationship between people in our company to be whether someone liked or disliked his colleague's wife. Wives, understandably, can have a narrow view of their husbands' role in a company. It's appalling but true that seemingly trivial social slights can start festering at home and the infection can be transmitted to working relationships. There's enough natural politics in the workplace as it is. My policy has always been to be friendly with the people at work and to have warm social contacts with their families outside work, but not to make the people in business the center of my social life. Indeed, a social life circumscribed by the limits of business associates is a pretty sterile and narrow one.

When Warren Askey moved to Pasadena as president, he had some trouble adjusting socially, but his primary problem was adjusting to the differences in culture between the two companies. First, there wasn't the comfortable "good old boy" network he was used to. Then there was Stan Krugman's almost palpable antipathy. Stan's anger was exacerbated by what appeared to him to be a situation in which his relationship with me was being displaced by mine with Warren. He was right—I went out of my way to defer to Warren publicly and in private. I was determined to demonstrate to the Pace people that Warren's appointment was not a surface appeasement—that I truly meant him to bring the two companies together and to mold them into a stronger one. (Warren stayed as president for only two years. The reasons for that and for subsequent management changes are described later.)

We benefited from a long period of expansion in the engineering construction business, enjoying a steady and satisfying growth for the next six years. In 1980 our after-tax profits were $5.5 million and in 1981 we made a peak of $9 million after taxes. It was easy to become self-congratulatory about such performance—and I freely confess that I was not immune. Those seven years up to 1982 were a period of unprecedented prosperity in the engineering construction business, and we were beneficiaries. The major firms in our business were busy in the Middle East and elsewhere overseas. The oil embargo instituted by the Arab countries in 1973 disrupted the world economy and started the enormous flow of petrodollars to the Middle East. The frenzy of capital spending by the Arab countries over the next 10 years was unprecedented, and the only engineering construction companies in the world capable of handling their huge projects were American. So our large competitors left most of the domestic American market to middle-sized companies such as ours. Toward the end of the seventies, the increased stranglehold of the strong OPEC cartel on our economy and the war between Iran and Iraq caused an almost hysterical (and not unjustified) reaction here. With rapidly rising dependency upon foreign oil at artificially high prices, the synthetic fuel era was upon us. Congress appropriated enormous sums of money for numerous mammoth synthetic fuel projects. President Carter rather grandly called them the "moral equivalent of war," but the program was so ineffectual that wags dubbed it "meow."

With their staffs swollen from their work overseas, the major engineering and construction companies began obtaining huge projects from our government and major private companies to convert oil shale to hydrocarbons, recover oil from oil sands, make synthetic natural gas and crude oil from coal, and so on. The engineering construction industry expanded in the late seventies and early eighties to a size that we now recognize as being abnormally large—probably twice its natural size. We, too, participated in all the activity and succumbed to the general euphoria in the engineering construction business.

In the early eighties I became an unwitting greenmailer—before the term was invented. Our business does not have much need for capital, so we built up fair amounts of cash in the late seventies and early eighties. I had admired the Turner Construction Co., the premier builder of office buildings in the United States. We started to buy its stock and gradually accumulated about 7 percent, at which point we had to file a notice with the SEC disclosing our ownership. Believing that our companies were complementary rather than competitive, I visited the executives to ask politely whether a merger between our companies would make sense. I was received rather coldly, and the fear in the managers' eyes was something to behold. The next week an investment banker called to say he was deputized to buy our Turner stock for Turner's own pension plan at a premium. He named a price, I accepted, and we made a nice profit.

I hadn't realized how intimidating my own stock ownership in Jacobs Engineering could be—especially for professional managers. It was startling to see the Turner executives impute malevolent motives to me. Instead of judging me after listening to my proposal, or considering how a merger with us might have helped their stockholders, they acted with an instinctive fear that was appalling.

Another more extreme example of management myopia occurred a few years later. In the late seventies Kaiser Industries, the holding company that owned Kaiser Engineers, was being dismembered for some complicated tax reasons. The prospect of buying my old friends, Kaiser Engineers, made the juices flow. I flew up to see Edgar Kaiser to suggest that we negotiate the purchase. He was a sad man, reminding me that Kaiser Engineers was his father's original company and the foundation of his family's business. Selling it was the last thing Edgar wanted. "But Joe," he said, "as much as I'd like to, I can't negotiate solely with you. Our board has insisted that investment bankers put the company up for auction." We submitted an offer of about $16 million. We weren't even close. Kaiser Engineers was bought by Raymond International (who had started years before as Raymond Concrete Pile Co.) at more than twice my offer. Raymond was headed by a rather pompous chief executive officer, Henry Le Mieux.

He was right and I was wrong. Over the next three or four years Kaiser made profits that more than returned the purchase price. But I was still fascinated by the prospect of a combination of Kaiser and Jacobs. "Perhaps it might be done through a combination with Raymond," I speculated. So we started to accumulate Raymond stock. Finally we bought a fair-sized block and filed a Form 13-D (a notice of ownership required by the SEC), showing that we owned about 7.5 percent of Raymond's stock.

I'll never forget the phone call from Le Mieux! "Joe, you're not going to take over my[!] company! I'm sitting in Joe Flom's office and we're ready for you." (Joe Flom is one of the two foremost takeover lawyers in the country; the other is Marty Lipton.) Henry was trying to intimidate me and was probably paying enormous fees to retain Flom. The defiance in his voice betrayed his underlying fear.

"But Henry," I said, "I'm not interested in taking over your company. I don't go where I'm not wanted. I think you did a smart thing to buy Kaiser. I think we'd do great if we combined, but I'm content to be a stockholder if you can't see the advantages of getting together."

The next week I got a call from an investment banker who said he had been authorized to offer to buy all our Raymond stock and mentioned a price. I was noncommittal and went to Marty Lipton for advice. I spent about an hour or so with him and put the matter in his hands. In two days Lipton called to say that he and Joe Flom had met over lunch and agreed upon a higher compromise price. "I suggest you take it," Marty said. The legal bill was $35,000, but we made more than $1 million on the transaction.

Ironically, only a few months later, Raymond borrowed an enormous amount of money for a leveraged buyout at a stock price substantially above what they had paid me. (I suppose we could have sued if, as I suspected, they were planning the buyout when they were negotiating with me, but we never considered it seriously.) Le Mieux controlled so little stock that he plunged the company into a staggering debt in his scared attempt to retain personal control of the company—the stockholders be damned! Under the weight of that debt, Raymond eventually went broke. The banks that loaned them the money lost over $100 million. It was a tragedy for the employees and it all arose out of a CEO's fear and ego. What stayed with me from the whole episode was Henry Le Mieux's palpable fear when he talked to me on the phone, and the way in which he plunged a large and successful company into crushing debt in order to avoid "raiders." Forgive my immodesty if I say that he might have been wiser to have invited us to help him run the business.

During the two decades over which our company culture developed, one project contained most of the elements that defined the personality of our company—the plant we designed and built for the Arab Potash Co. in the Kingdom of Jordan. It involved, again, enormous risk taking. It required almost spirit-crushing perseverance. More than 20 years elapsed between the time that the first contracts were made and the successful completion of the Arab Potash Co. project. Because of the emotional implications of working on an extremely large project in the land of my forebears, I took very personal interest in the project. Every emotional and motivational tool that I put into creating Jacobs Engineering I put into this project. The anatomy of the entrepreneur is laid bare in the creation of the company, and during its growth; but that single project in Jordan, 10 times larger than any other project we had done during the 20 years, had within it all of the forces and conflicts that characterized our struggle to grow and to succeed. That the plant we designed and built for the Arab Potash Co. in Jordan on the Dead Sea is now running successfully and in excess of design capacity is not fortuitous, for that project is but a reflection of the spirit of the company that bears my name.

# III

# Back to My Roots

FOURTEEN

# *Across the River Jordan*

The pride I have in my ethnic background was fostered by my parents and my adopting many of the values they brought with them from Lebanon. That pride was accompanied by an equally intense curiosity about the country of my forebears and, indeed, about the whole Middle East. Is the search for one's roots a universal yearning, or is it more pronounced in Americans?

At my father's knee, I listened for hours to stories of his youth in the Old Country. I heard how he constructed traps for birds out of a stiff sheet held up by a stick, which somehow had a trigger containing wheat kernels. The birds came to eat the wheat, triggered the stick, and the sheet then fell on the birds, which were a delicacy when roasted on an open fire. And the fruit! In my father's nostalgic memory, the apricots were as big as his fist and drippingly sweet. So were the grapes, the plums, and all the other fruits. It had always been a remote dream that I would visit there one day.

In 1961 I read in one of the technical journals that the Arab Potash Co. (APC) of Amman, Jordan, was requesting proposals for the design of a plant to recover potash from the Dead Sea. Because Jacobs Engineering was eminently qualified technically to contend for the job, my interest was piqued.

At the time of the formation of Israel by the United Nations, the truce line between the Kingdom of Jordan and Israel ran north and south through the center of the Dead Sea. The high salt content of the Dead Sea has been remarked upon for millennia. According to the Biblical account, Lot's wife turned into a pillar of salt as they left Sodom and Gomorrah, cities located on the edge of the Dead Sea. That story has a plausible derivation. Any object sprayed with Dead Sea brine will turn into a pillar of salt under the hot sun. Everywhere around the shores of the Dead Sea are pillars and domes of salt.

Besides table salt, the Dead Sea contains significant amounts of potash and magnesia (magnesium chloride). In the 1920s, the Palestine Potash Co. built a small plant at the north end of the Dead Sea to recover potash by solar evaporation. It was destroyed during the first Arab-Israeli war in 1947. In the late 1950s, the Israelis organized a project to recover potash from the Dead Sea brine. The project was fraught with technical problems, and the plant took almost 10 years to meet its original design capacity.

When I saw the announcement I thought we might have a chance to win the contract. Stearns Rogers Co., the premier potash experts and our primary competitor in potash technology, was working for the Israelis and so, as the Arab boycott was particularly virulent at that time, a major competitor was eliminated. Though we were a very small company then, we had outstanding technical credentials from our Southwest Potash work. I thought (naively, it turned out) that my Lebanese and Arabic-speaking background might give us a competitive advantage. Finally, having heard about it as a child from my father, I yearned to see Lebanon.

With great expectations, I booked plane passage directly to Beirut from Los Angeles with just a short stopover in London; it was 23 hours elapsed time to Beirut. It was foolish of me to book that way, less than a year after my first heart attack, but I did and arrived dead tired. I was welcomed at the Beirut airport by at least 20 people, including Vi's sister Flo. In those happy days in Beirut friends customarily joined the relatives in greeting a new arrival. I was a long way from home, but that smiling welcome from 20 total strangers was heartwarming.

Flo, the oldest daughter of F. M. Jabara, was born and raised in Brooklyn during the height of her father's affluence. She did not go to college (Vi was the only one of the daughters to go) but attended an expensive finishing school in Lausanne, Switzerland. In about 1930 Najib Khairallah, from a highly placed and respected Beirut family, visited the Jabara home in Brooklyn. His father had been one of the first students at the American University of Beirut and had converted to Protestantism, a rarity among the Christians of Lebanon. Najib courted Flo, who agreed to marry him in 1931, and they both moved to Beirut. Flo became a glittering hostess in Beirut; but after only eight years of marriage her husband died suddenly, leaving her widowed with two young daughters.

After Flo and her friends met me, she whisked me to her apartment, one of three in a building owned and occupied by the Khairallah family. Flo had the middle apartment. One widowed sister-in-law lived upstairs and her bachelor brother-in-law lived downstairs. Each apartment had a full complement of servants and a crude speaking tube between floors. Flo barely gave me time to unpack because, she said, we had been invited to a party at a friend's apartment. Tired as I was, I went along obediently.

Our hosts exemplified everything I had heard about cosmopolitan, cultured Beirut. Mohammed Adham, the son of one of the leading families in Baghdad, was a graduate of Harvard and had an additional degree from Columbia University Law School. His wife, Emily, an American from Philadelphia's Main Line, was the charming hostess.

The apartment we went to was recently built and luxurious by any standards: polished marble floors, enormous rooms, beautiful Persian rugs in abundance, modern appliances, and a very large terrazzo balcony overlooking the Mediterranean Sea. Servants were all about and exotic *maaza* (Lebanese finger foods) and whiskey were plentiful. In a slight daze I stood on that beautiful balcony (about 10 stories up), drink in hand, at sunset watching a giant orange ball setting over the blue-green Mediterranean, cutting orange, red, and pink stripes down the center of that ancient sea. As darkness approached, the calm water turned blue-black and stretched to the horizon to meet the sun, now blood red. I felt disembodied. This was a Hollywood movie—a dream! This was all the stories I had heard about beautiful Lebanon dramatically reenacted for me. Finally in a daze of both exhaustion and too many new and extraordinary experiences, I went back to Flo's apartment, where I collapsed into a bed shrouded in mosquito netting (malaria was still a problem then).

The next day I began to meet more of Flo's many friends—Lebanese, displaced Palestinians, Syrian, Iraqi, British, French and, of course, American. They trooped through her apartment from morning till night, paying their respects to Flo's brother-in-law from America. By Lebanese custom, they must never leave without being served something—coffee or tea and biscuits in the morning, an elaborate lunch at midday, tea and small sandwiches at teatime, cocktails and hors d'oeuvres at cocktail time, or finally an elaborate dinner that never started before 9:00 P.M. Exhausting, but they had a system to cope with the pace—everyone took a siesta. Men closed their offices at 1:00 P.M., went home for a heavy lunch and a two-hour nap, then went back to the office until 7:00 P.M. or so, before cocktails and a late dinner. The social whirl in that community was perpetual and tiring. In later years when Vi came with me on most subsequent trips, we were overwhelmed with hospitality. We were invited by so many people, all friends of Flo's who later became friends of ours, that we had serious scheduling and logistical problems. The Lebanese tradition of hospitality is well known, but it can be wearing.

The well-educated, urbane, and cultured Lebanese we came in contact with constantly over the next 15 or 20 years were a stark contrast to the milieu in which they existed. At that first party I mentioned, if instead of looking out to the Mediterranean I had looked straight down from the balcony where I stood to the street below, I would have seen a vastly different world. To the left, beyond the shiny Mercedeses and Buicks, there was an empty lot occupied by a few ragged tents belonging to Bedouins in dilapidated *aba*, and women carrying water in jars on their heads. There was dirt, filth, and garbage on the streets. Butcher shops were clouded with flies attracted to the fresh skinned lambs hung on hooks outside. The butcher would cut whatever meat you selected. Beirut was a city of romantic Hollywood images on the horizon and squalor right below.

At that first party and at others I attended were beautiful dark-skinned women with huge dark eyes, alongside many blond, blue-eyed foreigners and even blue-eyed Lebanese throwbacks to the Crusades. They were made up and coiffed beautifully and dressed impeccably in the latest fashions from Paris. As likely as not, they had just flown to Paris, or London, or New York to do their semiannual shopping for clothes. The men had been educated at the American University of Beirut, the Sorbonne, Oxford, Cambridge, Harvard, and Columbia. Their cultured and sophisticated conversation overwhelmed me. It was like nothing I had ever experienced in the United States, even though I was moving in reasonably cultured circles by that time. They spoke familiarly of hotels, shops, libraries, museums, and restaurants in Paris, London, New York, Washington, Rome, Amman, and Hong Kong and, to my consternation, were all fluently trilingual in French, English, and Arabic. Commonly they would switch in midsentence from one language to another in order to find the appropriate word, searching all three vocabularies in their minds simultaneously as I listened in awe. Was the romantic view from the balcony and those glittering trilingual people the real Lebanon, or was it the squalor and filth I saw when I looked straight down? To this day that question remains unanswered as the country has returned to tribalism and the "have nots" try to force their entry into the system with guns.

Because I was obviously a novice in the Middle East, one of Flo's close friends, Dr. Alfred Diab, who was the head of the department of ophthalmology at the American University of Beirut, offered to accompany me to Amman and introduce me to some of his friends who might help me find out about the potash project. He took three days away from his teaching just to do Flo and me a favor—what kindness! We checked into the Philadelphia Hotel—

at that time the best hotel in the city. The population of Amman was then about 250,000, having grown from 25,000 before the Arab-Israeli war in 1947 when many Palestinians migrated to Amman. Now I was in the Middle East of my imagination—hot, dusty, dry, on a high arid plain. In the noisy, breathing city with its narrow streets were women in embroidered, heavy gowns, many with veiled faces. Most men were wearing the *kheffiyah*, the colorful head kerchief held on with a head-sized girdle made of metal-threaded rope. Mosques were prominent and on a high hill was the palace of young King Hussein, the Hashemite descendant of Mohammed, whose grandfather, King Abdullah, had been the first king of Transjordan. Hussein's father, Talal, was confined to an institution, and when King Abdullah was assassinated, Hussein was taken out of Sandhurst and crowned king at the age of 18.

The Philadelphia Hotel (Amman was the site of an ancient city with a Greek name, Philadelphia) was crude by Western standards, but livable. Across the street a well-preserved Roman amphitheater was still used for outdoor concerts. On the porch, a black waiter took my order. When he spoke to us in Arabic, I was startled. I guess I expected him to speak with a southern accent. Such is our visual conditioning. Again I was almost disembodied as I sat there looking at a 2,000-year-old amphitheater. The romantic sights, smells, and strange costumes of the Middle East made me almost giddy with the romance of it, until once at about four o'clock in the morning I awoke to a booming Arabic call to prayer outside my window. I looked out across the street to the top of the needlelike mosque, shining in the moonlight, expecting to see a tall *muezzin* in flowing robes and with a long white beard calling his flock to face Mecca. My movie illusions were shattered. A large loudspeaker was trumpeting a taped recording of that beautiful bass voice over the city! Technology triumphed over tradition!

Alfred Diab introduced me to a classmate of his from the American University of Beirut, who was chairman of the Arab Potash Co. He was polite to me and suggested that the real decision maker was the managing director and that I should see him.

I'm not sure, in retrospect, that he was not dissembling. In any case, I arranged a visit with the managing director. He was a Circassian, light-skinned with blue eyes. In Amman there is a fair-sized colony of Circassians, who stand out dramatically from the swarthy Arabs. I later learned that their forebears had migrated south from the Caucasus in Russia in the nineteenth century and had settled near Amman. Though they are Moslem and speak Arabic, with their fair skin they are easily identifiable. It is startling to see the Circassian guards at the King's palace dramatically attired in Russian Cossack uniforms with crossed bullet belts over their shoulders, karakul hats, tunics, and flowing trousers tucked into black boots.

I told the general manager about our qualifications. He was impressed and seemed to enjoy being able to speak Arabic to me. He drove me to the north end of the Dead Sea where there was a small hotel for people who wanted sun and the unique experience of floating in the Dead Sea—a dubious adventure, I must say. Though it is true that you cannot sink, the high salt concentration will irritate any scratch in the skin and, if it gets in your eyes, is extremely painful. Nearby were a few acres of ponds in which the APC people had attempted to simulate an operation to recover potash from the Dead Sea water by solar evaporation. It was beastly hot there, about 120°F. Amman was also hot, in the nineties, but at least it cooled at night because it was at a much higher elevation—about 2,500 feet above sea level—whereas the Dead Sea was 1,300 feet *below* sea level!

I picked up a copy of the formal request for proposal and in a week prepared a submittal. The general manager looked at it and coolly remarked, "You know you have a lot of competition." It was the first of many hints I failed to recognize or respond to.

Later that week I received an invitation to visit the chairman of the company at home. We spent several hours alone at his palatial estate while he told me his interesting story. He had been a high school teacher in Jerusalem and eventually became head of the school board. He had also served on the Jerusalem city council with Golda Meir, but when the conflict began, he moved to Amman and, needing to make a living, started a business manufacturing cigarettes. By some chance or political circumstance, a high import tax was placed on foreign cigarettes and he became quite wealthy.

I had noticed that the Palestinians, or "West Bankers," in Jordan were far more affluent than the "East Bankers" or Bedouin Arabs. I asked him to explain the success of the Palestinians. "Simple," he said, "we came from British Palestine where, before the Zionist invasion, we were trained by the British and competed with the Jews. Can you think of a better schooling to explain our ability to prosper here in Amman?" We spoke at length about the Arab-Israeli conflict—a subject on everybody's mind and a favorite topic of conversation with any American who came along. After listening to the usual recitals of injustice and accounts of the chaotic days in Jerusalem after World War II, I dismissed his complaints and anger as a useless looking backward. I pleaded with him, as I did with all of my Arab friends, to come to an accommodation with Israel for, in my view, peace would yield more benefits for the Arabs than would their fermenting hatred and continual confrontation. He said simply, "We can't negotiate from our knees!" Even today, there is little appreciation in Israel of this simple stumbling block: dignity and pride are so important to the Arabs. To be treated as an inferior people by those who have suffered the same humiliation for 2,000 years is an irony often remarked upon by the angry Arabs. The Arabs, quite properly, remind everyone that during the dark ages when Europe was a squalid and brutish place, they produced scholar after scholar in poetry, medicine, mathematics, and the sciences. The libraries of Egypt provided the continuity of knowledge that had been virtually extinguished in Europe.

One evening in the bar of the Philadelphia Hotel, I told a justice of the Jordanian High Court that "if I were an Arab, or more important, a Palestinian, and had the power, I would recognize Israel immediately, open the borders, and start to trade. That's the only way you can win this war!" I have spent an enormous number of hours trying to persuade anyone who will listen that all the incendiary and inflammatory rhetoric should be dropped. Israel, from its position of enormous military strength, should also, in my view, reach out its hand and simply offer to talk to the Palestinians with no preconditions. Since those conversations in 1961, the blood that has been spilled and the anger that has been institutionalized are a tragedy and an abomination that sadly bear out my predictions.

When we finally got back to business at the chairman's house, he finished with an impassioned plea to me. "Jordan needs you and the APC needs people with your knowledge. This project is very important to us and we need the help of Arab-Americans to make it happen!" This corresponded so closely to my own romantic image of the role I could play in the land of my forebears that I promised to devote a lot of effort to fulfill Jordan's dream. In view of what happened later, that was either a hypocritical enticement or a second hint that I didn't recognize. Taking him literally, I left his house invigorated and filled with fervor to do something good in the land of my forebears.

Through friends at the hotel I learned that there was a representative of a British firm in town. The British Ambassador had put on a party in his honor and had invited all of the Jordanians connected with the potash project. I received no such help from the American Embassy. When I went to the embassy, they ushered me in to see the commercial attaché, a pimply-faced 22-year-old. When I asked for his help, he rather haughtily told me that he could show me no preference because other American companies were being considered. Through clenched teeth, I told him I wanted nothing special, just some guidance. He asked me whom I had seen and then dismissed me with, "I guess you're seeing the right people." I was furious as I walked out.

I suppose I was in Amman for about three weeks and, as is common in the Arab world, spent much of my time waiting. Arab bureaucrats have little compunction about having you wait half a day in their outer offices and then sending word that they can't see you—"The prime minister (or the crown prince) summoned me to his office" is the usual excuse.

Shortly after I arrived at the Philadelphia, I found to my surprise that one of the owners had been in China in the late thirties and knew my sister Helen, who was at that time living and working there with her husband, Dave. As Middle Easterners often do, we immediately became "cousins" and I was treated as a part of the family. One evening, sitting in the bar chatting with one of my "cousins," a group of dust-covered Americans trooped into the hotel. I learned that they were the crew filming *Lawrence of Arabia* at the Wadi Rum more than an hour's drive south from Amman. I subsequently met Alec Guinness and Peter O'Toole. Guinness I found to be shy and almost diffident but unfailingly polite—a pleasant man whose manner belied his status as a star. In contrast, Peter O'Toole's resonant voice could be heard throughout the bar lounge as he recounted story after story in a way only the Irish can. Having been there, knowing the area, and having met some of the principals, I found the film especially interesting.

Just before I was ready to leave Amman, I decided that our company's small size might count against us and that there were influences at work I didn't understand. The British company that was competing for the project was partly owned by the very old, large, and prominent British firm of civil engineering consultants, Sir Alexander Gibb & Partners. Because there was a large civil engineering component in the project, I decided to see if they would be interested in a joint venture—half a loaf being better than none. The British Embassy put me through to the counselor (second in command) who told me that the ambassador was in England, but he recognized my name and made an appointment immediately. He was fully informed about the project and could see the fit of the affiliation I proposed. He asked if I could arrange to go home by way of London so that he could set up an appointment for me with Sir Alexander Gibb. I was scheduled to leave Amman early the next morning to spend the weekend in Lebanon at my sister-in-law's mountain home, which had no telephone. He said I was not to worry, he would get a message to me somehow if the appointment were confirmed.

As I got up to leave, he asked how I was getting back to the hotel, and I said I would take a cab, as I had done from the U.S. Embassy. He wouldn't hear of it and ushered me to a Rolls Royce with a uniformed driver, sheepskin rugs on the floor, and the British flag on each fender, which was waiting to take me to the hotel in splendor. To cap it all off, on the following Saturday, a messenger drove all the way up from Beirut to Flo's mountain home to tell me that the appointment was all set, exactly as promised.

In London the senior partner at Sir Alexander Gibb readily agreed to join forces with Jacobs Engineering. I came home reasonably confident that we had put together a team with credentials better than anyone else's. To my surprise, we were not awarded the project. Some months later I received a call from my "friend" the chairman, who was in the United States to negotiate the contract with a company whose technical qualifications weren't even close to ours. Later a friend of mine met a Lebanese who boasted about having landed this large project for his client and receiving a nice fat commission, which he shared with the decision makers in APC. I also heard this later from other sources, and the stories all checked. Who got the money, I don't know; but I was shattered and disillusioned. I had heard of such things, but thought my sincerity in wanting to help, our outstanding qualifications, and my Arabic-speaking background would override such sordid doings. Wrong! I had ignored the hints.

Over the years I have come to understand the deep complexities of doing business in the Middle East. American companies operate under the constraints of the Foreign Corrupt Practices Act, which is an abomination. The moral and well-meaning motivations behind the act cannot be denied, but it is virtually impossible to legislate morals. It is not right to get business by bribery. However, the simplistic solutions offered by the self-appointed guardians of world morals often exacerbate the problems against which they express justifiable revulsion.

That disappointment might have been the end of this failed foray into the Middle East, except that, about a year later, I received a call from a Mr. George Novak of the Agency for International Development (AID), a part of the State Department. He explained that AID was funding the engineering work and that he was the project officer on the Arab Potash project. He said that everywhere he turned for the name of a potash expert my name came up. Unfortunately he had no funding available to hire a consultant, but he hoped I would help him on an informal basis.

His appeal to my patriotism was all I needed. It was arranged that whenever I flew East on business I would go to Washington for a day, talk to George, and advise him as best I could.

In early 1964 George called to say that he had the final report and was being pressed to arrange the financing for the construction of the plant. The project seemed to him to be on shaky economic and perhaps technical grounds. He wanted my opinion. The report indicated a return on the projected investment of somewhere between 4 and 6 percent—a woefully inadequate return for such a risky project. As I recall, almost $750,000 had been spent for engineering at that point. The pressure on the engineers from our State Department, the APC people, and the Jordanian government to recommend that the project be funded anyway must have been enormous. For Jordan the project was the cornerstone of employment, foreign exchange, and not incidentally, competition with Israel. I confirmed George's dim view of the report's conclusions and he then asked if we would undertake a paid critique of the project because the size of the needed investment now justified his hiring an independent consultant to review the project before recommending or rejecting the request to finance it. I was so anxious to sink my teeth into that project that I wanted to make it easy for George to get funding, so I quoted a giveaway price of $40,000 and we were awarded the study.

Back to Jordan I went with one of our bright young chemical engineers who was a veteran of the Vicksburg start-up. Sir Alexander Gibb assigned one of its senior engineers to accompany us. They rolled out the red carpet for us in Jordan, knowing our judgment could make or break their project. The U.S. Ambassador was then William McComber who, in contrast to my previous contact, took me in hand and arranged for me to meet the prime minister, Wesfy Tell (who was subsequently assassinated by terrorists). He also arranged for me to meet King Hussein, the first of many meetings we were to have over the years. The ambassador later described the king as being like a fighter pilot—highly intelligent, with quick instinctive reactions, and lots of guts even though he lacked much formal education. What a thrill to walk up the steps of the beautiful limestone and marble palace to meet the king, and what a man! His large, dark, penetrating eyes riveted directly on mine. In a deep bass voice, he spoke beautiful, only slightly accented English. With the touch of formality and courteous manner that is the hallmark of the desert Arab, he said, "Dr. Jacobs, this project is very important to us. We need it for practical reasons, jobs, foreign exchange, and, above all, for our dignity. I have heard very much about you and your dedication to the Middle East and to Jordan and this project. I'll help you all I can. I wish you success in your efforts." I have met with King Hussein a number of times over the past 20 years and have never ceased to admire him as a person and as a statesman.

The south end of the Dead Sea had been selected for the plant site rather than the north end—a conclusion with which we agreed. It made sense for a lot of technical reasons, but the proposed site was in the most forbidding location imaginable. Less than 50 miles from Amman as the crow flies, it required, in those days, a tough two-and-a-half to three-hour Jeep ride to get there. One traveled along the old Roman trade route that Lawrence of Arabia took from Aqaba north past the Wadi Rum and the Roman ruins of Jerash to meet General Allenby in Damascus during World War I. This ancient desert, littered with black flint, is about 2,000 feet above sea level. About one-third of the way to Aqaba one took a right turn on a road rising gradually to the Crusaders' castle at Karak. What an overwhelming sight! The castle, with its sheer, 100-foot-high walls of roughhewn stone, stands on a mountaintop 6,000 feet above sea level. Surveying, to the east, the desert plain and to the west the Wadi Karak—an awe-inspiring canyon as deep and spectacular as the Grand Canyon—one is dramatically reminded of the ubiquitous penetration of the Middle East by the Crusaders in the twelfth century. The rutted road followed the breathtaking canyon walls down to the Dead Sea. The only habitation at the southern tip of the Dead Sea was the small village of Safi, consisting of a few thatched stone huts that were virtually abandoned in the summertime when temperatures regularly rose to more than 140°F. The farmers who lived there grew vegetables in winter when the Wadi ("river" in Arabic) Hasa flowed, then retreated up to the town of Karak in the summer to escape the oppressive heat. The prospect of building a major industrial chemical complex there was daunting.

The prime minister arranged to make an army helicopter available to us so that we might have a good aerial view of the terrain in order to locate the plant site. Two handsome young Jordanian pilots flew us over the mountains and down to the Dead Sea, keeping carefully to the east to avoid Israeli air space. As we circled the area, I asked the pilots to come down to 500 feet to circle over the Lisan peninsula, a chalk and sand outcropping that almost reaches the eastern, Israeli shore of the Dead Sea. We wanted to see if the center of the Lisan could be used for the plant site. As we circled, I heard a sharp ping, then another, and then a string of Arabic curses from the pilots. I looked up at the rotor blades, assuming there was mechanical trouble, but the pilots were looking down. Suddenly we tipped at a 45° angle and circled again. To my horror I saw Jordanian soldiers shooting at us with army rifles. We quickly flew beyond a sand hill to a concealed spot where the pilots landed and told us to get out and crouch behind the helicopter. I feared we would be shot. The pilots jumped out and ran over the hill to a knot of soldiers and we heard a lot of shouting and cursing in Arabic. They finally came back red faced and cursing now in English. "Those bloody, stupid bastards! I wish I had worn my side arms, I'd have shot those idiots," one said. The soldiers, he explained, were from a lookout foxhole dug in the sand to forewarn in case of an Israeli attack. They claimed not to have been notified that we were coming and thought we were an Israeli plane! "But," said our pilots, "we practically turned the helicopter on its side so you could see the Royal Jordanian Army insignia." Their answer: "We thought you were an Israeli plane in disguise."

When we got back to Amman, most people were amused by our story. We were not, and neither was the prime minister. He called the army general and upbraided him. "Can you imagine the world reaction if two Americans and a Brit, flying in a Jordanian Army helicopter, were killed by Jordanian Army soldiers?" He was furious and we were too—after we got over being frightened.

After reconnoitering the situation in Jordan, we returned home to prepare our report. It took about four months, and we spent considerably more to produce it than we were paid. Because we were reviewing $750,000 worth of work by another highly reputable engineer, we had to be professionally unassailable. We pointed out a number of potential technical problems and a few assumptions that were clearly wrong and might have seriously affected the operability of the plant. On a larger number of issues, we had differences of opinion in interpreting the data and found that we could suggest several substantial technical improvements that made the process easier and more economical to operate.

However, the principal flaw could only have been spotted by a businessman, and that was my major contribution to the conclusions. The original proposal was for the design of a plant to produce 250,000 tons of potash per year. Even though the plant cost and production economics turned out to be marginal at best, the engineers had tried to force-fit a recommendation to proceed. The technical problems would still be monumental, but I was convinced that the key to economic production was an increase in the capacity of the plant. Depreciation was the largest factor in the costs. Labor was cheap and the use of fuel was minimal because so much energy was derived from the sun. As the capacity of any plant is increased, the building cost does not go up in proportion. Any increase in the plant size would lower the depreciation charges per ton of potash and thus improve the economics substantially. The rule of thumb is that a plant twice as big should only cost about 50 percent more to build. But could an annual production of 500,000 tons or more be sold? This was where our intimate knowledge of the potash *business* as well as our familiarity with the technology was crucial. Consequently, an important part of our report was a sketchy market study. We concluded that 500,000 tons, and perhaps more, could indeed be sold at competitive prices in India and Southeast Asia, as well as in the other Arab countries.

By this time AID had enlisted the interest of the World Bank in the project. Its large staff of experts agreed with our conclusions and felt that we had finally put the project on a sound basis.

They recommended that we be hired to rework the engineering to include our innovative ideas and to estimate the cost of a larger plant. Because AID and the World Bank were financing this second stage of engineering, they virtually demanded that the Jordanians select us as the engineers. In 1965 we were awarded the study contract by the Arab Potash Co. on a cost-reimbursable basis. We spent about $500,000 preparing our report, which was completed by the end of 1966.

We confirmed our original analysis; in fact it appeared that an even larger plant should be built. Our detailed market study showed that more than 1,000,000 tons of potash could be sold per year within an economical shipping range. Also we judged that the topography at the south end was such that we could build enough solar ponds for this higher production rate. We predicted that, with a 1,000,000-ton plant, we could produce some of the lowest-cost potash in the world.

By this time APC had a new general manager, but the real decision maker was the minister of industry in the Jordanian cabinet. He was a young Palestinian lawyer who was very close to the royal family. During the course of our work, I remarked privately to both AID and the World Bank that it was unlikely the Jordanians could operate such a complicated plant if it were built. It wasn't that they weren't highly intelligent and educated people, but the cultural differences, while subtle, were profound. In that society, it is considered demeaning for a man with a college degree to do any physical work. To get out and work around the clock, turning valves and checking instruments, as I had done many times at Vicksburg and other places, was unthinkable. On top of that, pragmatism or experimental testing were regarded as signs of weakness. All problems could be solved by logic, argument, and mental exercise.

This attitude was dramatized when I suggested a novel approach in the evaporation scheme to the Jordanian chief engineer (a chemical engineer with degrees from Louisiana State University). He opined that my idea would not work and we argued for several hours. Finally, in exasperation, I said, "Okay, let's stop arguing and go out to the desert, dig a hole, line it with concrete, put some Dead Sea brine in, and see if it doesn't behave in the way I suggest." He almost panicked. "No, no, let's continue our argument and simply decide who can persuade the other." I see this characteristic as a basic flaw in the Arab culture. Pragmatism, experimental testing, and the acceptance of reality over theory do not seem to come easily to Arabs.

The World Bank agreed with my concerns about operating the plant and persuaded the Jordanians that they should look for an experienced U.S. chemical company as a partner. Because I knew them all, I was asked to contact American companies at high levels to see if I could stir interest. Most declined because of political risk, but finally the president of W. R. Grace's chemical division concluded that it was worth investigating. A meeting was arranged between my friend, the president of the chemical division, and the Jordanian minister of industry. To my chagrin, I was not invited to the meeting. What went on at that meeting I'll never know because the talks were private, but a deal of some kind was struck.

The proposed contract faced strong opposition from the W. R. Grace board because of the political risk, but finally the project was approved. Two months later, on June 7, 1967, Israel made a preemptive strike against Egypt. Jordan was drawn into the war and the Israelis soundly defeated the Arab armies in the Six-Day War. Our project was aborted and, incidentally, the prescience of the opposing directors was proved.

With that project in limbo, we concentrated on our domestic projects until 1974, when we heard that Jordan wanted to revive the project. Back to Jordan I went. Amman now had the modern Jordan Intercontinental Hotel, a sharp contrast to the Philadelphia. Despite a population of more than 1.5 million people, Amman was still pretty primitive. The PLO had been defeated in their effort to overthrow King Hussein in the early seventies and had moved on to Lebanon. I visited H.R.H. Crown Prince Hassan (King Hussein's younger brother), whom I'd come to know well, and all of the government officials I knew.

Through a friend I was introduced to Hamad El Farhan. Well educated, influential, and eloquent, he was a self-appointed critic of the king. He had even been jailed for a brief time by the king, but was regarded as an absolutely incorruptible, though irascible, man. We retained him as our agent for a nominal fee. Even though he was critical of the United States and of Jordan's close relations with our country, we still became good friends. More important, we completed this mammoth project in Jordan without paying a single cent to anyone connected with it. The total commissions paid to Hamad over almost ten years did not leave any room to pay anyone else, and he provided services and conveniences for our people that were worth every nickel. Although we were squeaky clean, we paid a very stiff price by not recognizing some of the norms of doing business in the Middle East.

When the project was revived AID again asked us to prepare a paper study to determine how the project should go ahead and to update the economics. We recommended a cautious approach. We pointed out that, to insure the feasibility of such a project and to protect the enormous investment, we would need to collect much new data in the field to expand upon that already obtained. We estimated the cost of this preliminary work at $10 million. We had learned our lesson well at Vicksburg, Mississippi. We had to insure that, if the plant were built, we would not have extensive start-up problems.

There was much competition, but we were finally awarded the contract. The Jordanians, like most Middle Easterners, do everything by competitive bidding. They don't understand what a professional relationship is. They claim that they are avoiding corruption, when in fact a fixed-price bid is the best cover for a hidden "commission."

Just as we were starting on this contract, a new general manager of APC, Mr. Ali Khasawneh, was appointed. He was intelligent and extremely aggressive. We got to know him well as he shepherded the project almost to completion. He was an ambivalent mixture of Western businessman and Middle Eastern "rug peddler." For instance, halfway through the first phase, we convinced him that there would be tremendous cost and schedule savings if we could negotiate a continuance of our contract through to the completion of the large plant. His reaction was exactly that of a Western businessman. Though he had heated opposition within Jordan (it was not their way of doing things), he prevailed and AID and the World Bank supported him.

During that negotiation, Ali asked for a private meeting with me. I thought it was primarily to negotiate a reduction in price, so I concentrated on that and made some price concessions (typical Middle East haggling). Looking at it now, I believe I was expected to make some overture. Many times over the years, Ali would say to me, "You know I respect Hamad El Farhan very much; he was my teacher, but he is not a very good businessman!" Was he telling me that El Farhan was one of the few agents who did not cooperate with the decision makers? I think perhaps he was, and my inability to come to grips with the realities cost us millions of dollars and took a high emotional toll upon me and our people. Yet I've never regretted our stand.

We mobilized our team and started this enormously complicated project. While design work was being carried out in our Pasadena office, we sent a team to live at the south end of the Dead Sea to gather field data. It's difficult to imagine the primitive conditions under which they worked. The first crew, who did the test borings, lived in tents until, with great difficulty, huts and barracks were built. When summer approached, working hours were from 2:00 A.M. to 10:00 A.M. and the team slept during the heat of the day. Most of the land on which the dikes and ponds would be built either was under a foot of brine or was a soggy, sticky gumbo into which a man could sink up to his armpits. We actually lost one Jordanian laborer who fell off a platform and died of heat prostration before anyone could get to him. Some of the ground was so impossible to traverse that we had to use a hovercraft to support our drilling equipment.

A group of Irish engineers from our Dublin office lived on that hellish site for two years. I will not recite all of the things we studied, but the real success of this project was insured during those first two years of field research. The people who worked so hard and used their extraordinary ingenuity during the first phase were the real heroes. Though we had hundreds (perhaps thousands) of hurdles to overcome before the project was completed and running, it could all

*JJJ and Ali Khasawneh, general manager of the Arab Potash Co., signing the contract for construction of the plant in Jordan, 1976.*

have been for naught without the dedication of those men and their excellent work during the first two years.

During this period I remembered my original concerns about whether the Jordanians had the infrastructure or the cultural background to operate what would be an extremely sophisticated and complicated plant. The Middle East is strewn with complicated process plants of all kinds, designed by American engineers, that lie rusting after operations were turned over to local people. Though they had intelligent engineering college graduates running them, the Western overlay was just too thin. I have often said that to run today's modern plants you need a supply of engineers who as youngsters learned to fix their own automobiles. It was decided to solicit a company to operate the plant on contract for a fee rather than for equity. I had been able to read the proposed contract with W. R. Grace negotiated in 1967 and, in my opinion, APC had given away entirely too much equity—though W. R. Grace's concern about political risk easily explained their need to be paid handsomely.

The negotiation of the design, procurement, and construction contract was most difficult. Ali Khasawneh made demand after demand after demand—some pure bargaining, but most were totally unreasonable. He asked for impossible guarantees, not understanding that if guarantees were exacted, we would simply overdesign everything, making the project cost too much and causing it to be uneconomic. We maintained that we could guarantee nothing anyway because we couldn't control what happened during operations. So he countered by offering us the operating contract. With that, we agreed to certain financial penalties if the plant did not perform and some bonuses if we exceeded the guarantees. In retrospect, I laugh ruefully at my naïveté. They found thousands of ways to breach our contract to avoid paying us our due or to pressure us into giving up our contractual rights. The concept of "moral obligation" seems not to exist in their language. Unlike most American businessmen, they deemed the use of any device to avoid paying agreed-upon fees to be "smart business."

As the years went on and the project progressed, Ali Khasawneh's every success, as a result of our good performance, made him more and more arrogant. He developed the delusion that it was *his* project when in fact he was merely a Jordanian voice repeating what we told him needed to be done. Against our advice he gave interviews to the press, making wildly optimistic predictions about what the plant would do in the future. There was growing resentment in the Jordanian bureaucracy. By 1981 a cabal of important people was after his hide. I never did get a reasonable explanation of why—jealousy perhaps, envy, or resentment of his arrogance, or more simply they may have wanted a piece of the pie they suspected Ali was getting. When a new prime minister was appointed, there were rumors that Ali Khasawneh would be replaced. Though I was beginning to recognize that he had some serious deficiencies, I was also concerned that some bureaucratic bumbler might be appointed in his stead.

King Hussein visited the United States at about this time, and President Reagan invited Vi and me (among many others, of course) to a state dinner given at the White House for the king. For me, an unabashed patriot, it was thrilling. When we were announced at the reception before dinner, and Vi was escorted in

*The administration building of the Arab Potash Co. at the Dead Sea plant site.*

on the arm of a handsome lieutenant colonel of the Marines in dress uniform, I had goose bumps. The king and many of his aides greeted me as an old friend. When I had a few moments alone with him, I pleaded Khasawneh's case, saying that to remove him would disrupt the project.

Subsequently, I was invited to have lunch with the king at Blair House, where I met the new prime minister; he was obviously unhappy with Ali Khasawneh, but I presented my arguments to him too. "He'd better cut out this tribalism," was the prime minister's annoyed reply. My decision to defend Ali, even though at this time he was giving our people fits, was, ironically, used against us later. Many people took it as a sign that Ali was "in our pocket." When I heard that, I was furious because we had always been characterized as those naive Americans who didn't know how to lubricate the business process. Here was a perfectly valid and almost altruistic position being construed in the shadiest terms. I've never quite gotten over being angry about that.

*Laser-controlled harvester on the Dead Sea.*

While our data were being gathered, we prepared a detailed cost and construction schedule. We followed that with an exhaustive feasibility study that served as a basis for financing this $450 million project. Besides AID and the World Bank, several other sources of funds from various Arab countries, such as Kuwait, were part of the financing syndicate. With the financing in place, we transferred the detailed design and management of the project to our Dublin office and started full-scale construction early in 1978. When completed, there were 40 linear miles of dikes containing approximately 10,000,000 cubic yards of hauled-in rock and soil and enclosing 40 square miles of evaporative ponds.

The most serious technical difficulty was to prevent the evaporated brine from leaking through the dike. This was another case in which my instincts as a businessman really paid off. The Israeli dikes had been designed by Dutch engineers—for after all, who knew more about dike design? In looking at their specifications, we found that the leakage allowed by the Dutch engineers was minuscule. That was understandable, because any

*King Hussein greeting JJJ at the dedication of the Dead Sea plant, 1982; Crown Prince Hassan is in the right foreground.*

leakage of sea water in the Dutch dikes would quickly ruin their farmland. But we reasoned that leakage in the Dead Sea dikes was a purely economic decision: It was a matter of balancing the leakage against the cost of pumping in extra brine. We concluded that we could easily tolerate *five times* the leakage that the Israelis allowed without affecting the viability of the project. That purely economic decision must have saved at least $20 million in capital costs. It is rarely recognized that good engineering is as much about economic choice as it is about making accurate calculations or reaching the best attainable performance. The system worked as well as we had hoped.

The construction of this giant project in such a remote and barren place was a monumental task. There were thousands of logistical and technical problems to be solved during the four-year construction period. To illustrate the international nature of the project: A British company built the civil works and dikes; an Austrian company, the chemical and mechanical plant; a Swiss company, the power plant; a Korean company, the village and community structures; and a Taiwanese company, the highway extension.

*JJJ, Vi, and Linda at the Dead Sea plant site.*

In early 1980 we brought in the first Dead Sea water through a five-mile-long canal from north of the Lisan peninsula, where the depth was over 400 feet. South of the peninsula where our ponds were built, the sea was very shallow and flat, rarely over 15 feet deep (making it ideal for the evaporation ponds). We started the long evaporation cycle.

By 1982 we had completed the chemical plant and were starting to collect potash-bearing salts in our evaporation ponds. We had met our prescribed budget and construction schedule. A celebration was in order and Ali Khasawneh arranged an elaborate dedication ceremony. Preparation took months. Stands were erected, soft couches were brought in for the dignitaries, huge tents were put up, and food, literally fit for a king, was prepared. Guests from all over the Arab world came in their colorful flowing robes. The Duke of Kent came from England. And of course the king, the crown prince, and their aides. I brought Vi, Flo, and Linda, our daughter, who was working in Jordan as an archaeologist. Where once we slept on the bare ground in sleeping bags, we were sitting on plush, overstuffed chairs, next to a modern

40,000-square-foot office building and a new town accommodating 2,000 people. We looked out on a complex chemical plant as modern as any in Texas. In that setting, what a contrast it was to see the flowing robes of the desert princes and table after table piled with *mensaaf* (the Jordanian national dish of lamb, rice, wheat, and pine nuts). Sweets and fresh fruits were in abundance and 140 whole lambs had been roasted for this feast to which all of the neighboring Bedouin tribes were invited to help themselves after the official party was over.

The ceremony was filled with flowery rhetoric in Arabic and English. At Ali's request we had commissioned the famous sculptor, John Svenson, who rapturized over Hussein's classic Arab profile, to make a 15-inch gold-plated bas relief of the king to be set on an onyx base. Our company also commissioned a large Waterford trophy piece as our gift to the king. Because we were not on the program, we had no opportunity to make a presentation, so we asked Ali to give it to him. Afterward, as the king and I walked through the grounds, a wave of bearded and robed Bedouins (about 200 of them, I would guess) came rushing at the king. Many just wanted to touch him, or shake his hand, but many tried to hand him notes. He explained later that these were pleas for help, for the resolution of tribal squabbles, or for dispensations of various kinds. The jostling became so heavy that I was separated from him. He called out, "Dr. Jacobs, come next to me." He put his arm around me, commanded the people to step aside, and escorted me through the crowd, a very warm and typical gesture that I have not forgotten.

The whole ceremony is vivid in my mind—a colorful and brilliant panoply that compared with *Lawrence of Arabia* in its dramatic beauty. The contrast between the exotic and flowery Arabic rhetoric and the highly sophisticated plant that represented the best in Western industrial technology was a wonder to behold. Yet I found a worrisome undertone of uncertainty about the compatibility of the two cultures.

Twenty years after my second battle of Vicksburg and my first disappointing trip to Amman, there it was—a triumph of brains, heart, perseverance, and sacrifice. To have helped create this great industrial complex in the most inhospitable place in the world was a thrill never to be duplicated. Here is a summary of this great project of which Jacobs Engineering is so proud:

| | |
|---|---|
| Cost: | Approximately $450,000,000 |
| Capacity: | 1.2 million metric tons of potash per year |
| Township: | Residences for 800 families, supermarkets, churches, sports club, and other amenities |
| Evaporation ponds: | Total area enclosed by dikes is 40 square miles—twice the area of Manhattan Island. |
| Product: | Delivered to Aqaba by 100-ton trucks with air-conditioned cabs. The trip to Aqaba on the Red Sea was, of course, up hill (the concept of going up hill to reach the ocean is difficult to grasp). One truck leaves every half hour, around the clock. |
| Energy: | The evaporating power of the sun is the equivalent of burning 1.25 billion gallons of fuel oil per year, enough energy to heat 4.7 million homes in Los Angeles year round. |
| Economics: | One of the lowest cost producers of potash in the world. Shipping costs from Aqaba, the port on the Red Sea, are the only limitation to the markets that could be reached. |

After that climax, we began our operations contract. We had hired a man with many years' experience running a plant for Kerr-McGee at Searles Lake in the high California desert. We learned later that he had been eased out for some personal characteristics that later also became a problem for us. As his technical assistant we hired a consultant, Bill Stanley, whom we had known for years. Both of these men and the rest of the operating crew were to report to John Buehler, then a vice president of our company.

We urged John to move to the plant site for two years to provide the continuity and representation needed for the relatively new employees. John demurred—we guessed that his wife had declined to go to such a godforsaken place, which was understandable, but the decision was unfortunate for John and for the project. John believed that he could supervise the operations by commuting back and forth every other month—a distance of over 10,000 miles. We made a serious mistake in agreeing to that, as subsequent events proved. There is a traditional rivalry between operating people and the engineers who design plants. Operators are always muttering about the "dumb engineers" who design things people can't operate, and the engineers make similar complaints about the operators who can't understand the clever things that have been designed into the plant.

The two key operating men we hired were no exception. It takes a lot of hand-holding and day-to-day contact to reconcile this traditional rivalry. Furthermore, John was so much smarter than the operators that he tended to be brusque and intolerant, which aggravated the antipathy. Between John's sporadic visits they could and did undermine his decisions, and the physical toll on John of all that flying exacerbated the situation. Ali Khasawneh sensed the antipathy of the operating people to John Buehler and to our design team and, for his own reasons, exploited it to the fullest. With his newly developed arrogance, he was out to prove that *he* was making this project go in *spite* of us. The old psychological truism that the quickest way to turn a friend into an enemy is to make him obligated to you was exhibited here in starkest terms.

The leaders of our site team were new to us and had not had the tenure to develop any company loyalty. They did not hesitate to "bad mouth" the engineering to Ali Khasawneh every time a little bobble occurred. After all, they had not been there when the plant was designed so they felt no responsibility, nor did they understand the number of debates we had had that led to selecting one particular feature design rather than another. Ali simply reveled in supporting and encouraging the antagonism. The on-site people were beguiled into thinking they were cementing their relationship with the management of APC, but they were simply being used.

Because we had a poor evaporation season that first year (the sun wasn't as hot as usual), the thickness of the salt layer was less than we expected, and we were afraid we might lose a multimillion-dollar potash harvester in the mud if we started too soon. That harvester, designed by us, was unique, and much of the success of this project rode on the risk we took that it would work. We took the prudent view and decided to wait another season to get extra thick salt bottoms before starting to deposit the potash. The operation of the harvester was the greatest uncertainty we faced, but eventually it performed as well as we had hoped.

The same forces that had tried to remove Ali Khasawneh two years earlier finally succeeded. He was replaced by Ali Ensour, an engineer by training but essentially a bureaucrat. He had been in and out of government many times and his last post was as minister of electricity. It was a terrible time for us. Ali Khasawneh, in his arrogance, had turned against us completely, refused to pay our bills, and reneged on promises he had made. Ali Ensour viewed us as Khasawneh's ally. He took the position that we, as Ali Khasawneh's "lackeys," had done a poor job, and he used our ostensible shortcomings to discredit his predecessor. He spent a year hiring consultant after consultant who wrote reports saying that the plant would never meet its capacity goals. Ali Ensour's approach to business dealings contrasted sharply with ours. Americans are often beguiled into thinking that a Western education automatically implies the adoption of Western cultural values. That is a mistake. The climax came when Bill Stanley, the so-called technical expert on the site, wrote a memo stating that even though the plant was designed to produce 1.2 million tons, it would never make more than 900,000 tons per year. He turned out to be dead wrong, but at that time he posed as the preeminent potash expert—a stance he maintains to this day, although I don't recall that he had much experience with solar evaporation before coming to our project.

He concluded, properly, that a diversionary dike should be added to prevent short circuiting in the ponds and he proclaimed that the lack of this dike in the original design was a deficiency. He did not realize that, years before, during the design phase, we had carefully considered the need for a diversion dike or baffle and had decided not to spend the money constructing it until we had the operating experience to prove that need. When operating experience showed that a dike was indeed needed, he trumpeted his analysis of our "oversight" as proof of his own technical brilliance. Although the Dead Sea brine inlet was more than one mile from the place where the evaporated brine exited, the raw brine tended to go right to the outlet, without being thoroughly mixed. We had hoped that wind and wave action would provide sufficient mixing. The baffle forced the brine to mix and thus increased the utilization of the sun's energy. As in any startup, there were many other minor modifications made.

The management of APC was holding up payment of several millions of dollars rightfully due us. Maintaining that the plant was deficient and would not meet design capacity, they used that as an excuse for withholding payments in defiance of contract terms. Furthermore, they were making these claims a year before the plant was scheduled to reach the rated capacity. We kept asking why they didn't wait until the next year to see whether it produced the capacity we had projected. Here was that old Arab belief that, if you could "prove" that the plant was not going to reach capacity, then it was so—no recognition that the theory might just be faulty, as we maintained. Why wait to find out?

Unjustly, John Buehler became persona non grata with everyone. Ali Ensour insisted that I become involved personally, but when I did, he made promises to me that he did not keep. Again, the Arab mind could easily have viewed these actions as normal business conduct. By that time I was so angry and emotional that my effectiveness was curtailed. To introduce new players, I asked Warren Kane, one of our directors, and Noel Watson, then executive vice president of our company, to take over. They went through several rounds of negotiations trying to narrow the differences. Finally, I decided that the bad publicity was unjustifiably ruining our reputation; I had to do something drastic (an instinctive reversion to pride, reputation, and integrity). So I went to see the crown prince. I explained that APC management was withholding payments of millions of dollars owed us. He asked why I hadn't come to him before. I explained that I had not wanted to presume upon our friendship for what might appear to be personal reasons, but now I felt that the project, and therefore Jordan, was being hurt badly by a misinformed management that was trying to besmirch Ali Khasawneh by castigating us. I asked the crown prince the same question we were asking the management continually: "Why doesn't everyone wait until next year to see if the plant meets capacity before concluding that it won't?" Under indirect pressure from the crown prince (he never intervenes directly), we finally settled our claims, though we had to give up over $1,000,000 more than we had already agreed to. It was a bitter pill to swallow, especially when we felt, with good reason, that we had completed one of the most complicated projects in the region on time and on budget and deserved substantial bonuses and perhaps even accolades. It has been described by others as the most successful project of its size and complexity ever undertaken in the Middle East.

It is so easy to say "I told you so!" but, the next year the plant did produce almost the 1.2 million tons we had designed it for; the following year it produced more than that, and three years later, I understand that, with only a few minor modifications, it produced 1.4 million tons of potash. It was unfortunately too late to undo the damage that had been done to us.

With loyalty, dedication, and extraordinary talent, we created what is undoubtedly one of the most successful and complicated chemical plant operations in the Middle East. This was done despite mean-spirited political and venal hurdles imposed by those who should have been most grateful for our dedication—the Jordanian bureaucrats whose self-aggrandizement outweighed their loyalty to their country. What hurt most was the absence of respect for the Jacobs Engineering employees who had worked so hard over so many years to turn a dream into reality. The bureaucrats should have applauded loudly for a job well done. Despite all of that, the success of this project is the highlight of our company's technical accomplishment and an enormous source of pride for me.

FIFTEEN

# *Even Babe Ruth Struck Out 1,330 Times*

I have a marvelous cartoon mounted on a wooden plaque opposite the easy chair in my office. It shows a brawny baseball player holding a huge bat and his belly hangs over his belt. The bold caption is: Babe Ruth Struck Out 1,330 Times. What a story that tells! How many times have I looked at that wistfully as I "fanned" another one. I've sent replicas to friends and even to President Reagan when he had tried something I considered courageous and for which he had subsequently been pummeled in the press. He wrote me a nice note saying that he had decided to put it on his desk in the Oval Office. Ed Meese confirmed that it was indeed there on the left-hand side of the desk, and he had seen it every time he went in to confer with the president.

The significance of this cartoon is not lost on anyone familiar with baseball. Babe Ruth, the most renowned home-run hitter, also struck out a lot of times. Moral: If you swing for the fence trying to hit a home run, you'll also strike out a lot. So it has been for me. The path of any entrepreneur is strewn with strikeouts. To avoid giving the impression of self-satisfaction or smugness, I must tell of some of the many times I have "struck out."

Perhaps the best place to start is to describe the failed acquisitions we have made. My drive to grow in size led naturally to the path of acquisition, because I was too impatient to accept only internal growth. The series of acquisitions we made in the sixties added very little to the growth of Jacobs Engineering and more than likely diverted us from taking advantage of our internal growth potential. About the only thing we gained from these experiences was a vivid reminder of the pitfalls of acquisition as a route to expansion. Over those years the following lessons became painfully apparent:

- Never make an acquisition that is not enthusiastically endorsed by your operating people. Indeed, they should be pushing for the acquisition rather than the other way around. Otherwise they have little incentive to make it work.
- Beware of being beguiled by a well-known name and past glory. Companies are like people. If they are past their prime, you may wind up providing intensive, or even terminal, care.
- A cash buyout is often an invitation for the owner to retire, making the integration of the company very difficult.
- A small business founded by an entrepreneur has probably not developed a strong management succession.
- Diversification by the acquisition of very small companies in different markets will not necessarily provide an easier access to those markets than would building from within.
- Cultural differences between companies that merge or are acquired are always difficult to reconcile and may be well-nigh impossible in the case of small acquisitions.

Ironically, I tried for years to vault into the position of a major engineering construction company by making a major merger and never succeeded. Today we have achieved that goal in the old-fashioned way, for which I was too impatient. Though we made a few small acquisitions, we have grown mostly internally.

One strikeout was the decision to use a profit-center concept in running our business. We had a number of regional offices that, unfortunately, tended to have a provincial viewpoint. Each office thought of itself as a small local engineering company, and their connections to our whole company were tenuous. Profit-center accounting is supposed to provide incentives. For us it was a disaster! The bickering among offices and among lines of business competing for manpower in each office was endless. Rather than eliminate provincialism, it exacerbated it. There are many enthusiastic supporters of profit-center accounting, but it doesn't work where there is much interdependence among the groups. I am convinced that profit centers work only when each group operates as a virtually independent business and there are few, if any, business dealings between the various units.

Another serious mistake was our dividend program for the stockholders. During good years, we paid our key people generous bonuses, but I felt guilty about our stockholders, who had not received dividends. Not being a capital-intensive company, we were accumulating cash. I wondered whether I was being arrogant in thinking that I could invest the money more prudently than our stockholders could. In retrospect, I think that the honest answer should have been no. Consider that, after we paid corporate tax and the stockholders paid personal income tax on their dividends, we'd have almost four times as much money to invest as our stockholders would, and it did not take much ingenuity to get a better return with the larger sum of money that the company would retain. I did not think it through.

We had a long discussion about this at one of our board meetings. Some members argued for a dividend and, following the conventional wisdom on Wall Street, contended that it would improve our stock price (another investment banker's myth of dubious merit). With my unreasonable guilt feeling about "my friends" the stockholders, I was persuaded. Emotion overcame reason.

Our first dividend payment amounted to about $1 million in fiscal 1976 and, with stock splits and stock dividends, gradually increased to $1.7 million in 1981. In 1982, after a banner year in 1981, we paid $2.2 million in dividends. A dividend of 25 percent of earnings was not unreasonable, but we should have based it upon future earnings, not upon past earnings. Our after-tax earnings in 1982 were only $3.1 million, and yet we paid over $2 million in dividends when business was falling off!

I was intimidated by the stock market folklore that reducing or eliminating dividends would shatter the stockholders' confidence and cause the price of the stock to drop. Business was slowing down and I should have reacted with forthrightness. I didn't. Worse yet, in 1983 we paid out $2.2 million in dividends when we *lost* $5.5 million! The insanity of that action rankles to this day. The next year we lost even more ($8.9 million), and finally we stopped the dividends. What a horror! Between 1976 and 1984 we paid out a total of $12.5 million in dividends (out of after-tax earnings too), enough to have neutralized our losses in the two very bad years of 1983 and 1984.

In 1983 and 1984 I personally received approximately $800,000 annually in dividends. I paid approximately 50 percent in income tax, leaving me with $400,000. Having already paid approximately 50 percent in corporate income tax, the company therefore had to earn $1.6 million before taxes in order to enrich me to the tune of $400,000! Could the company have used $1.6 million more effectively than I could use $400,000? Of course it could! If I wanted to receive $400,000 from the company, why didn't I simply give myself a bonus of $800,000? That would have at least saved the company $800,000! But by my standards, a bonus of that size would have been a shameful imposition upon the stockholders.

The events leading to those traumatic years of losses for Jacobs Engineering in 1983 and 1984 are complex and intertwined, not only with general business conditions, but also with some personal idiosyncrasies. I have mentioned, without too much apology, my strong ego (large, inflated, overwhelming—choose your own adjective). But my ego had another odd twist to it that had plagued me for about 10 years. It stems from the often repeated question, "Is Jacobs Engineering a one-man business?" It's hard to imagine how much that question, and all it implies, has occupied my thoughts and led to a lot of management trauma that in turn contributed to those two terrible years.

I founded the business and my name is on the front door. Over the years I have projected a distinct personal image, that of a man who is aggressive, decisive, a penetrating questioner, a tough guy in a fight, persistent, a good salesman for the company and of myself as well. I pride myself on being considerate of people's feelings, but my friends have told me time and again how intimidating I can sometimes be. I do not intend to hurt, of course, but my questioning is persistent and my uncovering of incompletely thought-out ideas is quick. My facility with language can be overwhelming. I am not an "aw shucks" guy. I command attention, consciously or unconsciously. In meetings with clients I tended to overshadow my colleagues, as hard as I tried to do otherwise. That "name on the door" seemed to confer undue importance, beyond reason I think, to the things that I say, especially when compared with the things said by others in the company.

Is it any wonder that I've heard for years that Jacobs Engineering is a one-man company dominated by Joe Jacobs. Very rarely was it said critically; often it was said admiringly. But every time I heard it, I winced. I had seen many "one-man" companies and witnessed the unfortunate effects on their employees. Invariably, I admired the heads of such companies who were, without exception, enormously talented. But I cried for the employees, who not always, but often enough, got little credit from the outside for their contributions to the business.

I have read somewhere that a college professor claimed that the average life of an entrepreneurial enterprise is only 24 years because most entrepreneurs fail to attract or create a strong management to succeed them. "Not me!" I said "I'm going to show everyone that this is not a one-man company!" I had learned to consult and share decision making with our people. I rarely dictated to them. At least as I see it, and I believe it true, I did not lead our company by dictation or by fiat, but rather by forceful argument and persuasion.

Starting with the merger with Pace, I embarked upon a long quest to find a successor, intending to prove that I could delegate the responsibility to run the company. Warren Askey seemed to have all the right characteristics: He was intelligent, a chemical engineer, and a genuinely nice guy. He had helped build a fine company himself. When he moved to Pasadena and became our president and chief operating officer, I invested a lot of hope in him. I set tough goals for myself to try to make the transfer succeed. In writing and in words, I delegated the running of the business to Warren, and deferred to him in meetings. If I disagreed with something he was doing, I would do so only in private.

However, during the two years Warren was president, he became increasingly unhappy. There was the difference in social life between Houston and Pasadena. Then there was the problem with Stan Krugman. Warren couldn't fathom how to handle the strained relationship, although I'm not sure anyone could. Sensing that he was getting restless and uncertain, I finally had a frank talk with him. "Warren," I said, "are you happy in your job?"

"No, I'm not really."

"Warren, I know you feel an obligation to your colleagues in Houston and came up here primarily to insure that they would be treated fairly. You've done that."

We discussed it for awhile, and Warren said that he really wanted to go back to Houston and spend his time on personal interests. There, he would dabble in real estate, make investments, and "have some fun," a remark I interpreted as affirmation that he really wasn't enjoying his job. So he left after two years. Warren subsequently made some poor investments and suffered in the Houston real estate crash. Upon his recent sudden death, he had considerably reduced means. I felt sad for my friend.

What should I do after Warren left? Go back to running the company on a day-to-day basis? That would be a clear signal that I couldn't stand the competition. "Aha!" they would say, "it *is* a one-man company after all!" Had I made a mistake about Stan Krugman? After all, he had been the best operating man we had ever had. I knew I would get hell from the Pace people if Stan were perceived to have won what was clearly regarded as his contest with Warren. Even so, I made discreet inquiries among members of our staff who had worked for Stan during all of the growth years. I was unable to get support from any quarter. Everyone expressed admiration for his skills, but his comportment during Warren's regime was not admired.

In the late sixties we had done a survey of world potash markets for Allied Chemical Co., whose chemical fertilizer division used large quantities of this product. The company was considering integrating backward. Ed Korbel was vice president of this division. Though we did not support the idea, he and others admired the honesty of the study. Ed and I became friends and saw each other socially on my frequent trips to New York.

When I faced the problem of replacing Warren in 1976, I thought of Ed Korbel. Frequently when we saw each other, he would talk wistfully of his dissatisfaction with working for a giant company. He'd like, he said, to start his own business, as I had, or to work for a smaller company in which he didn't have so much politics and inertia to deal with. I thought that Ed would be less threatening to Stan because he would fill a role more nearly like mine, for Ed is a superb marketer. He had run a very large division with profit responsibility, and I was misled by this into thinking that he had talent for operations. I hoped that, being articulate and socially adroit, he could replace or supplement me as "Mr. Outside."

Perhaps he could persuade Stan to form a partnership with him similar to the one Stan had with me. In another frank talk with Stan I used my most persuasive skills to get him to accept what he did best. I asked that he help make Ed Korbel a success. I got a grudging agreement, but unfortunately it didn't work. I guess I wasn't as good a salesman as I had imagined, and as it turned out, neither was Ed as good a salesman as I gave him credit for. Ed Korbel came to work for us as president and chief operating officer in 1977, and by the latter part of 1979 it became apparent to us and to Ed as well that he was not cut out for operations of the type required in our company. Ed's real interest was in making deals.

When it became obvious there was a misfit between Ed's strengths and what we needed in the chief operating officer's job, several things were happening. The mix of our business was beginning to change. We were led in new marketing directions almost inadvertently when we bought a small laboratory in

Pasadena, run by a famous environmental and water quality consultant, Dr. Richard Pomeroy, who had ventured into environmental science well before it became an enormous market. Another by-product of this small acquisition was that most of the laboratory's potential clients were government agencies, either local or federal, and we had to learn to deal with them.

I had developed a deep-seated and unreasonable prejudice against dealing with the government. I was not prepared to put up with paperwork or to deal with government auditors and their allowances and disallowances of certain normal business expenses. (I was the "brilliant" prognosticator who predicted only disaster for a new company formed by Simon Ramo and Dean Wooldridge when they left Hughes Aircraft Co. in the late forties. The new company, Ramo-Wooldridge, was only going to do government work, principally to act as a "think tank" for the air force. I predicted that their dependence upon the vagaries of government funding would be disastrous. That company was the forerunner of TRW. Was I ever wrong!)

I was reluctantly persuaded that we must learn how to do business with the government. I saw our major competitors taking on large contracts with the Department of Energy, the Department of Defense, and other government agencies. With constant urging from Noel Watson, one of our younger "old timers," we hired Gary Allison, who had been working for a competitor in the government sector division. He helped teach us the subtle nuances of doing business with the government. It was different from our commercial business, but once the system was in place, it worked smoothly.

The necessity of finding a new chief operating officer was discouraging to me, to say the least. We happened to be doing quite well financially so there were no apparent ill effects from the lack of a clear operating head. A coterie of about 10 people who had been with us from the early days was experienced enough and loyal enough to operate the day-to-day business adequately. I didn't recognize it at the time, but many had probably assumed roles just a step above the point at which they operated best. I searched among them, but there was no real candidate for the job of chief operating officer. There were some younger, long-time employees that I considered comers, such as Noel Watson; but I judged them as not ready to skip over the 10 or 12 vice presidents who were contemporaries of Stan and myself.

Upon reflection, I wonder whether we were doing nearly as well as we should have. The profits from our real-estate and stock transactions were significant and perhaps masked the fact that the performance of our basic professional service business was only mediocre.

The old question came back. Were people saying, "Joe Jacobs doesn't want a strong player. He doesn't want the competition"? I knew I had given both Warren Askey and Ed Korbel every opportunity to grab the reins; but frankly, I was developing a bit of paranoia about other people's perception of what was happening.

I had met Dale Myers through Bob Barton; they were very old friends from their college days. Dale had a superb record, in both industry and government. He first came to public notice as manager of the Apollo program for North American–Rockwell. That series of space flights and missions was one of the great engineering management successes of our time. Dale's reputation was made with the Apollo project. When it started to wind down, Dale accepted an appointment as the number-two man at the National Aeronautics and Space Administration (NASA), the agency handling the space program. He spent a couple of years at the job, then returned to Rockwell as president of the North American aviation division. Then he went back to government service, this time as the deputy secretary of the Department of Energy until the end of 1978 when he resigned. By this time our government sector work was increasing and I had learned to accept the reality of the enormous market. Dale had impeccable credentials, and his experience with the government at high levels was an important asset. Though I knew he had never worked in our industry, I was persuaded that his nationally celebrated management credentials would override that. So Dale Myers came aboard as our third president and chief operating officer.

Jacobs Engineering was still not considered to be a major engineering and construction company and so was rarely prequalified for any of the "mega" projects, either in the private sector or the government, in spite of our fine reputation. Clients kept telling us, "You guys are good, but you need more system, more controls, and more specialists for these very large projects." To my protests that there was no mystery about these systems and that, given a project of that size, we would install those same systems, the not unexpected reply was, "We can't chance it. We've got to go to a known quantity. There's too much at stake." My ambition to join the ranks of the majors then led us to invest enormous sums to construct such systems without having the work to justify the expenses. And who was more skilled at gearing up for the really large or "mega" projects than Dale Myers? During the next few years, with this drive in mind, I made, supported, and encouraged many policy changes that turned out to be disastrous for our company. I was overconfident and became unrealistically ambitious to make a quantum leap in size. I gave Dale the green light to install the elaborate systems that were deemed necessary to qualify us for very large projects. We invested heavily in computers and computer programs; we added a whole layer of senior management and sailed blithely along into our most profitable year, 1981. At about that time I wrote a now infamous memo to key managers exhorting them to comport themselves and to think of themselves as part of a "major" engineering and construction company. I had ignored the lessons learned at Chemurgic and had allowed overhead to build up and assumed that sales would increase enough to justify it.

In 1980 OPEC had started coming apart. The new Reagan administration, in a move to curb the rampant inflation, permitted interest rates to rise astronomically. Capital spending stopped dead in its tracks and the inflated synthetic fuels and alternate fuels projects started to unravel. The change was so abrupt that I was unprepared for it, and competition for the few projects available suddenly became fierce.

Clients started to demand competitive fixed-price bids. Most of the work during the previous boom years had been done on a cost-reimbursable basis. I have written and spoken on this subject many times and have defended the thesis that the projected savings of fixed-price contracts are mostly a chimera. Many engineering and construction companies believe that they can make more money on fixed-price contracts than they can on the low fees that cost-reimbursable work carries. That is a myth. We have kept records for over 20 years. In calculating the costs of bidding on all the projects that were not awarded to us, our losses on many of the projects we *were* awarded, and the modest profits and even the bonanzas on some projects we did receive, we discovered that we *netted no profit at all* on fixed-price work over those 20 years. The wasted brainpower and energy is appalling to contemplate.

But we couldn't resist the trend. In 1982 and 1983 our salespeople were pleading with Dale to change our policy and bid fixed-price projects. I found out about this debate much too late because again, I was almost ostentatiously delegating the day-to-day operations. I was so busy in my self-assigned role of cheerleader, looking for new markets, and indulging in strategic planning for our future and also in my outside community interests that I wasn't watching the daily operations. Upon later review, I recognized every one of the symptoms and the skewed reasoning that led inevitably to bad decisions. It was entirely unreasonable for me to expect Dale Myers to have the sensitivity to see those hidden signals.

When business started to turn down in 1982, we reduced our staff modestly, but only by eliminating marginal, low-salaried people we had hired when manpower was short. So, when requests for fixed-price bids came in, our people argued that our experienced and proven staff could outperform the mélange we would have been forced to use the year before. Therefore, they claimed, we could bid on fixed-price contracts competitively and still make a profit, because we could assign our best manpower to the projects—a seemingly logical argument.

Unrecognized was the fact that subconsciously our people could see a bleak future for themselves if we weren't awarded these fixed-price projects. Isn't it natural that their judgment might be tilted or biased by the fact that, if we didn't bid on a project and if the project were not won, there might not be a job for them? Estimating is not an exact science—considerable judgment is needed. It is understandable that one who is facing a layoff if the project is not won might tend to make more optimistic assumptions.

In 1982, when our profits dropped to $3 million, I started to get worried and finally began probing into operations. Not only were we bidding fixed-price projects in an almost uncontrolled fashion, but also overheads had swollen beyond belief from that ill-fated decision to gear up for the "mega projects." We were overstaffed at the executive and other management levels. (We were waiting for those fixed-price projects to be awarded!) Headed for disaster and with our unfortunate dividend policy, our business might have been a candidate for bankruptcy except for the infusion of more than $20 million in cash from the sale of our headquarters building.

In 1983, after much soul searching, I told Dale I would have to get involved in the day-to-day operations, and in early 1984 I officially took over as chief operating officer as well as chief executive officer. I asked Dale to stay on the board and to remain as a consultant. I bore him no malice. It was too much to expect him to recognize such a complete turnabout, much less what to do about it—and I knew that my own contributions to the situation were more profound.

It was a terrible time for me. I was 68 years old, past retirement age for most people. I had struggled for 10 years to prove to the world that ours was not a one-man company. I had gone outside the company to bring in a chief operating officer and had failed three times. I had promoted the vision of our becoming a "major" engineering and construction company and had condoned the cardinal sin of building the overhead to meet expected sales, rather than the other way around. I knew I had honestly delegated thoroughly, and now I recognized that in my zeal to demonstrate my freedom from self-centered ego, I had delegated too much. I had delegated to the detriment of the company and the people in it, and above all, I had delegated to the ultimate detriment of those I had put into the job of president! I had, in an odd twisted way, repeated the errors of E. E. Luther that I had been so critical of when I went to work for Chemurgic Corp. 40 years before.

Then that old surge of pride came. My name was on the front door and I would not let it be besmirched. I would not let it be associated with failure. I had faced death, and I had faced business and engineering problems that seemed insurmountable and, by hard work, imagination, and sheer guts, had overcome them. I had the Kaiser project, Vicksburg, and the Arab Potash Co. in my history, but this was bigger than anything I had faced before; I must battle it through. I'm sure I subconsciously remembered that Mom would not let me quit college simply because of my unfortunate escapade in Iowa. "We will find a way for you to get that degree," she said. "You must not quit." Fifty years later I was responding to that same admonition.

In making the fateful decision to grab this problem by the throat, I swept aside all pretense. I worried not at all that people would say, "Aha, it *is* a one-man business after all." I had a challenge, and like a fire horse, I responded. I recognized and acknowledged the mistakes I had made and the warped reasoning that had distorted my need to delegate beyond prudence. Once I acknowledged that, I went into battle with a surge of self-confidence and energy that represented the best in my heritage, my training, and my essential fiber. As high as those mountains were, as scary as the danger of bankruptcy was, as physically and emotionally daunting as the prospects were, I confess I was almost exultant as I attacked that ever-present enemy—failure.

SIXTEEN

# *The Crash of '83*

To my mind, the term "restructuring" is a "nice nellyism." Read an article describing the restructuring of a company and pretty soon you'll come to a paragraph, tucked well below the lead, that calmly notes that there was a "staff reduction" of 10 percent or 1,000 people or whatever. That's the gut level of restructuring—a lot of people fired, laid off, retired, or put on "leave of absence." Concealed by that impersonal word is a lot of emotional turmoil, primarily, of course, for the people leaving their jobs, but the emotional toll on those having to do the restructuring should not be ignored.

What did I find when I got back into the details of the business? Chaos is the only way to describe it. It was difficult to know where to begin. Swollen overhead was the most obvious problem. We had too many people for the workload. How many of those people whose time was normally billable to clients were sitting around on an overhead account, waiting to be assigned to the next project we were awarded? Certainly unbillable overhead was quite high, but it did not explain completely the dramatic decrease in our profits.

The real culprit was the fixed-price bidding. We had good people sitting around. "Let's use them to prepare these bids," the managers said. As soon as it was decided to bid, a project number was assigned, people were taken off the overhead account, and it *looked as if* useful work were being performed. The fact that they were not gainfully employed was concealed. The total unbilled time was drowning us. "Time charged to overhead," did not tell the true story, but total unbilled time did. It took instinct born of experience to expose the underlying errors.

I discovered also that the management team that had grown up with us was not performing well. Why, when they had been such superb performers and contributors to early success and growth of our company? It was difficult to analyze. Was it the Peter Principle? Perhaps, in some cases. How much were the key people influenced by the fact that they were now relatively well off financially? Stock options, profit sharing, a pension plan, a savings plan, and a particularly generous "executive security plan" contributed substantially to their financial well-being, though each of them, I assume, made good outside investments as well. One could characterize our old reliable colleagues as no longer "hungry."

It is pretty obvious that the drastic restructuring required was no one-man task. Noel Watson was one of our bright younger people, and Dale Myers had made him an executive vice president at the end of 1980. Noel had worked shifts side-by-side with me during that tough startup at Vicksburg in 1962 and contributed significantly to our overcoming the problems there. I'd known him a long time and had been waiting for him to mature. This was my opportunity, at last, to test someone raised in the company. After three attempts, I recognized and accepted that it was unfair to expect anyone from the outside to understand the subtleties of our business.

So I started out with Noel and Jim Klohr helping me. Within a short while it became apparent that, emotionally, Jim simply could not handle the job, though he was loyal and dedicated. Jim was a nice guy who felt an enormous obligation to the people who worked for him; he couldn't bring himself to do the tough things that were required. I understood and sympathized, because it was not easy on any of us. Unfortunately, Jim's way of avoiding making demands upon his people was to try to do everything himself. For seven months or so I never saw him as he traveled interminably and worked inhuman hours. A big, robust man, he beat himself into exhaustion.

By this time the relative newcomer, Gary Allison, who had done an outstanding job getting us into government work and teaching us how to make money at it, was an executive vice president. He and Noel became my primary team. Meanwhile, I had assumed the title of president again, and we officially recognized our troika as "Office of the Chairman."

Here's the summary of what we did in the 17 months between May 1984 and September 1985.

- We eliminated one whole layer of management.
- We retired or otherwise eliminated 14 vice presidents.
- We reduced the total staff from about 1,800 people to 1,200, concentrating on highly paid people whose salaries were charged to overhead. By contrast, our peak permanent employment in 1981 was 2,300 people. (We do not include hourly paid craftsmen in our personnel count.)
- We reduced the general overhead from $42 million per year to about $28 million per year.
- We terminated our pension plan and, in all, we reduced fringe benefits from 32 percent of payroll to 25 percent. (We had already eliminated the dividend.)

That's a hard, cold recital of the facts, but the kind of determination, the emotional turmoil, the testing of our resolve, and the constant unpleasant choices we needed to make were debilitating to everyone.

No decision about reductions in staff was ever clear cut. We'd equivocate, saying "Maybe he's in the wrong job?" or "Can he be used elsewhere?" We recoiled from the hard decisions. It is easy to decide that, for the business to survive, we must cut overhead drastically; but such cuts are only the sum of separate, emotionally charged decisions. The general objectives were obvious, but the individual components were traumatic. Gary, when he participated, had less difficulty because he was a relative newcomer.

Noel Watson had perhaps a tougher emotional problem than I did. He had not only known these people for a long time, as I had, but also had worked *for* them as he climbed the management ladder. Now here he was firing them. In most cases it was much less brutal than that, though the final result was unmistakable. We retired people early. We gave generous severance pay. Some key people, seeing the situation, volunteered to take early retirement and some found other jobs. But Noel had the terrible burden of being pictured (unfairly, of course) as "ruthlessly" turning on his former mentors, presumably to further his own ambitions. In reality, I was the source of the drive to insure the survival of the company, and his loyalty was primarily to that basic requirement for survival. He was the instrument and had to take much of the direct confrontation. I mentioned frequently that we had a moral obligation not to make it easy on ourselves; that he had enough ego strength to do it and survive raised my already high regard for him.

Because I was at the crossroads in deciding who were our effective players and who were not, I enlisted the aid of our board members. I was no longer willing to trust my judgment alone, for I had so many emotional ties to all of the people. First, with Bob Barton's urging, I instituted a plan whereby I invited individuals from our top management to spend a long lunch hour with two of our directors (rotating) on a regularly scheduled basis. In that way I got an independent evaluation of each individual's personality, his knowledge about his job, and other factors. It was a two-way street—our directors learned more about the day-to-day problems our people faced. Over the next year these meetings were of incalculable value both to the board members and to me.

In addition, I asked Barney Bannan, my close friend and the director of longest tenure, to spend extra time looking at our management structure to try to identify the superfluous people. His experienced analysis helped clarify our thinking. Warren Kane, who had spent many years at Fluor Corp., one of the majors in our business, visited our outlying offices, criticizing our communications and our sales effort, and helping to identify the comers in the second layer of management. He argued philosophy and style with Noel to help shape his ideas about management. The wise counsel of our board members contributed substantially to the success of our restructuring. These were my friends helping me, and I will always be grateful.

Our decision to reduce fringe benefits for all employees raised predictions from all sides that we would have a mass exodus. Our personnel people were particularly concerned. Only two or three years earlier they had been scrambling to hire technical people, and during that time we added many fringe benefits, as all our competitors did. If we took many of those goodies away, everyone would leave, "they" said.

One of our major burdens was the pension plan. In some dim period of the past, we had converted our profit sharing plan to a "defined benefits" pension plan (a tax-driven decision, of course). Such a plan prescribed, in advance, the benefits employees would receive upon retirement, so the company was obliged to pay into the retirement fund an actuarially determined amount each year—whether we were making profits or not. Our contributions to this plan exceeded $1.5 million per year. Fortunately, we had overfunded the retirement plan in the lush years, so when we stopped contributing to the plan in 1984, no additional funding was necessary. But we faced millions of dollars of obligatory payments in the future. The decision to terminate our pension plan took guts. Fortunately, none of our employees lost anything as a result of this decision. The money vested in the pensions (all contributed by us) could be used to buy an annuity for the employee's retirement years, or could be transferred to a 401(k) plan. Though employees still could contribute to the 401(k) plan (tax-free), we also discontinued the company's contribution to it.

Then we modified our vacation policy and even reduced the number of paid holidays. Disaster was predicted at every turn. One could be cynical and say that all of our competitors were in a deep depression and jobs were not that plentiful. Some employees did leave and went to other businesses, but most stayed. They didn't like the changes, of course, but they saw that we were also cutting high-priced overhead without discrimination and picked up the sense of urgency. They may have understood that we were doing the things necessary to make the enterprise survive and to try to preserve their jobs.

A characteristic of our business is that there is a great reluctance to lay off highly skilled people when their time is not billable because, after all, they are our "product." That's what leads to the temptation to make fixed-price bids and to cut professional service rates to well below real costs in the hope of maintaining a stable of technical experts. The rationalization is obvious: Management says "Losing money on each hour we sell is better than retaining the people on unbilled overhead." All this to insure that we had the people to man new projects when they came. But what if the projects don't come? Nowhere in that rationalization is there mention of the third alternative—to lay people off. That's the trap many of our competitors fell into as they retained their manpower and sustained substantial losses for three or four years running. Our much larger competitors, with deeper pockets, only started to prune their costs in the middle of 1987. Many simply disappeared.

We made a spectacular turnaround and in 1985, 1986, and 1987 we were again making profits and began increasing our staff. In 1987 we equaled our highest employment peak of 1981. Today our total professional staff is more than twice what it was at our previous peak in 1981, and our profits in 1990 were more than 50 percent higher than our peak earnings in 1982. From 1985 to 1990 our profits increased at a compounded rate of 48 percent—an outstanding accomplishment that all of us are proud of!

The most surprising by-product of our traumatic and emotional "restructuring" was the enormous sense of pride it engendered in the people who went through it. During that time I heard, time after time, from our draftsmen, designers, and engineers, how "we did the tough things early. Our competitors are laying people off by the hundreds and we're now hiring." I suppose it is analogous to group identification and the pride of troops who've been through a tough battle and lost comrades, but had a leadership strong enough to help them survive.

In 1985 I had another experience (almost universally misunderstood) arising out of my highly personal viewpoint of our stockholders as my friends. With our losses in 1983 and 1984, our stock price had fallen to under $6 per share (at one time it had hovered between $25 and $28). We had discontinued our dividends and I had deep pangs of guilt that our stockholders' equity had eroded so much and that the stock options held by our loyal employees were now worthless. I had to do something for all of them.

Paul Hallingby, my investment banker friend, suggested that I offer to exchange the public holders' stock for a subordinated debenture that would have a substantially higher face value than the current price of the stock and would also pay an interest rate that was substantially higher than the dividend we had discontinued. The prime interest rate at that time was 9.5 percent. Paul's company evaluated the suggestion and recommended that a 10-year subordinated debenture with a face value of $9 be exchanged for each share of the publicly held stock, then selling for about $5.50 per share. The debenture would pay an interest rate of 12 percent, which would yield an income of $1.08 annually. To me this seemed a generous offer. We would exchange a low-value stock, paying no dividend, for a higher-value debt instrument that would pay good income—more than twice the maximum dividend we had ever paid!

Paul presented this proposal to our board and accompanied it with the professional opinion of his firm that it was a fair exchange for the stockholders. Though they respected Paul's opinion, the members of the board felt that they must get an independent opinion to protect the stockholders. They hired First Boston, a prestigious investment bank, and separate legal counsel. They were doing their proper duty and, understandably, protecting themselves against potential suits from stockholders. They were my friends and I understood.

But the introduction of the outside law firm and First Boston created a contentious and adversarial atmosphere that was exacerbated when First Boston sent in one of its young MBAs to crossexamine me as if I were trying to slip something past our stockholders. I proceeded to cut him up in little pieces as I exposed his ignorance about even the most elementary accounting and other practices in our business. Realizing that an incompetent was representing them, First Boston then sent out one of the senior partners from New York.

The atmosphere was abhorrent to me. Both the law firm and the investment bankers, it seemed, were trying to justify their substantial fees by trying to bargain me into increasing my offer. It appeared that in their "professional opinion," the face value of the debenture should be between $10 and $12, instead of the $9 I had offered, already at more than 50 percent above the stock price. For proof of the subjectivity and inaccuracy of their assessment, consider the 20 percent "range" of their suggested numbers, a range wide enough to belie the relevance of their supporting data. Why weren't they honest and straightforward? To justify their being hired, they had to avoid the appearance of having "rubber stamped" our proposal. I could help them prove their so-called objectivity by raising my offer slightly, and the fiction of an "independent" opinion would be preserved. Had they simply told me that, I'd have appreciated their candor. But their attitude was so fatuous and arrogant that I told them to go "pound sand." Paul Hallingby, who had every bit as much competence and mature judgment as the people from First Boston, was not persuaded by any of their arguments either.

By then two things had happened. Interest rates had started to fall and I became concerned that I might be burdened by paying too much interest. While I was concerned that I might be paying too much, they were implying that I wasn't paying enough! More important, I was getting some pressure from home—not so much from Vi, but from our three grown-up daughters. "Dad," they said, "why do you want to go in debt for more than $20 million at this stage in your life? Stop worrying about your stockholders and your key people so much!" Subsequently, it turned out that my concern about interest rates was prescient. By March 1986 the prime rate was down to 9 percent and by April (only four months after my offer) it was down to 8½ percent. In light of what actually happened, First Boston should have advised our board to grab my offer!

What bothered me most was the implication that I was trying to "steal the company," an idea as distasteful to me as it was an automatic assumption for them. I am almost certain that if I had raised the interest rate by 1 percent or the face value of the debenture by as little as $1 these "professionals" would have beaten their breasts in triumph and boasted that they had protected the stockholders! They never considered that, by conventional Wall Street wisdom, I had put the company in "play." Where were the investors or arbitrageurs to offer a higher price? None appeared. Their opinions were demonstrably dead wrong and unsupportable.

I abandoned the offer, partly because interest rates were declining, but mostly because I felt sullied by the suspicion. I regarded my offer as a sincere attempt to "rescue" our stockholders and to reward our employees. That may sound disingenuous, but I say it with mixed feelings and certainly not boastfully. Such a naive and idealistic viewpoint isn't particularly admirable in an entrepreneur. In the business world, my learned values of pride, reputation, and integrity are not always understood or appreciated.

The fact that Jacobs Engineering has subsequently gone from strength to strength tends to support the view that I knew something no one else did. I really didn't. Indeed, in the fiscal year ending September 30, 1985, we had already made our turnaround, earning over $2 million after taxes, and that was public knowledge. It wasn't something to come; it was there! Yet the price of our stock gave absolutely no recognition to that achievement. Our stockholders didn't benefit, and neither did our loyal employees, who had options. It was my frustration with the illogic of the stock market and its lack of recognition of the turnaround we'd made that impelled me to make the conversion offer.

When I inquired why our stock was at its all-time low, the "experts" who "understood" the stock market gave an answer that was as illogical and perverse as only Wall Street pundits could make it. They said, "Your whole industry is in a severe depression. Fluor, Foster Wheeler, and others are losing money hand over fist, so all engineering construction stocks are out of favor and your company is suffering from that."

"But," I protested, "we have turned our company around. We've gone from a $9 million loss to a $2 million profit. Shouldn't we be recognized as going counter to industry performance—and shouldn't investors be avidly buying our stock because we are outperforming the industry?" All I got was a shrug of the shoulders. Why aren't people on Wall Street honest enough to say that they simply don't know? Are the "seers" of Wall Street disciples of Hans Christian Andersen?

Even though I supported Paul's proposal for the debentures, I still thought, and my friends thought, and the people in the company thought that I was taking an enormous risk. It was by no means certain that the company's finances would continue to improve. As a matter of fact, in 1986 we made only $850,000 after taxes, not enough before tax earnings to meet the interest payments of almost $3 million that the proposed debentures would incur! The inference that I knew something the public didn't know was totally unjustified, as those reduced earnings figures show. Frankly, if I had known that was all we'd make in 1986, I'd never have made such a generous and economically unjustified offer.

My decision to abort the buyout turned out to be the right one for our stockholders. Our reduced earnings in 1986 and the dramatic drop in the prime rate made First Boston, in my opinion, look pretty silly. Fortunately, the stockholders who stuck with us are doing quite well—the price of our stock has now risen dramatically to an all-time high, and that's all I ever wanted. Furthermore, those of the management team who stayed with us during the traumatic restructuring were rewarded with substantial blocks of options at about $7 per share and, therefore, are also doing quite well now; at this writing those shares are worth more than 10 times that. I do not give First Boston credit for having been able to predict these outstanding results.

If I were motivated at all by the desire to accumulate more money, I should now regret that the buyout didn't go ahead: If I had been able to survive that first year (by no means a certainty), the subsequent years would have made me enormously wealthy. As it worked out, my primary motive of being able to do something for our stockholders and our key people has been fulfilled, and I am very pleased. If that sounds pious to the cynics, so be it.

There was one sad consequence of the incident. Seeing how angry I had become at being put on an unjustified defensive by the "experts," some of our board members seemed to feel some responsibility for what happened. Because they were, and are, my friends, this bothered them. Sometime after the proposal fell apart, Joe Platt, Art MacDonald, and Bob Van Tuyle resigned because they were well past the nominal retirement age of 70, and Barney Bannan, who had been on the board almost from the beginning, pleaded that he wanted to cut down on his commitments because his wife was seriously ill. I hope that I have misinterpreted their feelings because, as far as I am concerned, they only did what they had to do. Having selected their experts, they were as locked in and helpless as I was in the face of such arrogance.

There is also an interesting sidelight. After I had announced the convertible debenture offer, I received a call from one Siggi Wilzig, protesting vehemently that my offer was inadequate. Siggi Wilzig was a major stockholder and had previously filed a Form 13-D, indicating that he owned or controlled more than 5 percent of our stock. I thanked him for his call, politely disagreed with his opinion, and that was that. I had never met him, but did know something about him. I understood that he had made an "unfriendly" tender offer for one company and had finally sold his stock at a profit. He was a controlling stockholder of Wilshire Oil of Texas, and was also chairman of The Trustcompany Bancorporation in Jersey City, New Jersey. A mutual friend described him as "honest, a man of his word, but aggressive and combative to the point that some people resented his mannerisms." My friend went on to say, "But behind that brazen front is a guy I like."

After I dropped the conversion offer, both Wilshire Oil and the Trustcompany continued to buy our stock aggressively. Why Mr. Wilzig kept buying our stock was a puzzle; but I'd like to think that maybe he is a contrarian who defied the conventional Wall Street "wisdom." (In that respect, he and I think alike.) Perhaps he misinterpreted my debenture offer as evidence that I "knew something." Maybe he saw and appreciated that we were going counter to the industry as a whole—something no other investors on Wall Street were willing to give us credit for or had the intelligence to understand. As I have remarked to him since, "You sure showed a lot of faith in us, when no one else did. I'm pleased that we are justifying your confidence."

Shortly before our 1987 annual meeting, Mr. Wilzig called to tell me that he and his friends had accumulated a sizable block of our stock (just short of 20 percent), and he requested a meeting. When I reported this to our board, they expressed some concern. I told them to relax. "Let's hear what the man has to say before you make any judgments. After all, he represents a substantial stock ownership and has a right to be heard." The fact that my family and I controlled perhaps 40 percent of the stock made my position relatively secure, but even without that, my pride dictated that if I weren't the choice of all the stockholders to run the company, I wasn't interested in maintaining my position.

The episode with Henry Le Mieux and Raymond International ran through my mind as I went to meet Siggi at the airport and took him to dinner at Chasens. His first words were, "I may have a funny accent, but. . . " He certainly was verbally aggressive and talked continuously for the first half hour. Later I found that to be just a nervous habit. He had a slight German accent, but it didn't really justify any apology. He told me some of his dramatic life story. A victim of the Holocaust and a survivor of Auschwitz, where his family were all executed, he bears a tattoo that reminds him constantly of the horror of his youth. He came to the United States penniless and fought and scraped his way to considerable accomplishment and wealth. Understandably his outlook was shaped by the beastliness of the Holocaust and that explained (in my view) some of his aggressiveness and annoying mannerisms.

His story partly told, Siggi then said, "With my stockholdings I want two seats on your board." I think he was surprised when I said, "Of course." Perhaps he didn't know what to expect and had probably prepared himself for a rejection that didn't materialize. I went on to explain that we did not select our board members as advocates or to represent a given stockholder; our board members represent *all* the stockholders. I was prepared to nominate him for our board, because it was obvious that, with his broad business background, he could make significant contributions to the company. I had no objections if he wanted to suggest another director, as long as we felt the nominee could be a contributor—and that commitment still exists. He was satisfied and was elected a director. I've gotten to know him better. Siggi is intelligent. He has a quick and facile mind. His mannerisms and loud conversations can be annoying, but I've learned to look past the facade. Though my style is entirely different, our intuitive conclusions often match.

During the period of restructuring, I leaned heavily on Noel Watson and Gary Allison. Gary and Noel were put on the board. They shared the responsibility of reporting on our operations to our board. Half by design and half by inadvertence, I had created a horse race between the two for the position of president and chief operating officer that I was anxious to relinquish. Gary Allison is movie-star handsome, intelligent, and extremely articulate. He is an excellent salesman in the best sense of the word: He is not only likable, but also an imaginative strategist. His handling of our entry into the government market, which now generates close to 20 percent of our gross margin, was first rate. Noel Watson was the consummate operating man. He knew every aspect of our business. Articulate enough, he was not as polished as Gary was, but he inspired confidence in his people. Extremely ambitious, yet patient, he was ruthlessly honest.

Having set up the horse race, I found it interesting to hear the reactions of our board members as they slowly developed opinions. From the standpoint of presence and dealing with the public, Gary clearly had the edge. But he had a tendency to paint slightly fuzzy word pictures. He was prone to dissemble. He continually implied to me that he was well off financially. After hearing that he wanted to buy a large block of our stock, I suggested that he buy Dale Myers's stock. Dale had accepted a new appointment to be deputy director of NASA and had to divest his holdings. Gary quickly agreed, but then delayed and delayed before writing a check. Later someone told me that he had had to borrow the money.

Noel was conservative and careful, both in his personal affairs and in managing the company's business. The only criticism we had was that he seemed to go out of his way to be critical of himself and to accept personal responsibility for deficiencies in our operations. As a matter of principle, he never resorted to an alibi, even though in many cases he had good cause to. The difference between the two began to widen and harden. Finally our board was unanimous in its opinion that Noel should be president. Not surprisingly, when we told Gary he resigned. Soon thereafter he became vice president of sales for a large computer-related company at a salary and bonus far in excess of what we were paying him.

So, in January 1987, Noel became the president and chief operating officer of Jacobs Engineering. I have previously bemoaned the fact that I tended to expect too much of people. I have had some pleasant surprises, but I have also often been disappointed. I'm pleased to say that Noel has exceeded all my expectations. He wears the title of president with confidence and polish. His fluency of language now matches his honesty. He is rapidly growing into his job. Each of our board members has reaffirmed that we made the right choice.

With the current boom in the engineering and construction industry, our company has finally been recognized both in the stock market (our stock reaching new highs almost daily) and by our clients. All of my previously forced efforts to make us into a major having failed, we have now attained that status—and we did it the hard way. There was no spectacular merger or acquisition; we just persevered, plugged away, controlled costs, and delivered high-quality professional services. We are the essence of an entrepreneurial enterprise—the sum of thousands of small things done correctly and thousands more done less correctly but overcome and reversed by a company that operates according to its credo:

Pride without arrogance<br>
Professionalism without being hidebound<br>
Integrity without self-righteousness<br>
Daring without foolhardiness

SEVENTEEN

# *The Other Life of an Entrepreneur*

One-dimensional entrepreneurs whose every waking hour is spent in single-minded pursuit of their business are common, but I am not one of them. I believe that there are many more entrepreneurs like me who have full and productive lives running parallel with their business careers. I need to describe the "other life" that I have led to complement my entrepreneurial career. I have always had other interests—indeed I had to curb an inclination to be a dilettante. Going public and thus having my financial affairs exposed was a watershed in intensifying my outside interests. Here's the way it happened.

When our daughters read the prospectus that we were required to publish at the time we offered shares to the public in 1970, their wide-eyed disbelief led to one of the most poignant moments in my life. Our youngest daughter, Val, was 20 and in college, Linda was getting a master's degree in anthropology, and Peggy had graduated from Brown University and joined VISTA, the domestic peace corps. They were all home for Christmas. We were sitting at the kitchen table having dinner, and one of them, having just read the prospectus, said in genuine surprise, "Gee, Dad, you're rich!" I was stunned. It was almost as though I'd been slapped in the face. True, I would be receiving close to $3 million (minus taxes, of course). Add to that the value of the shares I still retained, worth about $10 million, and in 1970 that sum was impressive.

But me rich? Never! It couldn't be possible. I was still that struggling kid from Brooklyn working hard to "succeed." Had I succeeded already? No way! There was more to it than that. For some reason the very label "rich" had a bad connotation for me. One invariably coupled it with the adjective "filthy." Indeed for me and my friends, "rich" people were different. Rich people were spoiled; rich people were greedy. All the bad imagery that I had associated with the word—constantly reinforced by the demagoguery of some liberals and media—had conditioned me to react with feelings of guilt when described as rich. No wonder I was stunned when my daughters classified me that way, even though they said it admiringly. What exacerbated this negative image was their absolute astonishment when they came to that conclusion. I hadn't realized how unprepared they were for the facts about our financial condition.

Though that word repelled me so, in many ways I'm grateful that they used it. It had a profound effect upon my life, my philosophy, my values, and my family relationships. It affected Vi less because, as I have related, her view of money, wealth, and material things was so much less emotionally charged than mine was. As a matter of fact, therein probably lay the root of the problem we faced and the suddenness with which it was thrust upon us. Vi's conservative approach colored everyone's view, including mine. For that I'll always be grateful. I would describe most of our friends in Altadena as hard working, decent, and upwardly mobile middle class. That's the way we lived and that was the style with which we were comfortable. The monetary rewards of my business were never a topic of conversation at home, and certainly not among our friends.

Whether we could "afford" something never came up either, because we rarely, if ever, reached into any doubtful financial territory. Furthermore, I had never developed the habit of discussing "my day at the office" at the dinner table. If there were some unusual project, I might mention it, but even then only casually, and certainly never in terms of the financial rewards of what we were doing. My family time, which I protected jealously, was devoted to them, not to me. Therefore, our daughters' surprise was genuine and understandable.

But their recognition of the existence of a considerable sum of money forced us to answer the question of what Vi and I were going to do with it. Looming large within that context was the question of inheritance, of the estate, of how our daughters should participate. Would we accumulate a family fortune to be passed on to our daughters? If so, what would be the consequences? Should we follow the commonly accepted course and leave our daughters wealthy or (horrors!) rich? They were bright, intelligent, and aware of the amount of money in the trusts we had established for them, but it somehow never affected them or their view of the world. They never really considered it to be "their" money anyway.

The talks Vi and I had over the next few days (and nights) were intense and profound. Finally at dinner a few nights later, in our kitchen as usual, I told our daughters that we had something important to discuss with them. "Listen, girls" (they hated being called that—they were grown women!), I said, "your mother and I have had some serious and worried conversations over the past few days. To your surprise, you've discovered that we are lucky enough to have more money than you've imagined or suspected. You know where we started, and to the extent that it represents my accomplishment and that of your mother, I'm pleased and proud, and we hope you are. However, the thing we're proudest of is you and what you are making of yourselves. Because we love you very much, we have decided that we are not going to leave you a lot of money." Long pause, and to my inner joy, we got no special reaction, no disappointment, no "Why not?"—just interested attention. I can't say I didn't fear a strong reaction, for I am a realist. Encouraged, I went on.

"Your Mom and I have decided that we will leave each of you enough money so that, after we die, you will be able to be taken care of if you become sick or disabled—but that's all we are going to leave you. We have a number of reasons for making that decision. First of all, while none of you has ever given any evidence of being spoiled, there is at least an outside chance that it could happen, especially now that you are aware of how much money there could be. We wouldn't want that. Furthermore, you are attractive young women. We want you to be certain that anyone who courts you (I'm sure I used that old-fashioned term) is not influenced by the fact that you might inherit a large amount of money. You want him, and we want him, to marry you because you are a nice person.

"Finally, I tell you that the greatest joy I've had is the knowledge that your mother and I have made whatever we've made essentially by ourselves. We started with nothing, and the satisfaction of knowing that we were able to get this far is a special and very precious feeling. We do not want to deprive each of you of that same pleasure of making of yourselves whatever you choose. We do not want your accomplishments to be tainted by being seen by others, or even by yourselves, as somehow derived from a material inheritance from us. We have enough confidence in your innate ability to make your mark in life with or without inheriting a lot of money from us. We'd like to think that those accomplishments of yours will be the result of your own intelligence and of the values you've learned from us—and not from money or material things you've inherited!"

After a slight pause, the response from our three wonderful daughters made our hearts glad. They said, almost in unison and without hesitation, "We understand, Dad. What do you plan to do with the rest of the money?" What a reaction! Was I surprised? Of course I was, but with hindsight I realized that I did them an injustice. "We've talked that over too, and we have decided we will give it away, and furthermore we've decided not to wait to give it all by inheritance. We want to enjoy giving away that money while we are still alive."

I still get goose bumps as I recall the enthusiastic second response from our daughters, "Great, Dad! Can we help you and Mom decide where to give it?" Not a moment's hesitation—absolute enthusiasm and not a shred of disappointment! Is it any wonder that my eyes tear a little as I write this?

Most ideas one develops over the years are derived from scores of observations and judgments that finally coalesce into a course of action. I have seen many examples of thoroughly spoiled and overindulged children; I've seen rebellious offspring of wealthy parents; I've seen young people driven to overshadow strong fathers; I've seen dropouts from society; I've seen children overreacting with guilt to their parents' affluence. I knew the problems. However, fortunately, when the problem was focused for us, I had an excellent precedent to follow.

Jerry Sudarsky was my student. I enjoy telling people that when talking about this eminently successful man. Actually he's only a year younger than I am, but he was a night student in a class on thermodynamics that I taught at Polytechnic. Jerry is another entrepreneur and a very successful one, though in a different mold from mine. His is a long story, but briefly, he bought an abandoned milk processing plant near Bakersfield, California, on a shoestring in the fifties, converted it to make baker's yeast, a business his family had been in, and struggled with that prosaic business for a few years. Then he invented a process to make vitamin $B_{12}$. After fighting thousands of technical problems, he built a plant and went head-to-head against the gigantic Merck & Co., which dominated the field. With sheer guts and superior technical brains, he prevailed over this colossus and later sold his company for a substantial profit. Whoever said that big companies always crush little ones? Whoever said that a smart and determined entrepreneur cannot play against the giants of the business world? My friend Jerry Sudarsky single-handedly took on the largest pharmaceutical company in the United States and beat it! He retired at an early age a wealthy man. He too derived his entrepreneurial tools from immigrant parents. One day when Jerry and I were having lunch, he told me that he had redrafted his will. He and his wife, Millie, had decided to leave only a limited amount of money to their daughters and used the same line of reasoning that I ultimately adopted. I'm duly grateful to him.

What a send-off and launching pad for another important part of my life that ran parallel to my entrepreneurial efforts.

*Daughters Val, Peggy, and Linda.*

Without a doubt, my embarking upon a determined path of giving provided much more meaning and substance to my business career. Today, as I begin to minimize my day-to-day involvement in the business, it becomes even more important to me. In the intervening years since that important family meeting, I have spent an appreciable amount of time in public service and in helping finance worthwhile activities. My participation in public policy issues, foreign affairs—especially in the Middle East—and above all, in supporting engineering education, has occupied almost as much of my time as my business interests.

The first program we followed was to make regular contributions to our daughters' trusts, usually in the form of Jacobs Engineering Co. stock to start funding that minimum legacy we had promised them. The value of that stock has increased substantially over the years, so their holdings represent a tidy sum. As they became mature women, each selected a career to her liking: Peggy in various jobs serving the underprivileged in the slums and the barrios; Linda, with a doctorate in archaeology, digging all over the world; and Val, with a master's degree in psychology and counseling, developing a private practice. It was pretty clear to us that they were not spoiled; they handled money prudently and invested their spare cash wisely. We dissolved the trusts early and they now handle their assets themselves. For Vi and me those three women are a success story every bit as important as any business accomplishment of mine.

This diversion into a discourse on the alternate uses for money and the soul searching we went through is often neglected when entrepreneurship is discussed. Even if the theory that an existential view of the pleasures of being an entrepreneur is valid, there are always concrete goals, and those goals are very often finally defined in terms of money. Because we entrepreneurs are so involved in the process of attaining goals, we often neglect to consider what we should do with the fruits of our efforts. There are those who spend their money on ostentation, on possessions in an almost childlike binge of self-gratification à la Donald Trump, or worst of all, derive all of their pleasure from watching the number of dollars increase on a balance sheet. But most entrepreneurs are more thoughtful than that.

Unfortunately, the possibilities for the destructive use of money are infinite. It can be used to spoil children, to make people envious, to corrupt people, to make people be and feel dependent, to feed a sybaritic hedonism, or egregiously as a powerful force for the destruction of humanity or of human dignity. Most of these effects usually stem from inadvertence or thoughtlessness, though some are caused by an occasional, purposeful evil. Using wealth for human good requires every bit as much deep thought and planning as any entrepreneurial enterprise. It also needs the same dedication, commitment, discipline, and plain old hard work. Clearly I believe that entrepreneurs contribute substantially to the advancement of society, for it is the risk takers who provide the energy for progress. But the rewards for providing that energy and taking those risks can be used to nullify or mitigate the benefits.

I was lucky that my daughters said, "Gee, Dad, you're rich," because it shocked me into solving a problem I hadn't anticipated.

My solutions are not unique or even necessarily the best; but at least they are thoughtful and I am comfortable with them. I should mention that, although philanthropy in the broadest sense is my major thrust, I am also using a modest amount of the funds available as venture capital. The support and encouragement of entrepreneurs struggling with start-up companies serves a useful social purpose, and being able to recycle some of the money I have earned to support that process is, for me, a satisfying contribution.

There's a lighter side to the path I have chosen. I can't count how many people over the years that have said to me with real concern in their voices, "Joe, why the hell do you work so hard? You've got all the money you need. Why don't you take it easy?" I have two standard answers. One is, "Where is it written that you have to hate what you are doing? Did it ever occur to you that I might be doing something that gives me great pleasure?" The other is, "I'm working my ass off so that I can make more money, because then I can give more away and that's fun! Now do you understand?" Of course, most often they don't.

I have been fortunate to have been honored many times in my life with various awards, testimonial dinners, appointments to advisory groups, and so on. I have already mentioned the Newcomen Society (named after the English inventor of the reciprocating steam engine, an invention generally acknowledged as the foundation of the industrial revolution). Each year the society selects four or five companies to honor and organizes a black-tie dinner for that purpose. They invite the CEO to present the history of his company's growth. We were so honored in 1980, and it was then that I became aware of the unrecognized and pervasive influence of immigrants upon the business of America. Most presentations of a company's background refer to its obscure beginnings. Because I was the founder, I tried to reflect upon the forces that led to the formation of our company and influenced its growth. It was then that I crystallized the half-formed thoughts I had always had about the enormous influence of my ethnic background on my career. So I opened my speech with these words, "Let me tell you about my father. . ." and proceeded to speak admiringly of him

*JJJ receiving the Newcomen Award from Ernest Loebeke, chairman, and Charles Penrose, executive director, of the Newcomen Society, 1980.*

and how the high standards of our business were a reflection of his and our community's values.

What impressed me so much was the large number of leaders of our business community who came up to me later, saying things such as, "Joe, my story is exactly like yours. My father came from Greece (or Italy, or Germany, or Lithuania, and so on) and he taught me values that influence my business life today!" The idea of a biography reflecting that theme began to germinate then.

Another of those honors that I particularly cherish is the Hoover Medal. This award, made each year since 1930, is named for Herbert Hoover, the outstanding mining engineer who was the 31st president of the United States and its first recipient. To be included in a roster with Gerard Swope, Vannevar Bush, Karl Compton, Alfred P. Sloan, Jr., Charles Kettering, Dwight Eisenhower, Lucius Clay, and David Packard among other distinguished people, was thrilling. But what pleased me more about being selected by a board representing all of the major engineering societies was the criterion for deciding who should receive this medal. The award is not made for a distinguished engineering

*President Reagan awarding the Hoover Medal to JJJ, 1983. D. E. Marlowe, chairman of the Hoover Medal Committee, is at right.*

career but rather to honor the *"civic and humanitarian achievements"* of that engineer (my emphasis).

President Reagan invited Vi and me to the Oval Office for a ceremony recognizing the award. Knowing that I would not have deserved, or received, this medal if our daughters had not shocked me at the dinner table by pointing out that I was rich, I hope this recitation does not sound too self-congratulatory. They freed me to pursue the humanitarian and other activities that were the real reason for the award. A sidelight is that, the year before, the Hoover Medal had been given to Michel T. Halbouty, the famous geologist and oil wildcatter, who, like me, is a first-generation Lebanese American.

Until 1970 I'd virtually lost contact with my alma mater, Polytechnic. I was making small annual contributions, but that's all. Then they installed a new, dynamic, personable, and aggressive president, George Bugliarello, who visited with me. I was shocked to learn of Poly's financial condition—it was virtually bankrupt. He asked me to join the board. A year later I became

*JJJ, Vi, and George Bugliarello, president of the Polytechnic University, at the dedication of the university's Joseph J. Jacobs Building, 1985.*

chairman, and with my decision about handling our personal financial resources settled, I made a substantial "challenge" contribution. Almost simultaneously I was asked to join the board of Harvey Mudd College, a small, elite engineering school in Claremont, California, and I made a contribution to it too. Engineering education, and these two schools in particular, have been the recipients of much of our giving. While chairman of the board of trustees of Polytechnic University, I was honored a number of times with awards for creative technology, as a distinguished alumnus, and so on. Upon retirement after 10 years as chairman, I was presented with an honorary doctor of science degree.

Thus education and particularly engineering education, became a primary focus for me, not only in providing financial help, but also more directly in my trying to guide and modify the teaching to reflect what I had learned. The two schools represented opposite ends of the engineering education spectrum. Poly was primarily for bright disadvantaged kids, as I had been, who would be the hungry entrepreneurs of the future. In contrast, Harvey Mudd attracted a small selection of students chosen

*JJJ delivering the commencement speech at Polytechnic University, 1984.*

from the top 0.1 percent of high school graduates. They are being taught to be rounded members of society. Fully one-third of their courses are in the humanities—unheard of in the narrow technical concentration of most engineering schools. Most conventional engineering schools typically turn out far too many of what I sadly call "grunts"—inarticulate, introverted, computer-sharp problem solvers, who are unaware of and untouched by the beautiful, the ugly, and the imperfect world around them.

I had never been involved in politics, but I began to be interested in individuals and their views and to provide some of them with financial support. Needless to say, my views had become increasingly conservative, but not, as the popular canard would have it, because I became affluent. My conservative outlook flowed directly from the same compassionate concern for humanity that had fueled my radical and liberal views in college. My motivations didn't change but the prescriptions I chose to address those concerns, did. My current political positions evolved from a continuous examination of the methodology of the liberals and radicals and the realization of how often they failed to deliver the objectives of their laudable compassion. What was

*Dedication of the Jacobs Science Center at Harvey Mudd College, 1980. Left to right: Vi; JJJ; Ken Baker, president of Harvey Mudd; Henry Mudd, chairman of the board of Harvey Mudd.*

most often missing from many of the massive government programs they sponsored was a sensitivity to the self-esteem of the recipients of their largess and an indifference to the often undesirable secondary and tertiary effects of their shallow "fixes." Despite this I have not been narrow in my loyalties and have not hesitated to support Democrats I admire even though I may differ with their positions on some issues. Men and women of integrity and honesty deserve support, for only out of frank debate between sincere advocates can democracy be strong. I am not, however, a political "groupie." There are business people who support political figures in order to shine in reflected glory and to boast of their intimacy with them. I consider any support I give to be an obligation on my part rather than payment for access.

As a result of this political interest, I became at one time the chairman of the Institute for Contemporary Studies (ICS)—a

*JJJ with George Mitchell, Senate majority leader, 1989.*

public policy group that produces books with an indisputably conservative but scrupulously honest and scholarly viewpoint. One recent example is their publication, *Winning the Brain Race,* written by David Kearns, then chairman of Xerox Corp., and Denis Doyle, a fellow at the Hudson Institute. This is a much-needed analysis of the deficiencies of our educational system—a deficiency that threatens to make us a second-class nation.

ICS is a "think tank" that was organized at the request of Ronald Reagan when he was governor of California. Ed Meese and Casper Weinberger were the prime movers in establishing it. Governor Reagan was apparently interested in establishing a scholarly and thoughtful foundation for the conservative theories he had developed by trial and error. Despite the largely leftist thought that dominated sociology and political theory in colleges, ICS found a respectable number of academics who supported the free-market system. Arnold Harberger, for instance, an economist at the University of Chicago (now at UCLA), compared third world countries that had chosen managed economies with those that had free-market economies after World War II, and found that the latter spectacularly outperformed those with managed economies in providing the good life to their citizens. ICS organized the International Center for Economic Growth under the leadership of Nicolás Ardito-Barletta, a former president of Panama, to carry Harberger's message to policy institutes in developing countries around the world. Donald Rumsfeld, who has been a secretary of defense and chief of staff to President Ford, succeeded me as chairman of ICS's board.

For many years I participated in discussion groups organized by the Conference Board, which provides economic studies and forecasting to American business. Most companies of any size are members of this group. Besides making economic forecasts that are highly respected and often quoted in the media, the board sponsors three-day weekend discussions known as the "Yama Conferences," attended by leaders of major companies and, usually, with a notable political figure as a guest. I have found the format challenging and fun. About 40 people sit in a circle and the names of individuals are picked out of a hat. Each person chosen is given eight minutes to talk on any subject; all the remarks are completely off the record. Substantial discussion usually follows each speaker's presentation. I was in my element at these meetings, speaking on a wide range of subjects—the Middle East, the role of envy in business and politics, oil prices after the crises created by OPEC had peaked, and the pleasures of planned giving. I enjoyed myself thoroughly, but to judge from their reactions, it seemed that not everyone else did. No one knew when his or her name would be called and it was something to see these captains of industry nervously awaiting their turn and then being visibly relieved when they were finished. Some came with prepared talks, some had notes, and others talked extemporaneously—as I did. It was revealing to hear about the diverse interests of these people. Only rarely did they talk just about their own businesses. Most—but not all—of them were conservatives. I was mightily impressed with their concern about world political problems, prejudice, hunger, education, and other social matters. Their concern reinforced my opinion that most business people are probably more compassionate than they are given credit for. They were every bit as cultured and caring as their counterparts in academe and the media.

Because of my ethnic heritage, I have studied Arab-Israeli politics extensively. Though emotionally sympathetic to the Arab cause, I became convinced that the Arabs were all wrong in trying to convince people of the injustices that were done to them—no matter how valid their claims. I contend that, instead, they should make the case that it would be in Israel's own interests to make peace with the Arabs. The key to that, it seemed to me, was to persuade Jewish Americans that blind support of every Israeli political action—no matter how irrational—was wrong and counter to Israel's long-term self-interest; that they should be as critical in public of Israeli politicians as they were in private. Jewish supporters of Israeli policy have no hesitation about expressing their opinions about American politicians. Why shouldn't they apply the same standards to Israel?

I helped organize one of the first dialogues between important Arab Americans and Jewish Americans in 1983. Lawrence Chickering of ICS made the initial contacts and ICS sponsored the first meetings. The coordinator was Professor Steve Cohen of the City University of New York. For many years we met privately and off the record. The names of some of those who participated, though not always regularly, will be recognized by anyone interested in Middle East politics: Howard Squadron, Lester Crown, Larry Tisch, Steve Shalom, Professor Steve Cohen, Professor Henry Rosovsky, Lew Rudin, Arthur White, and Bob Arnow were Jewish Americans who participated. Najeeb Halaby, Al Tahmoush, Zahi Khouri, Jerry Haddad, Ambassador Philip Habib, and Jesse Aweida were among the Arab Americans. Our moderator was often the former secretary of state Cyrus Vance.

It was fascinating to watch the group dynamics develop. At our first meeting we circled one another like wary Indians and mouthed all the political clichés of the politicians. Dominated as the group was by business people, we quickly swept aside the useless rhetoric and got down to business—"How can we influence the peace process in the Middle East?" or, in business terms—"How can we make a deal?" As we grew to be friends, it was surprising how much we agreed upon among ourselves and how much we disagreed with our "cousins" in the Middle East.

Over the years it became apparent that our hopes to sponsor joint development projects in Israel and Palestine must await a political settlement. Finally, we realized that our influence behind the scenes was limited and that, to be effective, we had to go public. Here the Jewish members were under incredible peer pressure. The community threat of ostracism that pressures American Jews to avoid any public criticism of Israel—no matter how deeply they disagree with the political actions of the Israelis—is enormous. Only recently has the group made a public statement decrying the intransigence of both sides. In summary, it says: "Stop the rhetoric. Talk to each other. Stop using incendiary words such as occupier, terrorist, brutal oppressor, bomb thrower, conqueror, killer of innocents. Acknowledge that you have become enemies, but talk to each other, for only then can you find out how to stop hating and perhaps learn how to live in peace!" The group still meets sporadically. I'm not sure that we did any good, but the friendships we developed are deep and I cherish them.

Because of the unusual access of this group, we met several times with Shimon Peres when he was prime minister of Israel and with leaders in Egypt and Jordan as well. Indeed, once a group of us flew to Jordan and registered under assumed names at a hotel (except for me—I was too well known in Amman to get away with it). We had lunch and a long discussion with the king and his wife, Queen Noor (Najeeb Halaby's daughter). We also met for an afternoon with Crown Prince Hassan. At the time, King Hussein had proposed an initiative for a Palestinian state to be federated with Jordan—an idea that I think is one of the best solutions to that complex problem. Our small group was then escorted by the king's bodyguards to the Allenby Bridge, a puny two-lane affair over the River Jordan. In the exact middle of the bridge we were turned over to some high brass of the Israeli army. It was funny to watch Jordanian soldiers in training marching in formation to exactly the middle of the bridge, then halting, executing an about face and going back. It was like a comic opera or a third-rate spy movie.

We met with Mr. Peres that night about midnight, and I pleaded for King Hussein's plan. Shimon Peres has very sad eyes

*Delegation invited by Lebanese government to appraise reconstruction needs after the Israeli invasion of Lebanon, 1983. Left to right: Lela Hazaz, translator; Ray Irani, chairman of Occidental Petroleum; Al Tahmoush, then chairman of Frank B. Hall Co.; Bill Baroody, then president of the American Enterprise Institute; Sami Maroun, Lebanon's minister of interior; Alex Dandy, supermarket chain owner; Najeeb Halaby, former chairman of Pan Am; JJJ.*

anyway, but he was almost in tears as he wearily said to me, "Dr. Jacobs, I trust King Hussein and I think this plan has much merit, but I must deal with political realities. Yasir Arafat has a history of reneging on his promises or reversing himself as he tries to maintain his leadership of the many factions in the PLO. I could never get the agreement of my government to deal with a terrorist who has never recognized Israel's right to exist. Most of our people do not trust him to stick to any agreement he has made with the king—after all it was not too long ago that he tried overthrowing King Hussein." It was sad for me to see how years of hatred, of distrust, of incendiary rhetoric had almost institutionalized the continuing enmity between these Semitic "cousins." It was easy to romanticize my role of "secret emissary," but the forces at work were much too strong for my meager efforts to have any effect.

In the narrower sphere of my special political interest, I've devoted a lot of effort to the poor, embattled, war-torn, and chaotic country of Lebanon. In 1983, after Israel's terrible and unforgivable invasion of Lebanon, I was asked by the Lebanese government to join a group of prominent Lebanese Americans in helping them plan the rebuilding of their devastated country. Leading the group was Najeeb Halaby, a former chairman of Pan Am. We had Al Tahmoush, who was then chairman of Frank B. Hall Co.; Ray Irani, who is now chairman of Occidental Petroleum; Bill Baroody, then president of the American Enterprise Institute; and Alex Dandy, who owns a major grocery chain in the Midwest. This delegation was an outgrowth of a meeting of a group of Lebanese-Americans who, with their wives, had met at our country home in Pauma Valley, California. Bob Abboud, then president of Occidental Petroleum, had been asked by President Ameen Gemayal to organize Lebanese Americans to help Lebanon. Business commitments prevented him from joining us when our trip was organized.

The destruction we saw in Beirut was heart rending—the center of the city was nothing but rubble. American battleships were on the horizon and those towering apartments on the Mediterranean that I remembered so vividly were shell-pocked and unoccupied.

My memories of luxurious Persian rugs on marble floors, of beautiful dark-eyed women drinking, eating *mazza*, and talking in three languages were dissolved in my tears. The veneer of sophisticated, westernized Beirut was revealed to be paper thin.

We were there for a week. One day in the office of the prime minister, Shafik-al-Wazzan, we were almost knocked out of our chairs by a loud explosion less than half a mile away. In rushed a messenger with a note, and the prime minister informed us, "The American Embassy has just been bombed." Our next appointment was to be a meeting with ambassador-at-large Phil Habib, an indefatigable practitioner of shuttle diplomacy, at the American Embassy. We were relieved to receive a message from him that he was in fact at the residence of the ambassador to Lebanon, Robert S. Dillon, and that we should come there. Poor Phil was rushing around trying to find out where our ambassador and his wife were (they were found later, relatively unharmed). He was also trying to find a secure phone to let President Reagan know what had happened.

I came away from that visit to Lebanon sadly disillusioned. As members of his government pursued their own selfish ends in the same old way, President Gemayel missed a golden opportunity to rebuild a united Lebanon. Our offers of advice and counsel

*Officers of the American Task Force for Lebanon meeting with Senator Robert Dole in his offices. Left to right: Peter Tanous, Mounzer Chaarani, Sen. Dole, JJJ, Tanya Rahall.*

were brushed aside. We realized that we were being used primarily for image enhancement and public relations.

Today I am an active member of a group called the American Task Force for Lebanon, which was founded by Peter Tanous and is now chaired by Tom Nassif, former U.S. ambassador to Morocco. We are trying mightily to help bring Lebanon back from the edge of disaster. I oscillate between depths of despair and renewed hope, wondering if the Lebanese have the political resolve to save their nation.

Peter Tanous is the thread to another of my diversions outside my business. He is the executive vice president of Bank Audi–USA and came to visit me a number of years ago soliciting my personal account for his bank. Peter is the grandson of Salloum Mokarzel, a Lebanese-American journalist and author well known in the early twentieth century, who was a close friend of my father's. After a successful investment banking career, Peter joined this bank, which is affiliated with a group of banks that have Lebanese roots going back over a hundred years.

*Board of Directors of Jacobs Engineering Group, 1991. Back, left to right: JJJ, Noel G. Watson, Jerry M. Sudarsky, Robert M. Barton, J. W. Simmons, David M. Petrone, J. Clayburn LaForce. Front, left to right: Joseph J. Alibrandi, S. B. Wilzig, Peter H. Daily, Linda K. Jacobs.*

I gave the bank some business and found that their service and personal attention were outstanding. Peter and Joe Audi, a member of the banking family who is president of the bank in New York, became my friends. They had developed ethnic networking to a fine art and their clientele in California grew rapidly. When they asked if I were interested in investing in a new bank to be called Bank Audi of California, I said yes.

That bank is now established, doing well, and I am chairman of the board. The president and operating head is William Hanna, a well-educated and cultivated Lebanese American (he was actually born near Montreal, Canada). He has done a superb job. As I know nothing about banking, all I bring to that position is gray hair. However, I'm proud of my association with the bank because of its impeccable reputation and because its ethnic roots, culture, and ethical standards are even more directly traceable than my own. Through that connection I have come to know many more Lebanese-American entrepreneurs to add to the hundreds I have met in my travels. Every one with whom I compare notes repeats the same story over and over again. Lay their stories over mine and differences are only minor. Be they Maronite, Druze, Sunni, or Shi'ite, we call one another "cousin" as we talk about the brave immigrant fathers and strong mothers who implanted their own cultural roots in our psyches. The ethnic fibers that I share with them have not disappeared. They are with me always. They have become a thread "as strong as steel" in the fabric of this Lebanese-American entrepreneur. My observation that there is an extraordinary number of extremely successful Lebanese Americans has been repeatedly reinforced.

Needless to say, I have had many other outside interests, connected either with my profession or with the community. Though I will not list them here, all have contributed enormously to the rounded "other" life of this entrepreneur.

So this is an unfinished story. At the age of 75, I go to work every day and am still looking for ways to continue expanding our business. I'm getting a tremendous charge out of watching Noel Watson grow and his ambitious management team take on increasing responsibility. When I yell at him or criticize him he fights back, but always with good logic and good humor. He even wins once in a while! We are both trying to avoid getting "the big head," even though Jacobs Engineering Group has had an absolutely spectacular record for these past six years.

I'm still the consummate "idea" man. We have, without doubt, the best top management team in the business. They are able to sift and execute the few good ideas I come up with. My most important role, however, is to make good my oft-repeated boast: "I'm still the most ambitious man in the company." The aggressiveness, the willingness to take on new challenges, to say with confidence, as I did to Kaiser Engineers 40 years ago, "Yes, we can do it," is what I constantly project. It is my mission to preach this philosophy and attitude to our people.

Finally, I must relate what Vi and I have done recently about our other mission in life. Having provided for our daughters adequately, we formed the Jacobs Family Foundation, which we have started funding and which will get the residue (more than

90 percent) of our estate. Peggy, Linda, Val, Vi, and I constitute the board of directors. By its charter, the foundation is to support engineering education and education in general. It specifically refers to humanitarian help and education for young Lebanese people. It also is to be used to provide help to the disadvantaged, not as charity, but as support for self-help and training with particular concern about preserving the self-esteem of those being helped.

Peggy was elected executive director of the foundation. It's a running gag now that, when people approach me for a charitable contribution, my stock reply is, "I don't have any money—it's all controlled by Peggy. Contact her to evaluate your request." Peggy takes her role seriously and is much more disciplined than I have ever been in screening and considering requests. We derive the most fun, however, from our occasional family meetings to consider various projects. They're not without heat. Some of my "conservative" criteria clash with our daughters' more "liberal" ones. They outvote me as often as not.

So the saga goes on. I have the existential pleasure of watching Jacobs Engineering Group continue to grow, to explore new frontiers and new ways of doing things. Along with that, I have the parallel pleasure of using the fruits of my entrepreneurship for human good and to advance knowledge. Finally, I am proud of the legacy we have left our three daughters—the independence to be what they choose to be; the intelligence to appreciate whatever character traits they've inherited from us; and the opportunity for them to use the tangible rewards of their father's being an entrepreneur for human good. I suppose that's as close an approach to immortality that anyone is allowed, and that shall be my epitaph.

# *Appendix: Jacobs Engineering Group— Growth and Financial Performance*

## Historical Highlights

This appendix provides the reader with a historical perspective of Jacobs Engineering Group Inc. (JEG) and highlights important steps in its growth and financial performance.

The company (a Delaware corporation) is among the largest professional service firms in the United States providing engineering, design, and consulting services; construction and construction management; and process plant maintenance. It was originally incorporated in 1957 as a successor to a business organized by Dr. Joseph J. Jacobs in 1947. The company's common stock has been publicly held since 1970 and is listed on the New York Stock Exchange with the symbol JEC.

*Chemicals and Pharmaceuticals*

**1947** The company began by providing, in part, consulting services and continues to supply such services through its Pace Consultants and Zellars-Williams subsidiaries.

**1956** The company's first substantial chemical project was the engineering of a caustic-chlorine plant for Kaiser Aluminum. Eleven years later, JEG engineered a 300-ton-per-day expansion for the same plant.

**1963** Southwest Potash Co. received the Kirkpatrick Merit Award from the American Institute of Chemical Engineers in recognition of a novel process for the production of potassium nitrate. JEG developed the process with this client from pilot-plant through to commercial-scale production.

**1974** The company's first major chemical project abroad was the engineering and construction management of a $25 million pharmaceutical plant for Syntex in Ireland. The Dublin office, home of Jacobs International Ltd., has subsequently expanded considerably.

**1980** Inception of a multimillion dollar chlorinated organics incinerator project for Borden Chemical.

**1986** For Genetics Institute, the first of a series of biotechnology research and production facility assignments. Also designed 3 million-pound-per-year fermentation products plant for Phillips Petroleum Co.

**1988** Engineering, design, and construction of a new production plant to manufacture 40 million pounds per year of ammonium perchlorate for Kerr-McGee Chemical Corp. in Nevada. Ammonium perchlorate is an oxidizing agent used in solid-fuel rocket systems for the Challenger mission.

**1989** Engineering, procurement, and construction services for the expansion of a $135 million dyestuffs manufacturing facility for CIBA-Geigy Corp. in San Gabriel, Louisiana.

Acquisition of Camargo Associates, Inc., of Cincinnati, Ohio, an engineering company specializing in the pharmaceutical, chemical, and food processing industries.

**1990** Acquisition of Pegasus Engineering Holdings Ltd. of Cork, Ireland, to add to JEG staff in Ireland.

*Hydrocarbons, Petrochemicals, and Refining*

**1974** Jacobs Engineering Co. merged with The Pace Companies, petroleum and petrochemical specialists.

**1976** Expansion of Pennwalt Corp.'s alkyl mercaptans facility, increasing world production by 50 percent.

**1977** Engineering services for a $300 million petrochemical complex for Oxirane Chemical Co., at Channelview, Texas.

**1979** JEG performed engineering, design, and construction for the U.S. Department of Energy's $2.5 billion program to provide strategic oil storage in underground caverns. The company provided 1.5 million engineering man hours under the 5-year contract.

**1984** Award of two contracts for the design and construction of polymer production plants for Borg-Warner, now GE Plastics.

**1985** Completion of design and construction of two polypropylene plants for HIMONT U.S.A. The plant was delivered to the client in eleven months—an exceptionally fast schedule.

**1989** Contract to provide engineering services for the modification of a plant belonging to the Coastal Aruba Refining Company, N.V., in San Nicholas, Aruba. The facility, purchased by Coastal from Exxon Corp., had been shut down since February 1985.

**1990** JEG received a multimillion dollar contract from British Petroleum to provide engineering, design, and procurement services for BP to upgrade its petroleum refineries throughout the United States.

*Environmental and Hazardous Waste Programs*

**1976** JEG conducted the first nationwide study for the U.S. Environmental Protection Agency (EPA), an assessment of hazardous waste disposal practices in the petroleum refining industry. The company has since assisted the EPA in developing regulations, protocols, and guidance for various process industries.

**1977** For Lion Oil Co., a wastewater treatment plant that included a 1.8 million-square-foot rotating biodisc, the largest system of its kind in the United States.

**1982** JEG began work under a 7-year technical assistance contract to help the U.S. Department of Energy (DOE) remediate 24 low-level radioactive sites in 10 states. Awarded a 5-year follow-on to this contract in 1990.

Started work on the EPA's Technical Assistance Teams program, responding to hazardous spill emergencies.

**1986** Awarded a $74 million contract by the EPA to provide technical support services relating to its enforcement activities.

In conjunction with Morrison-Knudsen Co., undertook the remediation of DOE's mixed-waste site at Weldon Spring in Missouri.

**1989** Awarded a 10-year contract, worth more than $100 million, to support the Navy's Comprehensive Long-Term Environmental Action Navy (CLEAN) program.

*Facility Systems*

**1971** Acquisition of Design Sciences, Inc.

**1983** First contract from Lockheed Corp. that eventually led to the design of more than 1.5 million square feet of new and renovated space in Sunnyvale, California, and Austin, Texas.

**1984** First in a series of projects for the National Aeronautics and Space Administration (NASA) to upgrade and to provide increased security at Kennedy Space Center in Florida. Received NASA Public Service Group Achievement Award.

Began work on the 5-year, $150 million program to upgrade the U.S. Department of Energy's production facilities at Fernald, Ohio.

**1986** Provided automated systems for the production of rocket motors for Morton Thiokol.

**1987** Received a fourth contract from the U.S. Army Corps of Engineers to support their program for the destruction of chemical warfare munitions.

**1989** Provided architectural, engineering, and construction management services for a microcomputer system manufacturing facility being built in County Kildare, Ireland, for Intel Corp.—one of the largest facilities of its kind in the world.

**1990** Awarded contracts valued at more than $65 million by the Food Services Group of Borden's Grocery and Specialty Products division to provide services, from design through construction, for three "hyperplants," Borden's term for a state-of-the-art, high-efficiency facility, with low-cost production economics, for the manufacture and distribution of products for the food service industry.

*Minerals and Fertilizers*

**1955** JEG's first process engineering assignment was the alternative process studies of a potash crystallizer plant for Southwest Potash.

**1966** JEG built its first diatomaceous earth facility, for Eagle Picher Co., and then designed nearly all of the diatomaceous earth facilities built in the United States during the next decade.

**1974** Completed the world's largest granular fertilizer plant, for CF Industries, and provided four others in the United States, India, and Nigeria.

Designed and constructed copper ore leach, precipitation, and wastewater treatment facility at Ray Mines for Kennecott Copper Corp. In 1980, JEG designed a new solvent extraction facility, one of the largest in the United States, to produce high-purity copper, also for Kennecott.

**1975** Completion of engineering and construction of the 2.5 million-ton-per-year phosphate rock flotation plant, the world's largest, for Occidental Chemical at White Springs, Florida.

**1976** Contract for the design of the Mount Taylor, New Mexico, uranium mine mill for Gulf Mineral Resources Co., to have been the largest single processor of uranium ore in the U.S. The plant was not built because demand for uranium was severely curtailed as a result of opposition to nuclear power.

**1978** For Wyoming Mineral, Gardinier Inc., and Freeport Uranium, the company designed and built three of the first four U.S. plants that recover uranium from phosphoric acid.

**1980** Completion of a $66 million boric acid plant for United States Borax & Chemical Corp. Since 1962 Jacobs has completed some $100 million worth of projects for this client.

**1981** Completion of the ARCO Black Thunder Coal Facility in Wyoming, one of the largest coal handling and unit train loadout facilities in the United States. Similar facilities were provided for Shell Oil, NERCO Coal, and Pacific Power and Light.

**1986** Provided the engineering, construction, start-up, training, and operations management for a $450 million, 1.2 million-ton-per-year potash production facility in Jordan.

**1990** Completed the engineering, procurement, and construction of a $40 million clean acid manufacturing plant for P.A. Partnership in North Carolina. The facility uses a solvent extraction process to produce food-grade phosphoric acid for use in detergents, toothpaste, and soft drinks.

Providing engineering and construction services for a vacuum-distilled titanium sponge manufacturing facility for Titanium Metals Corp. (TIMET), at Henderson, Nevada.

*Construction and Maintenance*

**1960** The company's first combined design and construction project, a potash flotation plant for Southwest Potash.

**1974** As a result of the merger with The Pace Companies, JEG acquired several continuing maintenance contracts, including contracts at the Exxon Baton Rouge refinery and the Dow Chemical Plant at Plaquemine, Louisiana, that have been in effect for over 30 years.

**1985** Completed two polypropylene facilities for HIMONT U.S.A. JEG received the Corporate Safety Award for more than 400,000 construction man hours without a single lost-time injury.

**1986** Acquisition of Payne & Keller, specialists in the construction and maintenance of refinery and petrochemical plants, nearly doubling revenues from construction and maintenance.

**1987** Acquisition of Robert E. McKee, Inc., general contractors and specialists in the construction and construction management of municipal and high-technology facilities.

**1990** Awarded a 5-year contract to provide unconventional propellant and hazardous waste operations services to the U.S. Air Force's Western Space and Missile Center (WSMC) at Vandenberg Air Force Base near Lompoc, California. This project involves managing and handling unconventional propellants and cryogenic commodities—rocket fuels, liquid oxygen, and nitrogen—used to support space vehicle launch operations at Vandenberg.

Acquisition of the assets of Applied Engineering Company, of Orangeburg, South Carolina, which include Advanced Construction Technology (ACT®), an innovative offsite and modular construction technique that is gaining wide acceptance within the process industry.

*Growth and Performance*

Following is a presentation of financial performance and growth of the Jacobs Engineering Group over the past 20 years.

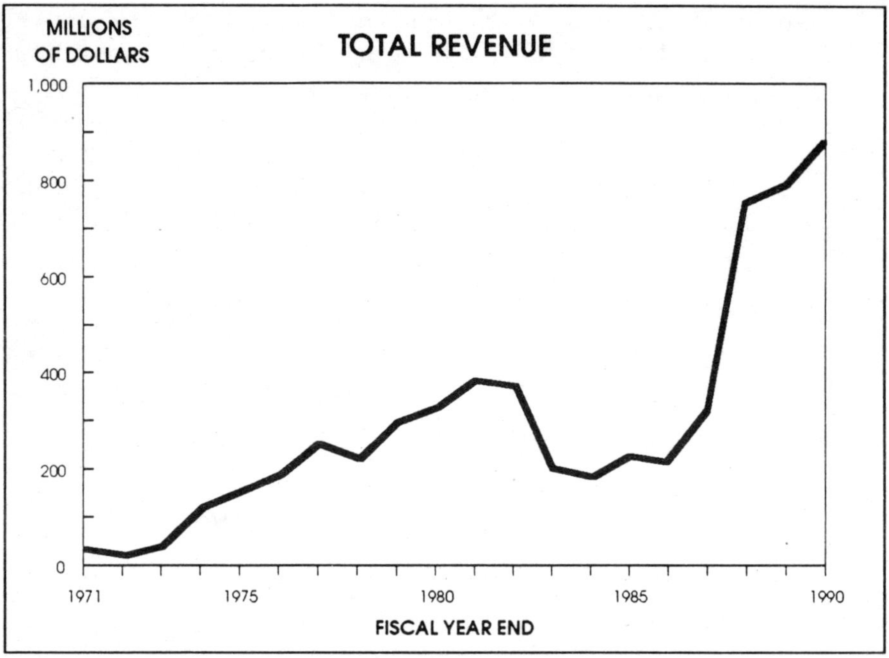
MILLIONS
OF DOLLARS
TOTAL REVENUE
1,000
800
600
400
200
0
1971
1975
1980
1985
1990
FISCAL YEAR END

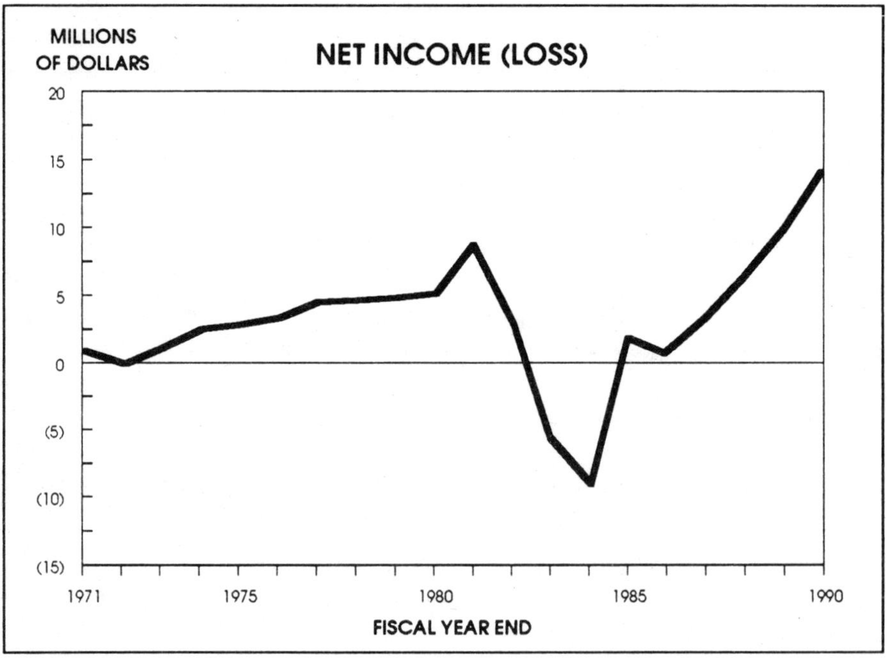
MILLIONS
OF DOLLARS
NET INCOME (LOSS)
20
15
10
5
0
(5)
(10)
(15)
1971
1975
1980
1985
1990
FISCAL YEAR END

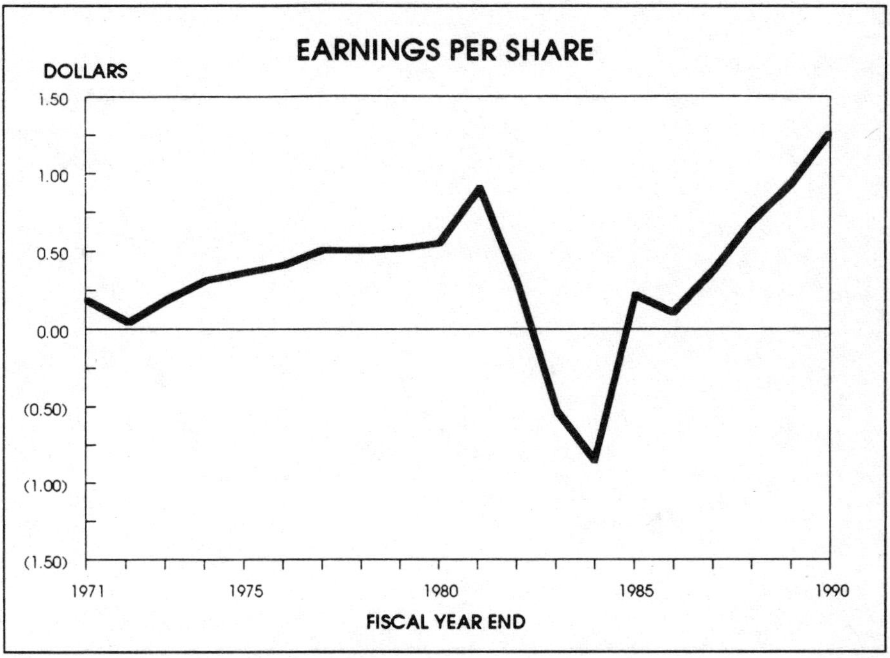
EARNINGS PER SHARE
DOLLARS
1.50
1.00
0.50
0.00
(0.50)
(1.00)
(1.50)
1971
1975
1980
1985
1990
FISCAL YEAR END

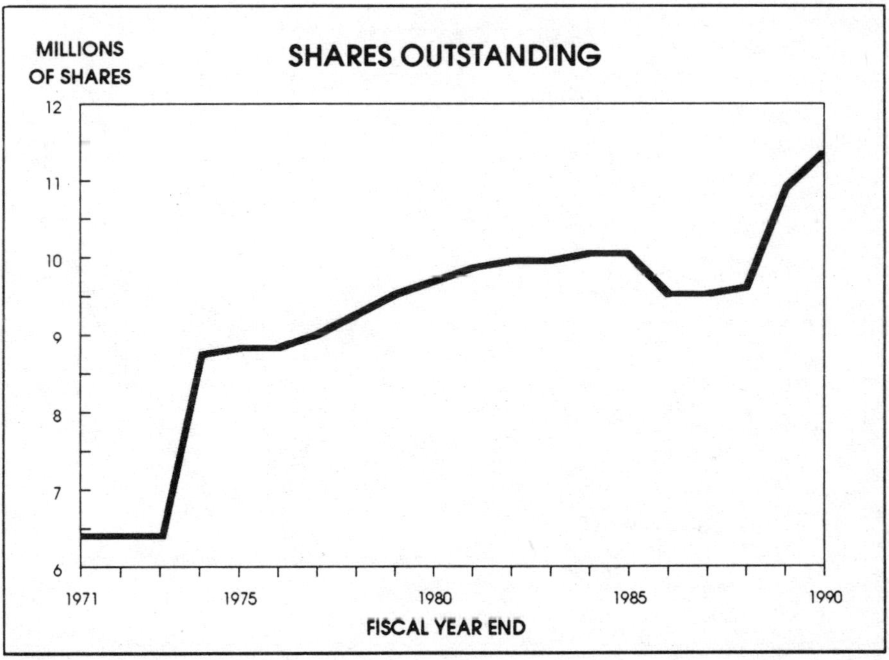
SHARES OUTSTANDING
MILLIONS
OF SHARES
12
11
10
9
8
7
6
1971
1975
1980
1985
1990
FISCAL YEAR END

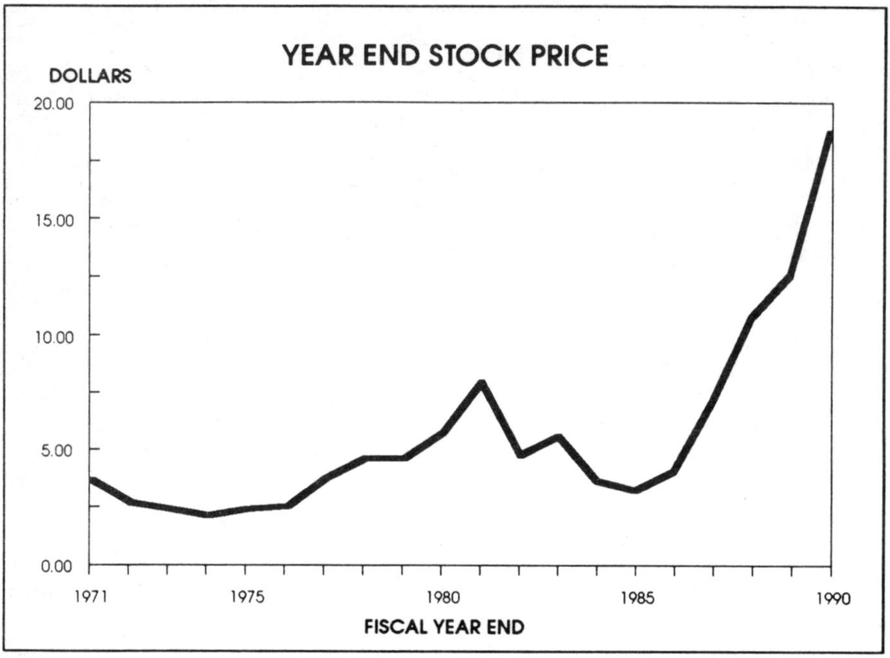
YEAR END STOCK PRICE
DOLLARS
20.00
15.00
10.00
5.00
0.00
1971
1975
1980
1985
1990
FISCAL YEAR END

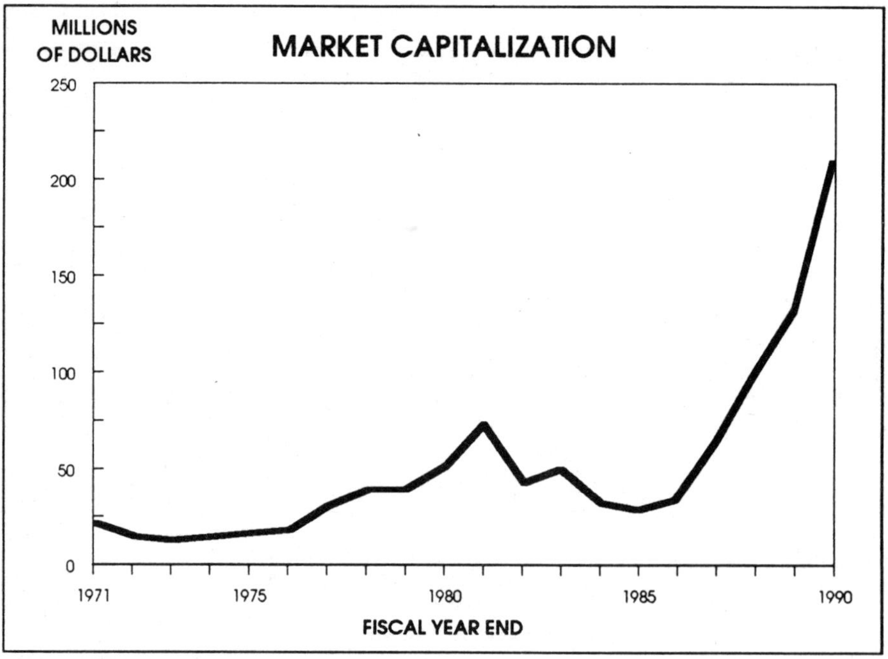
MILLIONS
OF DOLLARS
MARKET CAPITALIZATION
250
200
150
100
50
0
1971
1975
1980
1985
1990
FISCAL YEAR END

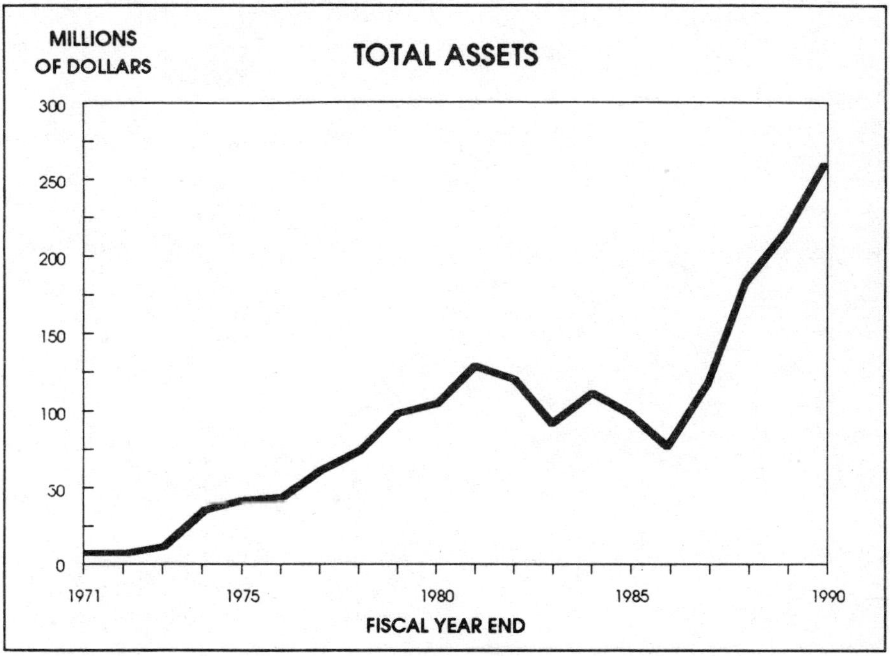
MILLIONS
OF DOLLARS
TOTAL ASSETS
300
250
200
150
100
50
0
1971
1975
1980
1985
1990
FISCAL YEAR END

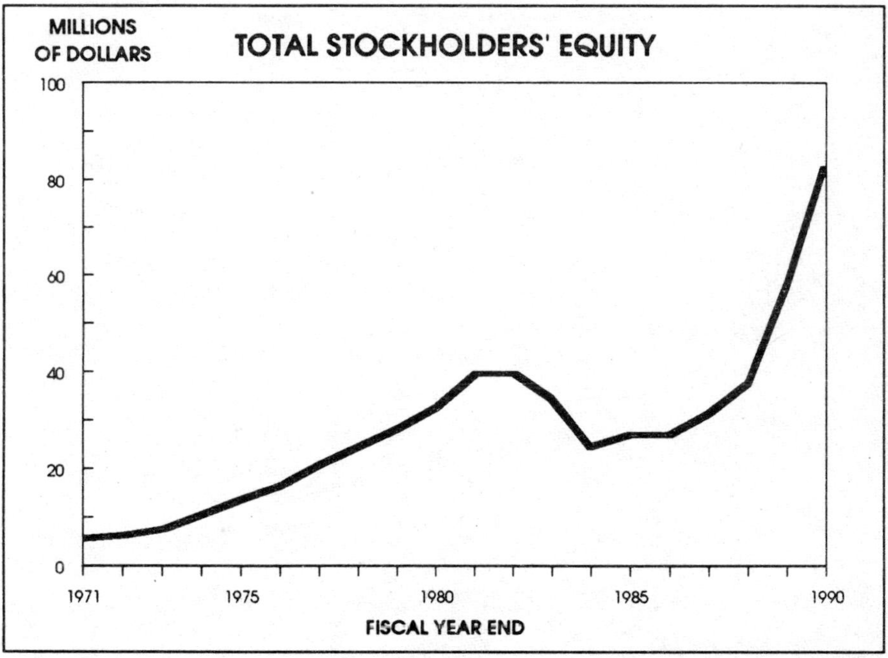
MILLIONS
OF DOLLARS
TOTAL STOCKHOLDERS' EQUITY
100
80
60
40
20
0
1971
1975
1980
1985
1990
FISCAL YEAR END

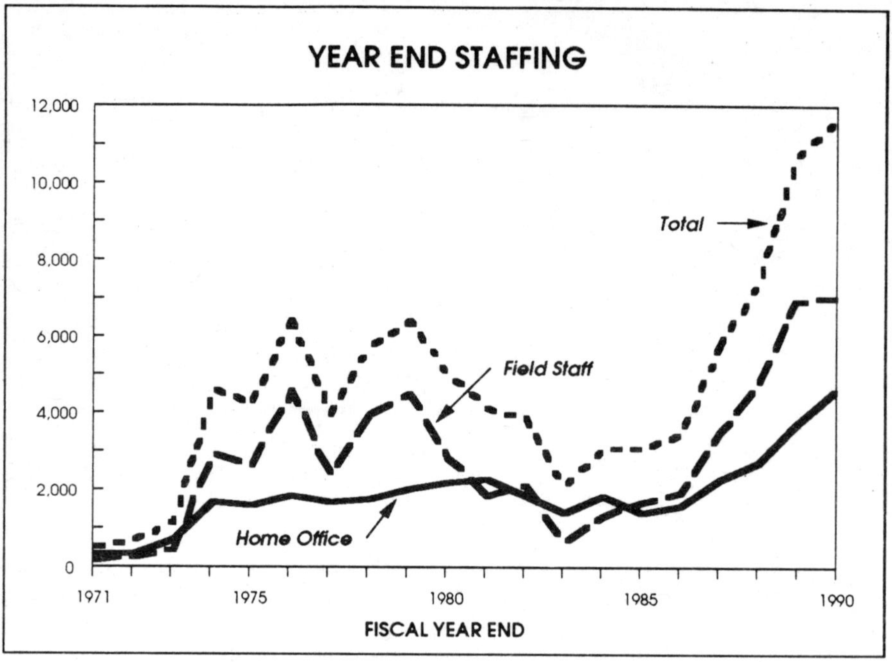
YEAR END STAFFING
12,000
10,000
8,000
6,000
4,000
2,000
0
1971
1975
1980
1985
1990
FISCAL YEAR END
Total
Field Staff
Home Office